MARKETING MANAGEMENT

TEXT AND CASES

MARKETING MANAGEMENT

TEXT AND CASES

David Loudon
Robert Stevens
Bruce Wrenn

ATLANTIC®
PUBLISHERS & DISTRIBUTORS

Best Business Books®
New York • London • Oxford

ATLANTIC®

PUBLISHERS & DISTRIBUTORS
7/22, Ansari Road, Darya Ganj
New Delhi – 110 002
Tel: 2327 3880, 2327 5880, 2328 0451
Fax: 91-11-2328 5873
E-mail: info@atlanticbooks.com
Website: www.atlanticbooks.com

Published in India by
Atlantic Publishers and Distributors, New Delhi
in association with
Best Business Books®, an imprint of The Haworth Press, Inc.
10 Alice Street, Binghamton, New York 13904-1580

First published 2005 by Best Business Books®
First Indian Reprint 2005

ISBN 81-269-0488-7

PUBLISHER'S NOTE
In some cases, names, selected data, and corporate identities have been disguised.

Printed in India by
Nice Printing Press, Delhi

CONTENTS

ABOUT THE AUTHORS

David Loudon, PhD, is Professor of Marketing and Head, Department of Management and Marketing in the College of Business Administration at University of Louisiana at Monroe. He has been a faculty member at Louisiana State University, University of Rhode Island, Hong Kong Shue Yan College, and the North American Executive Program in Monterrey, Mexico. He has taught a variety of courses but focuses on marketing management and consumer behavior. Dr. Loudon is the co-author of twelve books and has conducted research in the United States, Europe, Asia, and Latin America on such topics as consumer behavior, international marketing, services marketing, and marketing management. He has written more than 100 papers, articles, and business cases, and his research findings have been published in a number of journals and in the proceedings of numerous professional conferences. He is co-author of *Marketing Research: Text and Cases.* He also is co-editor of Best Business Books, an imprint of The Haworth Press, Inc., and co-editor of *Services Marketing Quarterly.*

Robert Stevens, PhD, is Professor of Marketing in the Department of Management and Marketing at University of Louisiana at Monroe. During his distinguished career, Dr. Stevens has taught at the University of Arkansas, the University of Southern Mississippi, and Hong Kong Shue Yan College. He teaches marketing management, business research, statistics, marketing research, and strategic management. The author and co-author of 20 books—including *Marketing Research: Text and Cases*—and more than 150 articles, he has served as a consultant to local, regional, and national firms for research projects, feasibility studies, and marketing planning, has been the owner of a marketing research company, and is currently the owner of two small businesses. He is co-editor of the *Services Marketing Quarterly* and serves on the editorial review boards of four other professional journals. He was selected as Northeast Louisiana University's Outstanding Professor of Business Administration in 1997 and has been selected as the College of Business Administration's Outstanding Researcher on five separate occasions.

Bruce Wrenn, PhD, is Professor of Marketing in the School of Business and Economics at Indiana University South Bend. The author of several books on marketing management, planning, and research, and two books on marketing for religious organizations, Dr. Wrenn has also written numerous articles on marketing strategy, research, and marketing techniques for nonprofit, for-profit, and health care organizations. He is co-author of *Marketing Research: Text and Cases.* He spent several years with a major pharmaceutical company performing market analysis and planning, and has served as a consultant to a number of industries, religious denominations, and organizations in the food, high-tech, and health care industries.

CASE CONTRIBUTORS

Rochelle R. Brunson, Alvin Community College, Alvin, Texas.

Richard W. Coleman, Texas A&M at Kingsville.

Philip C. Fisher, University of Southern Indiana.

Phylis M. Mansfield, Associate Professor of Marketing, Penn State University, Erie.

Cara Okleshen, University of Georgia.

Marilyn Okleshen, Minnesota State University at Mankato.

Marlene M. Reed, Professor of Management, Samford University, Birmingham, Alabama.

Jacquelyn Warwick, Associate Professor of Marketing, Andrews University.

Bruce E. Winston, School of Business, Regent University.

Janet Bear Wolverton, Oregon Institute of Technology.

Preface

This book is intended for use in undergraduate and graduate marketing management courses. We have tried to prepare a text that covers all of the essential managerial elements of marketing with sufficient detail to provide a review for marketing, background for nonmarketing majors in a case-oriented teaching environment, and challenge to take students to the next level of understanding marketing.

The selection of cases provides a wide variety of managerial situations for small, medium, and large companies. Also included are several entreprenurial cases that focus on the issues of product or business start-ups to expose students to the types of analyses needed for these decision-making situations.

Chapter 1

The Marketing Management Process

This chapter provides an overview of the marketing management process. It focuses on the tasks marketers must perform to manage the marketing activities of their organizations and the environment of marketing decisions. First, we will review the definition of marketing, the marketing concept, and the focus of effective marketing before turning our attention to these tasks.

WHAT IS MARKETING?

The American Marketing Association defines marketing as follows: "the process of planning and executing the conception, pricing, promotion, and distribution of ideas, goods, and services to create exchanges that satisfy individual and organizational goals."[1] Several key ideas are expressed in this definition. First, marketing is a managerial function involving both planning and execution. Thus marketing is not a group of unrelated activities but tasks that are planned and executed to attain identifiable objectives. Second, marketing involves the management of specific elements or functions: product, pricing, promotion, and distribution. These functions constitute the work or substance of what marketing is all about. To be involved in marketing means being involved in the planning, execution, and/or control of these activities. Third, marketing is goal oriented. Its aim is to create exchanges that satisfy individual and organizational objectives. Marketing's concern is with customers and meeting a need in the marketplace. However, its concern is not just with any customers or all customers but those preselected by management as the market segment(s) on which the company will concentrate. Thus, specific customers with their specific needs become the focal point of an organization's marketing activities.

THE MARKETING CONCEPT

The marketing concept is a business orientation that focuses on satisfying customers' needs at acceptable levels of revenues and costs. In for-profit organizations, acceptable levels of revenues and costs are defined in terms of a target return on investment; in not-for-profit organizations, the focus is on achieving a balance between revenues and costs.

Organizations having a true "marketing orientation" focus on addressing the needs and wants of one or more targeted segments of the market. However, other business philosophies may be put into practice by managers with marketing titles, which in reality do not reflect authentic marketing thought. Table 1.1 shows five different business orientations that have been used as the operating philosophies behind management decision making. The term *dominant* in the table identifies the core objective which gives the orientation its name. *Present* means that the orientation includes that objective but does not use it as the centrally controlling goal in orienting the manager's thoughts about his or her company, its products, or its customers. *Not pertinent* means that objective has no relevance, pertinence, or connection with the orientation described. This table makes it clear that the production, product, and selling orientations are internally driven. Managers

TABLE 1.1. Business Orientations

Characteristic	Production orientation	Product orientation	Selling orientation	Marketing orientation	Societal marketing orientation
Desire to capitalize on synergies and efficiencies in production process	Dominant	Present	Present	Present	Present
Attention to designing and production of a quality product	Not pertinent	Dominant	Present	Present	Present
Dedicated resources to stimulating interest and desire for product purchase	Not pertinent	Not pertinent	Dominant	Present	Present
Focus on identifying and satisfying needs and wants of customers	Not pertinent	Not pertinent	Not pertinent	Dominant	Present
Consideration of the short- and long-term effects of actions on customers and on society	Not pertinent	Not pertinent	Not pertinent	Not pertinent	Dominant

using such orientations determine what they want to dictate to the market. Only the last two orientations—marketing and societal marketing—contain the elements of an "outside-in," "market-driven," or "customer-oriented" philosophy which stresses discovery of market opportunities, marketplace input regarding the organization's claim of a competitive advantage, and the integration of effort across all aspects of the organization to deliver customer satisfaction. These two orientations reflect the competitive realities facing organizations of all types as a new millennium begins.

The societal marketing orientation is particularly well suited to internal and external environmental forces currently facing managers. It includes all of the positive contributions of the other four philosophies but adds concern for the long-term effects of the organization's actions and products on its customers, as well as the desire to consider the effects of the organization's actions on society at large. In other words, it recognizes the sovereignty of the marketplace and uses as ethical framework both deontological (rights of the individual) and teleological (impact on society) views in the decision-making process. Putting this philosophy into practice requires a planning procedure that transforms the consumer orientation into marketing activities.

The societal marketing orientation believes that the only social and economic justification for the existence of a business enterprise is the satisfaction of customer needs, at a profit, and with due diligence for the long-term welfare of the customer and of society. A firm's existence is justified socially in meeting customer needs—directly through provision of goods and services, and indirectly through being a good citizen of its operating environment. In the U.S. economy, this philosophy is exactly why businesses were given the right by society to own and use resources to produce goods and services. A firm finds economic justification by making a profit. Profit rewards the owners' investment in the organization and assures continued availability of funds. Customer needs become the focus of firms that operate under this philosophy.

Managers adopting the marketing philosophy must continually survey the environment to detect changes in consumer needs or other related variables that warrant altering their marketing activities. Sales revenues, in effect, become votes to help management judge the effectiveness of its efforts in meeting market needs compared to those of competitors; profits serve to judge the efficiency of management in this attempt.

MARKETING MANAGEMENT IN THE NEW MILLENNIUM

In recent years, marketing management has increasingly focused on four key elements to enhance market share, profits, and efficiency. These elements are quality, value, relationships, and customer satisfaction.

Product Quality and Value-Based Marketing Strategy

One of the most significant trends in recent marketing practice has been the emphasis on *value*—the right combination of product quality, service support, and timely delivery at a reasonable price. This concern with value by customers has forced many firms to reconsider their views of product quality and customer service in order to meet the demands of a global marketplace. For example, consider the differences between the traditional view of product quality and the total quality management (TQM) approach (see Table 1.2). Marketing plans must reflect the emphasis on value demanded by the market with respect to the quality of product and level of customer service.

Firms adopting a societal marketing orientation are interested in understanding how their customers perceive and define quality as well as making sure that their products are fully capable of generating customer satisfaction in both the short- and long-terms. Thus, product quality is not primarily internally determined but is rather centered around customer perceptions and evaluative criteria. The Strategic Planning Institute's procedure for assessing perceived quality may be instructive:[2]

1. A group of managers from different functional areas of the business meet to identify the nonprice attributes of the product or service that influence consumer choice.
2. The group assigns weights to the attributes to reflect the importance each attribute plays in consumer decision making. The weights must sum to 100 percent. This is done on a market segment by market segment basis when the weights differ by consumer segment.

3. A quality score is created for the company's product as well as its major competitors by multiplying the product's rating (determined by the management team) on the attribute by the importance weight and summing for all attributes.
4. The quality score along with other competitive comparison measures (e.g., pricing, share of market) and financial performance measures, i.e., return on investment, return on sales, and internal rate of return (ROI, ROS, IRR, respectively), are validated by comparing them with benchmarked data for similar business.
5. Finally, the team develops budgets and plans for improving quality relative to competition and to marketplace needs and perceptions, and calculates the financial payoff.

Whenever possible, the team's judgments are compared to and modified by information collected from customers.

TABLE 1.2. Traditional versus TQM Views

Traditional view	Total quality management view
Productivity and quality are conflicting goals.	Productivity gains are achieved through quality improvements.
Quality is defined as conformance to specifications or standards.	Quality is defined by degree of satisfaction of user needs.
Quality is measured by degree of conformance.	Quality is measured by continuous process/product improvement and user satisfaction.
Quality is achieved through inspection.	Quality is determined by product design and is achieved by effective process controls.
Some defects are allowed if the product meets minimum quality standards.	Defects are prevented through process-control techniques.
Quality is a separate function and focused on evaluating production process and output.	Quality is part of every function in all phases of the product life cycle.
Workers are blamed for poor quality.	Everyone is responsible for quality.
Supplier relationships are short-term and cost oriented.	Supplier relationships are long-term and profit oriented.

Source: Adapted from V. Daniel Hunt, *Quality in America* (Homewood, IL: Business One Irwin, 1992), p. 72.

The key to successful implementation of a quality strategy is teamwork and cooperation. Everyone should see his or her job, whatever the functional area, as a "value-added" role in the delivery of a quality product. Team members must be cognizant of what constitutes quality in the customer's mind, feel that the quality is everyone's responsibility, and be empowered to make decisions which affect the value delivery chain. Keys to successfully achieving world-class quality include the following:[3]

1. Top management must provide unequivocal support for the quality effort.
2. Close contact must be maintained with customers in order to fully understand their needs.
3. To avoid untimely delays, reaction time must be reduced when definitions of quality change over time.
4. People should be empowered to utilize their best talents
5. Reward systems should be assessed and adjusted to recognize efforts that are consistent with quality objectives.
6. The total quality program has to be viewed as an ongoing concern by everyone in the organization.

Service Quality Strategy

Companies have been concerned with delivery of a satisfactory level of customer service for decades, but it is safe to say that the level of concern has increased. Competitive forces and the more demanding nature of customers have combined to put customer service at, or near, the top of most marketers' lists of important issues. Research has revealed five dimensions used by customers to define perceived quality of service (see Table 1.3).

Further research has revealed that while respondents rank all five dimensions toward the "important" end of the scale in defining service quality, when asked, they said that reliability was the most critical. This suggests that firms must accomplish the following tasks with regard to their service strategy:

1. Determine the specific service expectation of the target market.
2. Design a service strategy grounded in meeting or exceeding those expectations.

3. Deliver on those promised service levels consistently when dealing with customers.
4. If steps 1 through 3 are performed better than competitors, a competitive advantage exists in the area of customer service and should be exploited as such.

Improving Customer Perceptions of Service Quality

The most vexing problem for management, given the importance of reliability in defining service quality, is to close any gap that exists between expectations and ultimate delivery of service to customers. However, four service-related gaps should be of concern to marketing planners:[4]

1. *Gap between the customer's expectations and the marketer's perceptions*—Research into what customers are actually thinking is needed. Marketers cannot assume that without such research they know with clarity what those expectations are.

2. *Gap between management perceptions and service quality specifications*—Knowledge of customer expectations is the first link in a chain of steps leading to customer satisfaction with service delivery. Specifications of policies and tasks of service delivery must be developed based on that knowledge and communicated to employees. Employees must understand that their job performance will be based in part or in whole on meeting those specifications.

3. *Gap between service quality specifications and service delivery*—Highly motivated, well-trained, and well-informed employees are needed to actually perform the tasks specified as necessary for delivery of quality service. Control systems that are capable of measuring any gap between desired and actual service delivery should be in place to indicate where excellence or shortfalls are occurring.

4. *Gap between service delivery and external communications*—Excellent delivery of service specifications can still disappoint customers if marketers have caused those customers to have unrealistically high expectations of service. For example, promotional photos that suggest the accommodations at a resort are more spacious or luxurious than they really are will likely raise expectations higher than can be delivered, resulting in disappointed customers.

Product quality and customer service decisions should be the cornerstone of product decisions in the marketing plan.

TABLE 1.3. Dimensions of Service Quality

Dimension	Components
Tangibles	Physical appearance of facilities, equipment, personnel, and communications materials
Reliability	Dependability and accuracy of promised service
Responsiveness	Willingness of providers to help customers and give prompt service
Assurance	Employees' knowledge, courtesy, and ability to convey trust and confidence
Empathy	Providing care and individualized attention

Source: Adapted from Valarie A. Zeithaml, A. Parasuraman, and Leonard L. Berry, *Delivering Quality Service: Balancing Customer Perceptions and Expectations* (New York: Free Press, 1990), p. 26.

Relationships

Another key element of effective marketing is relationship management. The word *relationship* means connection or closeness, and marketers must develop relationships with suppliers, intermediaries, other colleagues, and customers. The focus of relationship management is on building and maintaining long-term relationships with all the parties that contribute to the success of the organization.

The power of strong relationships can be seen in moves made by General Motors to revitalize and update their dealerships. GM has been slowly trying to remake its distribution system, including relocating dealerships to reflect shifts in population and merge dealerships from 9,500 to 7,000.

This $1 billion dollar project has already shown signs of paying off. In Bergen County, New Jersey, sales rose 42 percent after half of the dealerships were upgraded or moved. In addition to new and larger dealerships, consumer amenities such as playrooms for children and Internet access are available in some waiting rooms.

Not all dealers are happy with the changes, however. A move or merger that helps one dealer may hurt another, and this could result in broken relationships, i.e., lawsuits. Most industry experts feel that this is a move they must make to catch up to what other automakers have already done.[5]

Customer Satisfaction

An organizational emphasis on quality should result in increased customer satisfaction. Customer satisfaction is the result of a company's ability to meet or exceed the expectations of the buyer. Increased customer satisfaction results in retention of existing customers. Since it is cheaper for a company to retain an existing customer than attract a new one, customer satisfaction becomes a focal point for maintaining sales and improving profitability.

Organizations who want to improve customer satisfaction must implement systems to, first, measure current levels of satisfaction against established customer satisfaction goals, and, second, develop action plans to alter operations if goals are not being met. For example, a bank may have a goal that customers should wait no more than five minutes before accessing a teller for a transaction. Studying waiting times within the bank and at drive-through operations could provide measures of the bank's performance. If the goal is not being met, the bank might implement changes to reduce waiting time such as increasing the number of open teller windows, changing operating hours, or improving ATM accessibility. The overall process used to improve customer satisfaction is shown in the following list:

1. Determine relevant attributes and characteristics of customer satisfaction based on consumers' perspectives.
2. Establish customer satisfaction goals for each of these attributes.
3. Develop the measurement processes to assess performances on each of the attributes.
4. Analyze differences in goals and performance to determine where improvements need to be made.
5. Develop and implement an action plan to bring performance into alignment with goals.

Developing and implementing such a process leads to *continuous quality improvements* (CQI). This means the organization is always in the process of analyzing and implementing policies and procedures to improve service quality and customer satisfaction. Meeting these challenges in the new millennium requires effective marketing management processes.

THE EFFECTIVE MARKETING MANAGEMENT PROCESS

Effectively undertaking the marketing management process involves steps that are easy to describe but considerably more difficult to perform. The challenges of hypercompetitive markets and the demands of successfully addressing the four key elements of quality, value, relationships, and customer satisfaction can be daunting to marketing managers. However, experience has shown that effective marketing managers should follow the steps of the model shown in Figure 1.1. The remainder of this chapter briefly discusses the steps of the process; the remainder of the book discusses the steps in detail.

Societal Marketing Orientation

The process begins with the recognition that effective marketing management is driven by a distinctive orientation of the marketing manager toward the customers, the company, and the company's products. Although this orientation can take several forms (see Table 1.1), *effective* marketing managers will more often than not adopt a societal marketing orientation as a guiding philosophy. In fact, studies have shown a strong correlation between marketing orientation and profitability.[6] Companies without an authentic marketing orientation are more likely to have: an unfocused competitive position; a "me-too" approach to delivering customer value; excessive customer

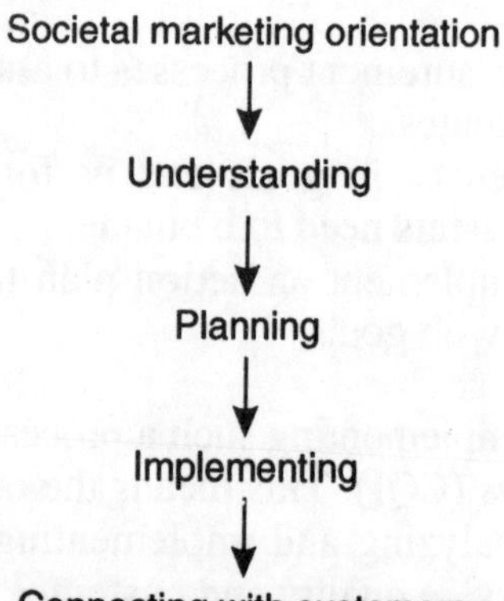

FIGURE 1.1. The Effective Marketing Management Process

turnover; market-share instability; a high cost of customer retention and acquisition; sporadic business unit profits and stagnant shareholder value; and managers under constant pressure to generate short-run results.[7] One can easily see why companies would want to become marketing oriented. However, committing to a societal marketing orientation is not a trivial undertaking. For many companies it means making a major philosophical shift in their thinking throughout the organization—not just among marketing managers. In fact, three fundamental forces drive the degree to which an organization actually does adopt a marketing orientation:[8]

Marketing knowledge—The extent to which managers and employees throughout the organization have been educated in marketing thought. For example, the Walt Disney Company requires all new employees to take a four-day course in how to treat customers, even if they are hired to sweep the streets at Disney World.

Marketing leadership—Being marketing oriented begins at the top of an organization. If senior management merely gives lip service to a marketing orientation, but manages with a product orientation, for example, it will be next to impossible for a true marketing orientation to flourish in that company.

Employee satisfaction—Employers cannot expect employees who are ill-treated to go to heroic lengths to satisfy customers (top management speeches on customer service to the contrary). Sears, for example, found a high correlation between employee job satisfaction, customer satisfaction, and store profitability.[9]

Practicing a marketing orientation demands a restructuring of what is considered most important in the organization's operations and changing how things are done. One of the most obvious pieces of evidence that an organization has adopted a marketing orientation is the emphasis managers place on the next step in the process.

Understanding

Organizations practicing a societal marketing orientation "determine the needs, wants, and interests of target markets and . . . deliver the desired satisfactions more effectively and efficiently than competitors in a way that preserves or enhances the consumer's and society's well-being."[10] Therefore, organizations guided by this philosophy make it a high priority to *understand* before they develop and implement plans. They understand the market, their competition, and the financial consequences of different marketing programs before settling on a planned course of action.

At the heart of the marketing manager's role in an organization is analysis of the firm's operating environment. The manager must understand the forces that influence the actions that can be taken by an individual firm. This is accomplished through research and analysis. The marketing research function is at the core of marketing analysis. Marketing research includes procedures and techniques involved in the design, data collection, analysis, and presentation of information used in making marketing decisions. The purpose of marketing research is to reduce uncertainty or potential error in decision making. The degree of uncertainty surrounding a decision, the importance of the decision, and the amount of uncertainty the information will reduce give information value.

Two basic types of data can be used in decision making: secondary and primary. *Secondary data* have been collected for another purpose and already exist. *Primary data* are collected for a specific purpose or research project and are used if no appropriate secondary data exist.

Some organizations have focused attention on creating marketing information systems (MIS) that provide a continuous flow of information to managers. Marketing research projects, the company's internal system of reports on sales, orders, receivables, etc., environmental input, and computerized decision-support systems can help in decision making. The marketing information system can provide insights on market segmentation, customer profiles and relationships, and products to assist in obtaining additional profit from a company's existing base of customers. A company's marketing database can provide timely, comprehensive information about current or prospective customers in order to maintain closer customer relationships and increased sales. Desktop marketing communication systems allow companies to communicate through microcomputer-based publishing. Database marketing research was designed to facilitate marketing functions such as direct mail, telemarketing, cross selling, and target-marketing research.

The understanding of such research and information processes is intended to include an understanding of market segments, competition, and the financial implications of management decisions.

Market Segment Analysis

A firm needs to identify the most attractive market segments that it can serve effectively. Instead of trying to be all things to all people, marketers must identify broad classes of buyers who differ in their product requirements and/or marketing responses and develop marketing mixes aimed at these buyers. This involves market segmentation and target marketing.

Consumer and organizational markets can be segmented in many different ways. When segmenting consumer markets three approaches are used:

1. Research-based segmentation
2. Existing segmentation services
3. Managerial judgment

Once segments have been identified, distinct marketing mixes can then be used to target different markets. All market segments are not equally attractive.

Target marketing involves evaluating the market segments, selecting appropriate segments, and positioning. When evaluating segments the marketer must consider size and growth patterns, attractiveness, competition for each segment, and potential profitability of the markets. After evaluating the different options, a company must decide which segments, if any, to select for targeting its marketing effort. The final step involves positioning. Product positioning is the act of designing the company's offering to attract customers in the chosen segment.

Competitive Analysis

Understanding competitors is crucial to effective marketing. A company must compare its products, prices, distribution, and promotion with those of close competitors to discern areas of potential competitive advantage and disadvantage. A company should take five steps in analyzing its competitors.

First, a company should identify its competitors. A competitor can be a company that offers similar products and services, makes the same product or class of products, manufactures products that supply the same service (i.e., addresses the same need), and/or competes for the same customer dollars (i.e., addresses the same customer need).

Competitors can be identified from industry and market points of view. An industry is a group of firms offering products that are close substitutes for one another. Industry performance is based on industry conduct, which is influenced by industry structure. The market approach to competitor identification deals with companies that are trying to serve the same customer group. The key to identifying competitors is to link industry and market analysis to products used to satisfy customer needs by segment.

Second, a company should identify competitor strategies. The more a firm's strategy resembles another firm's strategy, the more closely they compete.

Third, a company must determine competitor objectives. Knowing competitor objectives allows a company to know whether the competitor is satisfied with its current financial results and how it might react to certain types of competitive attacks.

Fourth, a company needs to assess competitor strengths and weaknesses. This involves analyzing competitor sales, market share, profit margin, return on investment, cash flow, new investments, and capacity utilization.

Finally, a company should try to determine competitor reaction patterns. Some industries are characterized by little direct competition; others experience fierce competition.

Information about a company's competitors must be collected and disseminated within the firm. The company must design an intelligence system to constantly analyze competitors and provide information to managers who use the information as an input to planning.

Financial Analysis

Marketing managers must also understand the financial impact of different marketing decisions intended to put the societal marketing orientation into practice. Financial analysis of marketing programs covers three different facets: revenue, cost, and profitability. One way to combine these three elements is to use a pro forma income statement, which is a projected statement for a specific time period using estimates of revenues and costs. It provides an estimate of future cash flows by a given market segment which can be discounted to determine the present value of the cash flows and the return on investment.

Revenue analysis involves trying to determine how many consumers will buy a product or service offering. For established markets, anticipated market share can be estimated and converted to a unit quantity and dollar amount. This is the sales revenue expected in a given time period. The key to obtaining an accurate estimate is careful judgment based on an analysis of your own offering versus competitive offerings. Competitive strengths and weaknesses in the market will be reflected in this basic estimate.

Cost analysis must be based on dependable estimates and a clear understanding of the different cost categories: period, product, fixed, variable and semivariable, direct and indirect, controllable, sunk, differential, and opportunity.

A company's historical records can provide much of the cost data needed for this analysis. Many other resources can provide information to form the basis of a reliable cost forecast. For example, trade publications, time studies, experiments, pilot plant or process activities, historical cost data, and interviews are all reliable data sources.

Risk analysis is the process used to identify and assign a degree of likelihood to changes in important variables that may be essential in determining the feasibility of a project or venture. Risk analysis includes the process of cost forecasting and forecasting procedures. The process of cost forecasting includes establishing a forecasting checklist and a project cost summary. Forecasting procedures include judgment techniques, survey techniques, historical data techniques, trend analysis, multiple regression, and percent of sales.

Profitability analysis defines the exact nature of an opportunity. One of the major objectives of all the time, energy, and resources used for a project is to generate a "good" profit. Two basic types of profitability analysis may be conducted: *return on investment,* which is how much the investment returns on an annual basis; and *financial analysis and capital budgeting,* which consists of the process of selecting among alternative investments in land, buildings, productive equipment, or other assets on the basis of future gain.

Many methods are available to evaluate investment alternatives prior to making the capital budgeting decision. They can be divided into two categories, nontime methods and time-value methods. Nontime methods include payback period (how long it will take for the investment to pay for itself); simple return on investment (the desirability of an investment in terms of a percentage return); and average return on investment (the measure of the estimated profitability of an investment).

Planning

Classes in marketing planning or strategy are required course work for aspiring marketing managers at accredited business schools. Likewise, books and seminars intended to aid practitioners in the development of marketing plans are very popular. This is because development of a well-grounded marketing plan is believed by most successful practitioners and theorists to be a prerequisite for success in today's hypercompetitive global marketplace. Although most marketers acknowledge the importance of effective planning, the model in Figure 1.1 indicates that this is the third stage of the process, not the first. Furthermore, such an orientation requires that the understanding about the marketplace must have a direct material influence on the content of those plans. Without the commitment to implementing the prior steps in the model, it becomes very easy to become so embroiled in the planning process that the voice of the market can become drowned out by all the "good creative ideas" spontaneously emerging during the process. Although not all ideas must have marketplace studies as their genesis, good ideas owe their "goodness" to the fact that they will ultimately help the company connect with the market, which reinforces the need for both accurate understanding and effective planning.

Marketing planning is conducted at two levels: the strategic level and the operating level.

Strategic Planning

Strategic planning is the responsibility of top management. Operational marketing plans are the direct responsibility of all marketing managers and involve short-term actions that help achieve long-term objectives.

Because strategic decisions have a long-term impact on the organization, strategic management is needed. Strategic management involves a three-step process. Step one defines the corporate purpose or mission with a written statement which spells out the uniqueness that has led to the creation of the business.

The second step is to develop a set of corporate objectives. An objective is a statement of what is to be accomplished by an organization. Three basic objectives are (1) to engage in a business activity that is economically and socially useful, (2) to maintain and survive as a business entity, and (3) to grow in size of operation.

The third step is to determine the overall corporate strategies which will be used to accomplish objectives. The organization tries to match its capabilities and skills with the key requirements of the market in order to take advantage of an existing opportunity. Designing strategies involves identifying options, assessing these options, and selecting the most appropriate strategy or strategies.

Several techniques are available for more effective planning of strategic business units (SBUs). For example, a matrix developed by the Boston Consulting Group classifies SBUs on the basis of their reiative market share and growth potential and offers guidance in assigning resources to each unit. General Electric pioneered a more comprehensive matrix based on long-term market or industry attractiveness and the business strength or competitive position of each SBU. The GE matrix provides nine cells and three zones by which SBUs may be classified leading to appropriate marketing decisions for the portfolios based on each unit's status or ranking.

Operational Marketing Plans

The operational marketing plan contains the overall strategic approaches to marketing within an SBU. It is derived from the corporate strategic plan. Several steps are involved in preparing an operational marketing plan. First, a detailed analysis of the SBU's situation should be done. This includes the product-market definition, customer analysis, key competitor analysis, environmental analysis, and marketing strategy assessment.

Second, management should indicate objectives for each market target. Firms also need various operating objectives to provide performance guidelines for each marketing mix component.

Third is the development of the marketing strategy. This involves deciding on the specific way to combine the marketing variables to satisfy the needs of market targets and accomplish the objectives of the organization. The selection of a marketing strategy moves the planning process to preparation of the actual plan and its supporting sales forecast and budget. Preparing the plan involves selecting the planning cycle and frequency, deciding the nature and use of the annual plan, choosing a format for the plan, and forecasting revenues and estimating expenses. To satisfy customer needs, marketers must develop a marketing strategy consisting of a combination of marketing variables called the marketing mix. The marketing mix is the set of controllable variables generally referred to as the four "Ps" of marketing—product, place, price, and promotion.

As shown in Figure 1.2, marketing mix decisions are made with a particular market segment in mind. Marketing effort is targeted at the selected segments by blending the elements into a cohesive strategy aimed at satisfying those specific segments. Organizations targeting several segments must develop an overall marketing program that includes all of its marketing activities.

Implementing

A good plan with great implementation is better than a great plan with only good implementation. Putting well-conceived plans into effect is one of the most demanding aspects of marketing management. No customer is satisfied, no contribution is made to the betterment of society, and no organization makes a profit by *developing* a plan. It is only when the well-conceived plan is *implemented* that all these objectives are possible. However, there is a huge difference between just doing something and doing the right things well. Implementation consists of putting into practice those strategies developed from an understanding of the market. That understanding occurs because the philosophy makes its achievement mandatory.

Implementation involves organizing the marketing effort, selecting the right personnel, and creating a culture of teamwork and achievement.

In organizing the marketing department, four basic dimensions of marketing activity must be accommodated: functions, geographic areas, products, and customer markets. The most common form of mar-

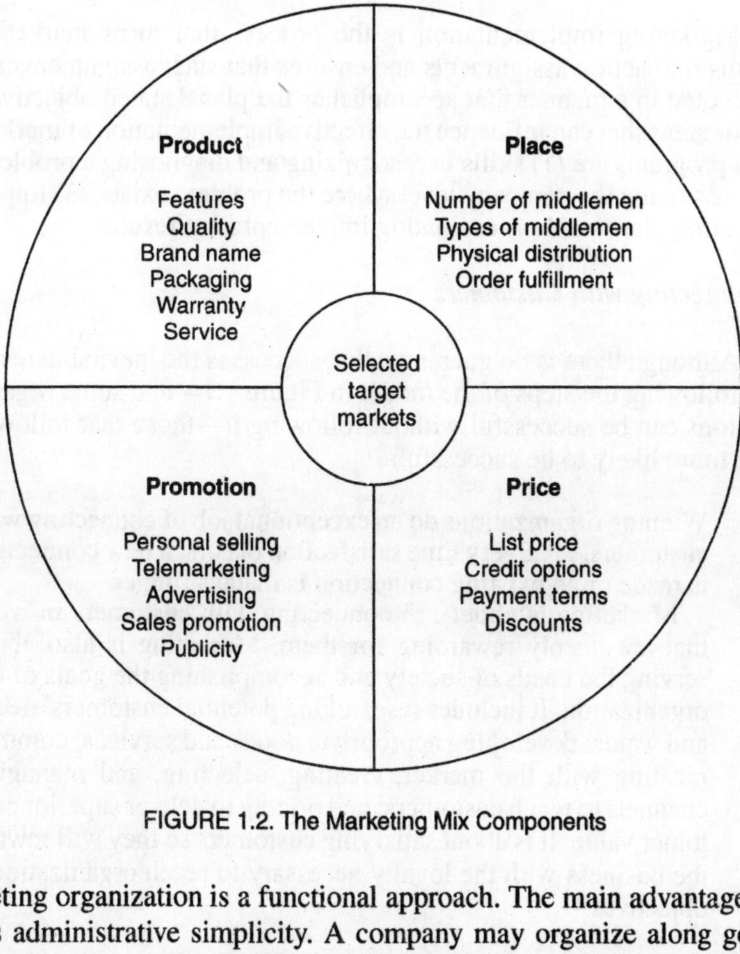

FIGURE 1.2. The Marketing Mix Components

keting organization is a functional approach. The main advantage is its administrative simplicity. A company may organize along geographic lines such as setting up its sales force by region when it is selling in a national market. Companies producing a variety of products and/or brands often establish a product or brand management organization. In order to make the product management system work better, a company can use a five-step approach, or it can switch from a product manager to a product team approach, with vertical, triangular, or horizontal product teams. A market management organization sells products to a diverse set of markets. Companies that produce many products flowing into many markets can use a product-management or a market-management system.

Marketing implementation is the process that turns marketing plans into action assignments and ensures that such assignments are executed in a manner that accomplishes the plans' stated objectives. Four areas that can influence the effective implementation of marketing programs are (1) skills in recognizing and diagnosing a problem, (2) assessing the company level where the problem exists, (3) implementing plans, and (4) evaluating implementation results.

Connecting with Customers

Although there is no guarantee that success is the inevitable result of following the steps of the model in Figure 1.1—and some organizations can be successful without following it—those that follow it are more likely to be successful:

> Winning organizations do an exceptional job of connecting with customers. . . . Every time satisfaction occurs, a new connection is made or an existing connection is made stronger.
>
> Marketing is about . . . connecting with customers in ways that are deeply rewarding for them. Marketing is also about serving the needs of society and accomplishing the goals of the organization. It includes researching potential customers' needs and wants; developing appropriate goods and services; communicating with the market; creating, selecting, and managing channels to reach customers; and pricing to deliver superior customer value. It is about satisfying customers so they will reward the business with the loyalty necessary to reach organizational objectives.[11]

Connecting does not happen by chance; it is the end result of a series of complex activities in which marketers engage because they are committed to a philosophy that highly values that connection and its salubrious impact on society.

Marketers are responsible not only for ensuring that the organization successfully connects with its target markets but also for determining *how well* the organization has connected. This involves evaluation and control of marketing activities.

The marketing department must engage in continuous monitoring and control of marketing activities. Despite the need for effective control, many companies have inadequate procedures. Marketing evaluation and control are needed in three areas: sales, costs, and profitability. The overall effectiveness of the marketing function can also be evaluated through a marketing audit.

By using sales analysis, market-share analysis, marketing expense-to-sales analysis, and financial analysis, management can do a performance diagnosis and then take corrective action to close any gaps between its goals and performance.

Companies must measure the profitability of their various products, territories, customer groups, trade channels, and order sizes to help management determine whether any products or marketing activities should be expanded, reduced, or eliminated. Firms should attempt to develop profit-and-loss statements by products, territories, etc. Then the best corrective action can be evaluated.

Companies should periodically review their overall marketing effectiveness with a marketing audit. A marketing audit is a comprehensive, systematic review of a firm's marketing environment, objectives, strategies, and activities with a goal of determining problem areas and opportunities and recommending a plan of action to improve the company's marketing performance.

An expanded version of the effective marketing management process model appears in Figure 1.3 with corresponding chapters and topics.

THE ENVIRONMENT OF MARKETING DECISIONS

Marketing decisions are made within a specific operating environment influenced by several factors. These factors can be divided into two groups: internal and external. The internal factors include the resources and objectives of the organization, organization purpose and strategy, and values of top management. The external environmental factors include social and cultural climate; the economic competition; the state of technology that affects its products and services; political/legal climate; and demographics. Some of the potential inputs of these external factors on marketing decisions are shown in Table 1.4.

The sociocultural environment of the organization is made up of the cultural and social structure of the countries where the organization markets its products. These influences include social institutions,

Societal marketing orientation
Marketing management orientations: Chapter 1

↓

Understanding
Customers (market segments): Chapter 2
Competition: Chapter 3
Financial implications: Chapter 4

↓

Planning
Strategic planning: Chapter 5
Operational planning: Chapter 6

↓

Implementing
Implementation issues: Chapter 7

↓

Connecting with customers
Evaluation and control issues: Chapter 8

FIGURE 1.3. The Effective Marketing Management Process

values, beliefs, and behaviors. Marketers must study these elements of the environment when developing marketing strategy.

The demographic environment is comprised of the size, distribution, and composition of people and organizations. Market growth, movement, buying behavior, and delineation by age, sex, education, marital status, and occupation must be studied and reflected in the choice of market segments and marketing strategy.

Technology affects marketing programs in three important ways: research and development (R&D) to develop new products, R&D to improve the designing and manufacturing processes, and the development of new means for performing the marketing functions themselves.

The economic environment consists of the changing patterns of government, industrial, and consumer expenditures, income and savings, and investment levels. These patterns are determined by level of personal incomes, consumption expenditures, changes in levels of personal savings, inflation, prosperity and recession, and interest rates. The competitive environment consists of the number, nature, and strategies of competitors and their actions and reactions. All these must be analyzed to determine their effect on marketing programs.

TABLE 1.4. External Environmental Influences on Marketing Decisions

Environmental factor	Marketing areas affected	Examples
Sociocultural	Consumer behavior—products and services consumed, collection and use of information, values, and ideas or product/services	Health consciousness, environmental awareness, use of language and symbols
Demographic	Target market—size, income, location, expenditure patterns, decision makers	Growth in the Sunbelt states, higher median age, graying of America, higher median incomes
Economic/competitive	Consumer behavior and marketing strategy—employment, inflation, industry growth or decline, new competitors, markets sought, marketing mix changes	Increased expenditures on leisure activities, high consumer confidence, new forms of competition
Technological	Consumer behavior and marketing strategy—acquisition and use of information by consumers, changes in marketing mix variables	Development of database marketing, Internet marketing, and electronic banking
Political/legal	Marketing strategy and specific variables—price changes, labeling, product testing, promotional techniques, marketing, etc.	Bans on tobacco advertising and antismoking campaigns, nutrition labeling of products, and control on Internet marketing

The political and legal environment affects marketing in a variety of ways. The legal environment consists of laws and regulations that affect the operations of firms. Laws and regulations govern product safety, warranties of products and services, pricing of products and services, the granting of credit, advertising and promotion, and distribution of products.

GLOBAL ORIENTATIONS TO MARKETING DECISIONS

Globalization of business activities has caused a change in market decisions. Marketing managers must learn to think and act in a world that is continually being connected through product and information flows. The importance of global markets to some U.S. firms can be seen in Table 1.5. This table shows that many U.S. companies derive a significant share of their revenues from foreign markets. As international markets account for larger and larger shares of many organizations, marketers must learn to adapt their strategies to compete effectively.

The external environment must be thoroughly researched to ensure that effective strategies used in one country are appropriate for other countries. Product designs, promotional appeals, distribution strategies, and pricing strategies may require considerable adjustment prior to entry into the international market.

For example, a Wendy's restaurant in the Orient may add local products such as noodles or rice to its menu to satisfy consumers. Failing to do so may result in a loss of business because it does not reflect the local culture and its values.

TABLE 1.5. Percent of Total Revenues from Foreign Sales for Selected Companies in 2002

Company	Total sales from foreign markets (%)
Compaq Computers	71.5
GE	69.7
Xerox	66.0
Coca-Cola	59.3
Lucent Technologies	59.3
IBM	56.9
American International Group	50.1
Hewlett-Packard	49.4
Intel	49.9
Motorola	47.3
United Technologies	47.2
Procter & Gamble	45.9
Johnson & Johnson	41.5

Source: Company data.

ETHICAL ORIENTATION TO MARKETING DECISIONS

In recent years, increasing attention has been focused on creating an organizational environment with a high concern for ethics. Ethics are principles of right or good conduct, or a body of such principles. Ethical issues in marketing can be categorized in one of two areas: individual-marketing-decision-related and collective-marketing-decision-related issues. Some individual marketing decisions may lead to unethical practices, although they may help the company. Collective marketing decisions may result in no ethical infraction in and of themselves. However, they may contribute to problems in combination with similar decisions over time or by other marketers such as the environmental impact of packaging.

The American Marketing Association (AMA) has led in the development of ethical standards of behavior among its members through the use of a code of ethics. Not only are general areas covered, such as honesty and fairness, but specific attention is devoted to the marketing mix variables.

The growth and the impact of the Internet on marketing activities have prompted the AMA's development of a code of ethics dealing specifically with this marketing tool. The code focuses on privacy, ownership, and access to infrastructure. These are the key areas of concern for ethical standards of conducting marketing or marketing research on the Internet. Both of the AMA Codes of Ethics may be found at <http://www.marketingpower.com>.

E-COMMERCE AND MARKETING PRINCIPLES

Conventional wisdom might suggest that the advent and growth of e-commerce or Internet marketing has altered the rules of the marketing game. Although successful use of the Net has been a challenge to all types of marketers, marketing principles have not been fundamentally altered as a result. Marketers are still trying to factor the use of the Internet into marketing programs and their marketing mix (e.g., product, price, promotion, and channel of distribution decisions), and efforts to integrate the Internet into marketing planning come with their own set of unique challenges and opportunities. However, marketing management principles are flexible enough to accommodate something as radically influential as e-commerce without losing their basic validity. For example, marketing management tasks consist of understanding, planning, implementing, connecting, and control; effective marketing management focuses on quality, value, relationships, and customer satisfaction. These are enduring principles that remain unchanged by the growing importance of the Internet. Rather, modern marketing management must find ways to creatively merge the use of the Internet with marketing strategies grounded in an understanding of consumer behavior, marketplace dynamics, and environmental influences. This book focuses on modern marketing processes that provide a foundation for future marketing managers. As with all learning, an individual's success will ultimately depend upon how well he or she can apply knowledge.

SUMMARY

The effective marketing management process is simple to describe but considerably more difficult to perform. A focus on quality, value, relationships, and customer satisfaction in the new millennium has resulted in a highly competitive marketplace. More than ever, marketing managers must effectively execute the stages of the marketing management process if organizations are to connect with customers. The environment, global concerns, and a need to practice ethical marketing provide the backdrop for this process. Chapter 2 begins the three-chapter sequence of *understanding* the market, competition, and financial implications—the first steps that marketing-oriented managers take in their efforts to ultimately connect with customers.

Chapter 2

Customer Analysis

This chapter, as are Chapters 3 and 4, is devoted to the second step of the successful marketing management process: understanding (see Figure 2.1). These three chapters encompass the market analysis phases of the marketing process and the relationship between these phases is shown in Figure 2.2. Chapter 2 introduces the concept of identifying and selectively marketing to market segments. Chapter 3 discusses the analysis of competitive forces, and Chapter 4 discusses the financial analysis of marketing decisions.

INTRODUCTION TO MARKET SEGMENTATION

Our discussion of market segmentation begins with the following somewhat surprising bits of due diligence:

- Nobody makes money by segmenting a market (except for marketing research suppliers). You make money by establishing profitable, long-term, highly satisfying exchange relationships with brand-loyal customers. Market segmentation is merely a device created by marketers to more efficiently and effectively generate such relationships.
- Market segments do not actually exist. Or perhaps it is more accurate to say that marketers try to impose their approach to structuring a market upon a market that has no universal, naturally occurring structure to it. Markets are not like the animal kingdom with its universally understood natural "segments" of genus, subgenus, and species. If segments exist in a market, they are there because a marketer has constructed them, hopefully by tapping into marketplace realities.

Societal marketing orientation

↓

Understanding

Customers (market segments): Chapter 2

Competition: Chapter 3

Financial implications: Chapter 4

↓

Planning

↓

Implementing

↓

Connecting with customers

FIGURE 2.1. The Effective Marketing Management Process

Identify market segments
and develop a profile of each segment

↓

Develop a forecast of market
potential for each segment

↓

Analyze competitive forces
in each segment

↓

Analyze sales, costs, profitability,
and return on investment
for each segment

↓

Select target marketing segments
and develop positioning and
marketing mixes for each group

FIGURE 2.2. Market Analysis Process

The truthfulness of this second point is supported by your own experience as a consumer: You have been classified by domestic and foreign marketers into hundreds, if not thousands, of market segments, yet you do not define yourself in any way by these segment memberships. For example, you are simultaneously a member of the heavy-use ice-cream-eating segment, the price-shopper clothing segment, the outdoor-sports-activist segment, and hundreds of other segments because marketers have found it useful to categorize you in such a way for marketing planning purposes. Sometimes you are grouped in the same segment as your peers or neighbors; sometimes you are put in different segments. In every case, marketers understand how to better think about a market's structure in ways that reflect the realities of how consumers can be grouped together so that a marketing appeal can connect with the people in the targeted segment. The rationale for segmenting a market as a prerequisite for marketing planning is therefore based on the following assumptions:

1. Not everyone in the market is looking for the same things from the product or service. That is, a specific marketing appeal will not connect equally well with all consumers in a market.
2. It is better to establish very successful connections with a portion of the people in a market than to only marginally connect with everyone.
3. To be very successful with your portion of the market you must be able to identify them, understand them in-depth, and then use that understanding to develop highly satisfying goods and services.
4. People prefer to give their business to companies who seek to understand the consumers who occupy the market segments, and then develop satisfying marketing offerings upon that understanding.

If any of these four assumptions is invalid, market segmentation may not prove as profitable as mass marketing appeals (i.e., treating all consumers as the same and marketing the same product to everyone). However, these assumptions hold true for the vast majority of markets, whether business to consumer (B2C) or business to business (B2B) in nature.

In addition to these assumptions, marketers also use a set of criteria to determine whether segmentation, targeting, and positioning are worthwhile exercises in developing marketing programs.[1]

1. *Sizable*—Any segmentation of a market must generate segments of a size (sales revenues) sufficient to be of interest to the marketer. If the resulting sizes are too small, segmentation may not be worthwhile.

2. *Identifiable*—Segments arising from this process should have characteristics that allow for easy description and correspond to the marketers' general observations. For example, if a study of the toothpaste market generated segments that could be described as "cosmetic" (seek dazzling white teeth), "economy" (look for lowest price), "worrier" (want decay prevention), and "sociables" (want fresh breath), then marketers have identified those characteristics of segments that make it easier for planning purposes.

3. *Reachable*—Marketers want to be able to identify the segments but also to reach them *selectively,* that is, without having to talk to the entire market to reach a particular segment's consumers. Therefore, if "romantic couples" is the target segment, the marketer would look for media patterns that these couples have in common within the segment. This allows for a promotional campaign that could speak to them without wasting resources on people who have no interest in the market offering.

4. *Respond differently*—Marketers want to develop a segmentation scheme for the market that results in different "sweet spots." In other words, what appeals to the members of one segment will be common within that segment but different from what consumers in another segment find appealing.

5. *Coherent*—Ideally, members within a particular segment are homogeneous along several attitudinal, behavioral, and other dimensions, which are useful in developing marketing programs, but they are heterogeneous with respect to other segments. In this way a marketer can maximize effectiveness by choosing a customized appeal for each segment that is uniquely capable of connecting with its members.

6. *Stable*—Although this criterion is not absolute (no segment will remain perfectly stable forever), hopefully, the formation of the segments and the resulting marketing programs will have a lifetime sufficiently long to allow for profitable connections over a reasonable length of time.

If, by segmenting a market, the marketer is correctly assuming that the four assumptions hold true, and he or she finds that the resulting segments pass these six criteria, then segmentation can lead to several benefits:

Effectiveness—Marketers can better connect with a group of consumers whose common needs are better understood and are not highly diffuse.

Efficiency—Marketers get more "bang for the buck" when they can concentrate on smaller, more responsive segments instead of larger diverse markets.

Loyalty—Developing marketing programs that communicate to the consumer that the marketer really understands them and has used that understanding to deliver highly satisfying offerings leads to loyal consumers seeking to maintain long-term relationships.

Now that we have established a strong theoretical support for the value of segmenting a market, the natural question is, "Does segmentation really work in the real world? Are companies that segment markets actually better off from having done it?" Consider the following case of Mobil Oil (prior to its merger with Exxon), a company selling gasoline, a product that is best described as an undifferentiated commodity.[2]

Mobil Oil Company had always assumed it was marketing gasoline and related services to a mass market of consumers whose sole motivation for choosing where to fill up was finding the lowest price. Losses in its retailing business forced Mobil to challenge this conventional wisdom for explaining marketplace behavior, and led it to conduct a survey of 2,000 motorists. Among other things, the study revealed that five segments existed in the market:

Road warriors: They are higher-income males of middle age who drive up to 50,000 miles per year, use premium gas, use the car wash, and buy convenience food items from the service station (16 percent of the market).

True blues: Men and women with moderate to high incomes, brand loyal, pay for premium gas with cash (16 percent of buyers).

Generation F3: They want fuel and food fast; these upwardly mobile males and females are constantly on the go, are young (under age twenty-five), and buy a lot of snack foods at the service station (27 percent of the market).

Homebodies: The second largest segment, these are usually "soccer moms" who buy gas wherever they are when they need it (21 percent of market).

Price shoppers: These buyers are not brand loyal, are on tight budgets, and do not buy premium gas (20 percent of the market).

Strategic analysis of these five segments resulted in targeting only the first three segments. This meant that Mobil was trying to improve its profits by ignoring 41 percent of the market! Its strategy was to raise prices but improve services ("friendly serve"). Revenues improved as much as 25 percent at some of the stations implementing the new strategy.

This case illustrates the dramatic positive effect that can occur in both strategy and financial results when a company seeks to understand a market through segmentation analysis and then uses that understanding to develop plans to improve the satisfaction of consumers in the targeted segments.

So segmentation works. We now describe how segmentation is done.

METHODS OF SEGMENTING MARKETS

Segmentation uses one of three methods:

Research-based segmentation—The Mobil case was an example of this approach. Consumers are screened to ensure they are members of the market under study, then surveyed to determine their attitudes, behaviors, motives, preferences, etc. Multivariate statistical analysis of the research results is conducted to then reveal the number and characteristics of market segments.

Existing segmentation services—In this approach, the marketer uses an existing segmentation service or system to identify market segments that can be evaluated for making targeting decisions. These systems may either be commercial systems, such as the geodemographic systems, or governmental, such as the North American Industry Classification Systems (NAICS). In either case, the segments are already established before the marketer buys the information, so this approach lacks the customization of the research-based method.

Managerial judgment—In this approach, the marketer uses his or her knowledge of the market and industry to identify segments. The marketer's insight and skill at using existing information are key in generating good results from this approach.

Each of these approaches is successfully used by firms in a variety of industries for segmentation purposes. Although each has its advantages and disadvantages, no single approach can be said to be best under all circumstances. Each of these methods is described next.

RESEARCH-BASED SEGMENTATION

Although it offers a highly customized method of segmentation based upon extensive up-to-date market data, research-based segmentation demands a high degree of expertise in research methodology and analysis, and can be very expensive and time-consuming. Typically, for first-time market segmentation, the process begins with qualitative market research followed by a large-scale quantitative survey (Mobil's study of 2,000 consumers is typical of research scope), which is analyzed using multivariate statistical computer software packages. Worthington Foods' study of the vegetarian market exemplifies this approach.

A Case Study in Research-Based Segmentation

Worthington Foods, now owned by Kellogg, produces a line of prepared foods from textured vegetable protein (TVP) (primarily made from soy). In more than fifty years of serving the vegetarian market, the company had never performed any studies to determine whether the market structure was best thought of as a mass market or if distinct segments existed within the market. Whether one thinks of the vegetarian market with segments, or the vegetarian segment with niches, the question remains the same: Would mass marketing or a segmentation, targeting, and positioning strategy be best? If the four segmentation assumptions apply and the six criteria fit in this case, the company would in all likelihood benefit from market segmentation. Worthington decided to conduct a research study of vegetarians and people who do not classify themselves as vegetarian but who are cutting back on the amount of meat they eat to lower their cholesterol intake. A series of focus groups helped to identify the kinds of questions that should be included in the quantitative survey. Because these two types of consumer groups may be hard (i.e., expensive) to find in the general population, Worthington used a consumer panel (i.e., 50,000 members of Market Facts consumer mail panel of over 600,000 U.S. households) to first screen for vegetarianism or reduced meat consumption, and then sent a twelve-page questionnaire to 2,000 of those people fitting these characteristics. Segmentation studies of this type typically ask questions intended to determine respondent attitudes, behaviors, preferences, motivations, benefits sought, psychographics/lifestyle questions, satisfaction with current products, intentions to try new products, shopping and media patterns, sources of information, and demographic data for households. In the Worthington case, five vegetarian and four meat-reducing segments were formed based on an analysis of attitudinal questions that were answered on a six-point scale:

Agree completely	Agree somewhat	Agree slightly	Disagree slightly	Disagree somewhat	Disagree completely
6	5	4	3	2	1

Table 2.1 shows the resulting segments and the percentage of the market each segment comprises. The term *meat alternatives* is the name given to the TVP products made by Worthington and other companies marketing these types of prepared foods.

How did these segments form? In the research-based approach to market segmentation, the questions about respondent attitudes, behaviors, motivations, demographics, etc., become "candidates" for being the basis of the segmentation scheme. Sometimes the marketer uses a statistical program such as regression to sort through these sets of variables to discover the set that does the best job of explaining a dependent variable of interest, such as consumption rate or likelihood

TABLE 2.1. Segments of the Vegetarian and Meat-Restricting Markets

Vegetarian market	% of market	Meat-restricting market	% of market
MA advocates	20	MA fans	26
Convenience driven	19	Time savers	26
Reluctant vegetarians	21	Meat lovers	29
Animal lovers	24	Natural nuts	19
MA opponents	16		

Note: MA = meat alternative

of purchase, which would have been included in the same survey. The set that has the highest explanatory value is then used as the basis for segmentation. Sometimes, based on past experience, the marketer will select one of the sets of variables as the segmentation base. In the Worthington case eighty-eight attitudinal questions were chosen as the segmentation base. Typically, once the variable set has been selected, it is processed through a data reduction program such as factor analysis that looks for response patterns in the way the questions were answered in order to group questions together that appear to be addressing a common theme. This accomplishes several worthwhile objectives. Instead of having to look at how 2,000 respondents answered eighty-eight attitude questions, eight different factors may arise from the factor analysis of the questions. Factors may, for example, include an emphasis on "convenience," another on "antimeat," another on "natural diet," and so on. One could try to eyeball the questions and group them together, but the factor analysis program processes the actual way the respondents answered the questions and determines the groupings.

Another benefit is that it is possible to compute a factor score for each respondent to each factor. For instance, respondent #1019 has a score for the convenience factor, the antimeat factor, and so on, which indicates how much he or she agreed to each of the sets of questions that constitute each factor. A high score for the convenience factor would indicate that respondent #1019 values the convenience of preparation of these food items to a significant degree. Factor analysis processes the scores for eight factors instead of eighty-eight questions. This determines how people can be best grouped together so that they are maximally similar to other people in terms of their factor scores and maximally different from the people in another group. In other words, the factor scores for the respondents become candidates for creating segments. For example, if you were a vegetarian respondent to the survey and you were put in the convenience-driven segment, the analysis would indicate that your desire for convenience dominates the way you think, feel, and act (the tricomponents of attitudes: cognitive, affective, and conative) toward these food products and your vegetarian lifestyle more than any of the other factors revealed by the data. Other people in your segment are very similar to you in this regard. This similarity pattern holds true for other respondents' memberships in their segments. Following are the questions that the factor analysis program grouped together for the convenience-driven factor (the questions were responded to with the six-point agreement scale previously shown):

________ I buy a lot of foods that are quick and easy to prepare.
________ I prefer buying products which can be cooked in a microwave.
________ I eat a lot of fast food.
________ There aren't enough prepared vegetarian foods available in grocery stores.
________ It's hard to find prepared foods for meat-restricting people.
________ Prepared foods are as healthy as meals made from scratch.
________ It's hard to find prepared foods for people on a vegetarian diet.
________ Vegetarian foods take a lot of time to prepare.

The label "convenience driven" for this segment seemed apt, given the high agreement with this set of attitudes that respondents in this segment had in common. The cluster analysis program seeks to find the smallest number of segments that group people around common responses within the segment, and maximize the differences with people in another segment (our homogeneous within, heterogenous between segment objective). In the Mobil case, a similar procedure was used to form the segments, then a descriptive label was used to capture the unique attributes of people in the segment.

Once segments have been grouped based on the variable used to form them (again, attitudes in this case), all the other variables can be used to profile the members of each segment. Although the members of the convenience-driven segment belong to that segment based on their answers to the attitude questions, we can see how members answered questions about behaviors, preferences, demographics, and intentions to determine if they have some of these things in common as well. Usually they do, which just confirms marketers' generally held belief that there is a strong connection between attitudes and behaviors (and lifestyles, preferences, etc.). The value of profiling of segments will be discussed in Chapter 6.

Worthington discovered, as did Mobil, that what was previously thought of as a mass market was really a market with distinct segments. Each segment is different from the others in ways significant for targeting and marketing planning purposes. This leads to effectiveness, efficiency, and brand loyalty if the company can capitalize on this new understanding of the market.

Clearly, the research-based approach to market segmentation can be a powerful tool in providing an understanding of the market, which leads to better planning. However, for this approach to be of maximum value in its contribution to the goal of connecting with customers, it must be based on good research—proper identification of the right research design, good questionnaire design, right sampling method and selection, proper use of statistical analysis, correct data interpretation—which require time, money, and expertise. Also, management must be willing to make targeting and positioning decisions based on the results and then quickly implement those decisions. If decision makers do not trust the research results to guide their decisions, one of the other methods for segmenting should be used.

EXISTING SEGMENTATION SYSTEMS

Managers who want to segment their markets for planning purposes but who do not have the resources or inclination to use a customized research study to identify segments can use existing segmentation systems. These systems have been developed either by commercial firms to sell to companies for use in making marketing plans or by the government. In either case, companies buying these services get "standardized" market segmentation schemes—the segments do not vary in composition by market or product type (e.g., you get the same segmentation scheme whether you are selling bicycles, wireless communications, or real estate). The advantage to using such a system is the wealth of information available describing the people or firms that occupy each segment. The best known of these systems for the consumer market are the geodemographic systems and SRI Consulting Business Intelligence's (SRIC-BI) Values and Lifestyle Survey (VALS) system. These two systems are described next, followed by the federal government's NAICS system for companies doing B2B marketing.

Consumer Markets

Geodemographic Systems

Claritas' PRIZM is perhaps the best known of the geodemographic segmentation systems that divide the U.S. population into specific lifestyle segments. All of these systems begin with U.S. census data and then add other databases to develop detailed descriptions of consumer segments. The PRIZM system divides the U.S. adult population into sixty-two separate lifestyle segments or "clusters" and ranks these clusters in socioeconomic order. They are given snappy names that reflect their ranking, such as Blue Blood Estates, Kids and Cul-de-Sacs, Bohemian Mix, and Shotguns and Pickups. Each residential address in the United States is classified into one of the segments based upon what the census data and other databases indicate as the socioeconomic, housing, and aggregated consumer demand information for that household. A Young Literati household in Portland, Maine, is more similar in the lifestyle to a Young Literati household in Portland, Oregon, than it is to a Shotguns and Pickups household located two miles away in the same city. Marketers can identify segments they wish to target and then get a map that shows the geographic areas where those segments are in highest concentration. They can also identify specific geographic areas they are desiring to penetrate and get a profile of the segments located in those areas. For example, PRIZM identifies the following segments present in the zip code 90210, Beverly Hills, California:

PRIZM rank	Segment name
1	Blue Blood Estates
2	Winner's Circle
7	Money + Brains
10	Bohemian Mix

The Blue Blood Estates are described as follows:

Elite, superrich families
Age group: 45-64
Professionally employed
1.2 percent of U.S. households belong to this segment

They are likely to:

- belong to a health club
- visit Eastern Europe
- buy classical music
- watch *Wall Street Week*
- read *Architectural Digest*

This is merely a sampling of the detailed information available for the segments.

Over 20,000 companies have used Claritas' PRIZM system to identify segments for target marketing purposes. Cox Communications is an example of how one company successfully used PRIZM.

> Cox Communications is a nationwide cable TV service that wanted to increase the number of households using its pay-per-view (PPV) service. It decided to launch a direct mail campaign in 12 of the cable TV geographic markets it serves. Of the 12 markets, most simply sent a mass mailing to those households which had never ordered PPV. In the Phoenix, AZ market Cox used Claritas' PRIZM segmentation system to help identify segments to target with its mailing. PRIZM analysis identified 14 of the 62 clusters (segments) that had high PPV usage. They created a mailing list of 41,000 of their 600,000 customers that belonged to these 14 clusters, and sent either 99¢ or $1.99 coupons to those targeted households. The coupons were coded so that responses to the campaign could be tracked. Results? The PRIZM targeted households in Phoenix had the highest response rate of all 12 markets involved in the campaign, even though the Phoenix market had considerably fewer direct mail pieces sent than in the other markets. Also, nearly 20 percent of the responders were repeat buyers in the following month.[3]

Some companies have found even greater value from using PRIZM when they combine it with segmentation information discovered in their own market surveys (i.e., combining the research-based approach with the existing segmentation system approach). Sodexho Marriott is an example of this hybrid method.

> Sodexho Marriott, a food service provider, used the PRIZM segmentation system for a nationwide college food program. Since there were no "off-the-

shelf" segmentation systems for student populations, Sodexho crafted its own—called LifeSTYLING—linking into PRIZM's household clusters to quickly and easily identify student segments by plugging in their zip codes. Adding customized information developed from a series of student surveys, the system identified the predominant food and dining preferences within a school's diverse population.

The mix of student segments, unique for each campus, was used to shape a particular school's meal services—including menus, dining environments, branding, development, product selection, marketing, and merchandising. Sodexho has used its LifeSTYLING segmentation system at more than forty colleges and universities and the student segments have proven to be on target regardless of the school's geographic location or focus. It has also uncovered some surprising niches.

At one university in the rural northeast, LifeSTYLING revealed a strong showing of students interested in foods and dining options with a global flair. So, at Sodexho's recommendation, the university's food service program installed a Starbucks coffee and pastry kiosk that gained immediate popularity among students.[4]

Claritas and its geodemographic competitors have developed a variety of proprietary software programs to help clients customize the segmentation systems to fit their needs. A detailed discussion of Claritas' segmentation services can be found at <www.claritas.com>.

VALS

SRI Consulting Business Intelligence's VALS was first established in 1978 as a consumer segmentation system based on lifestyle characteristics. In 1989 VALS2 was established to focus on consumer purchase behavior for advertising and marketing applications. VALS2 categorizes the U.S. adult population into eight mutually exclusive groups based on their psychology and several key demographics. They promote their segmentation service as allowing marketers to:[5]

- identify who to target;
- uncover what your target group buys and does;
- locate where concentrations of your target group live;
- identify how to communicate with your target group; and
- gain insight into why the target group acts the way it does.

A survey of thirty-five attitudinal and four demographic questions is used to classify people into one of the eight segments. Product usage and media data for the segments are available through VALS' link with the database from Simmons Market Research Bureau and other consumer databases. VALS differs from the geodemographic segmentation systems by classifying people into segments based upon attitudinal surveys of a sample of the population which permits classification into the eight segments. However, the geodemographers have up to sixty-plus lifestyle segments, which offer finer distinctions among segments, compared to the eight offered by VALS. The choice between VALS and PRIZM would depend upon the particular product and market, as well as the future segmentation needs of the marketer. Both systems have been used successfully for market segmentation, targeting, and positioning purposes.

Business Markets

NAICS

The North American Industry Classification System (NAICS, pronounced "nakes") replaced the Standard Industrial Classification (SIC) system in 1997. NAICS was jointly developed by the United States, Mexico, and Canada to provide comparable business statistics for these three North American Free Trade Agreement (NAFTA) countries. A North American Product Classification System (NAPCS) will initially focus on service industries, and will later include manufacturing products. The NAICS covers over 350 new industries, such as fiber optic cable manufacturers, wireless communication companies, HMOs, and bed and breakfast inns that have been grouped into twenty broad sectors (the SIC had ten sectors). The new six-digit codes (SIC used four) provide more detailed segmentation of businesses. The 1997 Economic Census serves as the starting point for NAICS. The Census Bureau will provide data that allow comparisons between the SIC and NAICS for several more years to facilitate companies making the transition.

Following is an example that will illustrate how a company might use the NAICS for segmenting business markets. If a company that sells hand tools were using NAICS to segment the market for prospective buyers, they would be interested in the following breakdown of one submarket:

Code	Definition
81	Other services
811	Repair and maintenance
8111	Automotive repair and maintenance
81111	Automotive mechanical electrical repair and maintenance
811111	General automotive repair
811112	Automotive exhaust system repair
811113	Automotive transmission repair

The government data for segment 811111 would indicate, for example, how many establishments existed in a particular geographic area, such as in Berrien County in the state of Michigan, that were categorized as general automotive repair businesses. Other information on the sizes of the businesses (number of employees) and other data of interest would be provided. See <http://www.census.gov/epcd/www.naics.html> for more information on NAICS.

The NAICS is the largest and best known of segmentation systems available to B2B companies in either goods or service businesses. Quite often, marketers in B2B industries will use the NAICS in combination with the managerial judgment method of segmenting markets, which is described next.

MANAGERIAL JUDGMENT

The third approach to segmenting markets is managerial judgment. This is not to suggest that using a research-based or existing segmentation system method does not also involve the judgment of marketing managers, because clearly marketers must make choices in either of those approaches. Managerial judgment in this approach means that managers use their judgment, based upon experience with the market in question, to identify the base for segmenting markets and for the number of segments the market contains. Some typical bases for use in specifying market segments are shown in Table 2.2.

Table 2.3 shows some possible bases to use in segmenting B2B or industrial markets. It lists major questions that industrial marketers

TABLE 2.2. Segmentation Bases—Consumer Markets

Bases	Examples
Geographic	
Region	Pacific, Middle Atlantic, New England
Metro size	Under 5,000, 500,000-999,999, 4 million +
Density	Urban, suburban, rural
Demographic	
Age	18-25, 65+
Gender	Male, female
Income	Under $10K, $30K-45K, $100K+
Occupation	Professional, technical, unskilled
Education	Less than high school, graduate school
Social class	Lower lower, upper middle, lower upper
Psychographic	
Lifestyle	Outdoor, sociable, sedentary
Personality	Compulsive, authoritarian
Behavioral	
Occasions	Regular, special
Benefits sought	Quality, economy, speed
User status	Nonuser, potential user, regular user
User rate	Light, medium, heavy

Source: Adapted from Philip Kotler, *Marketing Management,* Eleventh Edition (Upper Saddle River, NJ: Prentice-Hall, 2003), p. 288.

should ask in determining which customer they want to serve. In going after segments instead of the whole market, a company has a much better chance of delivering real value and receiving a premium price for its close attention to the needs of those segments. Thus, a tire company should decide which industries it wants to serve, noting the following differences: Automobile manufacturers seeking original equipment tires vary in their requirements; luxury car manufacturers want a much higher grade tire than standard car manufacturers. Tires needed by aircraft manufacturers have to meet much higher safety standards than do tires needed by farm tractors.

TABLE 2.3. Segmentation for Industrial Markets

Segmentation basis	Implications
Demographic factors	
1. Company size	Should we target large, medium, or small organizations based on number of employees, dollar sales, or number of plants/locations?
2. Type of industry	Do we target virtually all companies in many industries (horizontal market) or most all companies in a single industry (vertical market)?
3. Stage in life cycle	Should we focus on new or older, established organizations?
Geographic factors	
1. Location	Should we target companies in local, regional, or national geographic markets? Domestic or foreign markets?
Company style and culture	
1. Corporate culture	Should we target companies that place emphasis on technological superiority? Innovativeness? Market leaders or followers? Risk takers or risk avoiders?
Usage behavior	
1. Volume	Should we target heavy, light, or nonusers?
2. Size of order	Should we focus on large-order or small-order buyers?
3. Loyalty	Should we target buyers who exhibit high or low brand or company loyalty?
4. Situation	Should we target buyers seeking certain product applications? Those who need quick response?
Purchasing behavior	
1. Tasks	Should we target segments who exhibit a more scientific, high-quality approach to their buying tasks and decisions?
2. Organization structure	Should we focus on organizations with buying structures that are centralized or decentralized? Formal or informal? Specialized or generalized?
3. Technology	Should we target buyers with more sophisticated buying processes or systems?
4. Buying center	Should we focus on targets based on buying roles played by members and their power relationships?
5. Benefits sought	Should we focus on targets who seek low cost or price? High product quality? Excellent service?

Segmentation basis	Implications
Individual factors	
1. Motivation	Can we target segments based on their "hot buttons"?
2. Perception	Should we target customers based on risk tolerance? Importance of supplier size or image?
3. Learning	Should we focus on buyers with routinized purchase patterns?

Source: Adapted from David Loudon and Albert Della Bitta, *Consumer Behavior: Concepts and Applications*, Fourth Edition (New York: McGraw-Hill, 1993), pp. 661-675.

Within a chosen target industry, a company can further segment by customer size. The company might set up separate systems for dealing with large and small customers. For example, Steelcase, a major manufacturer of office furniture, divides its customers into two groups:

1. *Major accounts:* Accounts such as IBM and Prudential are handled by national account managers working with field district managers.
2. *Dealer accounts:* Smaller accounts are handled through field sales personnel working with franchised dealers who sell Steelcase products.

Within a certain target industry and customer size, a company can segment by purchase criteria. For example, government laboratories, university laboratories, and industrial laboratories typically differ in their purchase criteria for instruments. Government laboratories need low prices (because they have difficulty getting funds to buy instruments) and service contracts (because they can easily get money to maintain instruments). University laboratories need equipment that requires little continuous service because they do not have service people on their payroll. Industrial laboratories need equipment that is highly reliable because they cannot afford downtime.

In general, business-to-business marketers do not focus on one segmentation variable but instead apply multiattribute segmentation.

Marketers using a managerial judgment approach typically select one or more of the bases in Tables 2.2 or 2.3 and then use a market grid analysis to form the segments.

Market Grid Analysis

Marketing planners can use data collected from customers and prospective customers to segment their markets, then offer products aimed at specific needs. This is like using a rifle rather than a shotgun to shoot at a target. Specific products are developed for specific segments.

One basic tool that can be used to segment a market is a market grid. A market grid is a two-dimensional view of a market which is divided into various segments based on characteristics of potential customers. There are two important concepts in grid analysis. First, characteristics of potential customers are used to segment the market rather than product characteristics. This ensures a customer-oriented view of the market rather than a product-oriented view. Second, characteristics of *potential* customers rather than existing ones are used to focus on customers the organization may not currently serve.

Normally, a series of grids must be used to describe a market completely. Therefore, the planner must begin with a set of characteristics thought to be useful in differentiating consumers' needs. Each characteristic must be analyzed to determine its probable effect on consumers' satisfaction.

The types of characteristics used in the analysis may be those described previously: demographic, geographic, usage, benefits sought, or psychographics. Using these characteristics to divide a large group into smaller subgroups enables the planner to isolate the needs of very specific segments and then design products for them.

The examples previously discussed are not all-inclusive but are intended to illustrate the types of characteristics that can be used. A planner may begin with a relatively long list of characteristics. The characteristics chosen from the list are those which not only differentiate among groups of customers (i.e., customers can be grouped by that characteristic into segments that are homogeneous within and heterogeneous between segments), but which also are instrumental in some way in affecting consumer response to marketing programs.

For example, company size may vary among customers, but does it matter? That is, will companies have different needs and respond to different appeals based upon factors that vary by company size? If not, then the mere fact that we can group companies by their size is insufficient justification for the use of company size in the grid analysis. Managerial market experience is used to choose characteristics. Selection of characteristics is accomplished by assessing the impact of the characteristic on buyer need satisfaction. Only those characteristics useful in differentiating needs are used in the market grids. For example, a clothing manufacturer might develop a list that includes age, sex, income, geographic location, shopping behavior, and activity engaged in by consumers. The primary impact of each characteristic might be assessed as shown in Table 2.4. The consumer's age would certainly influence his or her needs, e.g., the styles the consumer is interested in, the person who actually is the decision maker, and the types of retail stores shopped.

Grid Construction

Once a list of potential consumer characteristics has been developed, the next step is actual grid construction. Tables 2.5 and 2.6 illustrate the process. Each section within the grid is actually a market segment for accounting services. As each characteristic is used to identify a specific segment it becomes possible to determine the nature of the products, place, and promotion most likely to satisfy needs in each segment.

TABLE 2.4. Consumer Characteristics for Grid Analysis in Clothing Purchases

Characteristic	Probable impact on need
Age	Style, who decision maker is, type of retail outlet
Sex	Style, type of retail outlet, motives for purchase
Income level	Price of quality, type of retail outlet, motives for purchase
Geographic location	Style, material used
Shopping behavior	Promotion, type of retail outlet
Product usage	Style, materials used, durability, colors

TABLE 2.5. Market Grid for Individual Income Tax Services

Ethnic Group	Income		
	Low	Medium	High
Hispanic			
Non-Hispanic			

TABLE 2.6. Market Grid for Corporate Accounting Services

Location	Company size (sales)		
	Under $5 million	$5-$100 million	Over $100 million
Regional			
National			

The shaded areas in Table 2.5 represent two rather different market segments. Needs of these groups would be different and different marketing strategies must be used to satisfy the clients in each segment.

In Table 2.6, it is also apparent that the needs of users represented by the two shaded areas (segments) would be different. As market segments emerge through the analysis, a potential group of consumers with similar characteristics can be seen. Planners can then select specific target markets. For smaller firms, only one or a few segments may be of interest, whereas a large firm may develop or already have a complete line of products and therefore select several segments as potential target markets. This type of analysis is needed regardless of whether one or many segments is selected.

An alternate approach to the representation of a market is a buildup grid or diagram. This approach involves identifying the individual market segments and then putting them together to represent a mar-

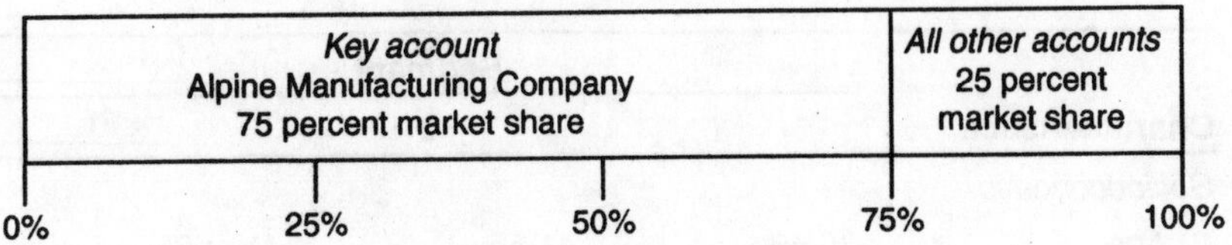

FIGURE 2.3. Market Segments for Industrial Product

ket. The result is the same: a recognition of the differences in needs of different consumers.

An example of this approach for an industrial product is shown in Figure 2.3. This shows the market for component parts of mud pumps used on oil rigs. In the consumer analysis, it was found that the market was dominated by one firm, which accounted for about 75 percent of the original equipment manufacturers' (OEM) sales in this market. The rest of the sales volume was divided among four other firms. The large manufacturer was designated a *key account,* meaning it was a very significant buyer and, therefore, a different marketing effort would be directed at this segment.

Consumer Profiles

As the process of developing market grids continues, a profile of the consumers in each segment emerges. This profile should be as complete as possible for each segment and should include all three types of characteristics (socioeconomic, behavioral, and psychological). The results of the analysis can be used in subsequent time periods so they should be easily accessible. In fact, if this type of analysis has already been completed, it can be updated or expanded.

The results of the analysis may be summarized as shown in Table 2.7. This approach allows a comparison of the characteristics for each segment in which a planner is interested.

Most of the information needed for this type of analysis can be obtained through secondary data. The most difficult data to obtain from secondary sources is psychological data. Unless the firm has previously conducted research to collect these data, a new study will be

TABLE 2.7. Consumer Characteristics by Segment

Characteristics	Segment 1	Segment 2	Segment 3
Socioeconomic			
Age	26-40	41-65	Over 65
Sex	Male	Male	Male
Income	Upper	Middle	Lower
Location	Southwest	Southeast	Southwest
Behavioral			
Shopping behavior	Specialty store	Department stores	Discount stores
Purchase rate	High	High	High
Psychological			
Opinions	Fashion oriented	Comfort oriented	Economy oriented
Awareness	High brand-name awareness	Some brand-name awareness	Low brand-name awareness

needed to collect them. For firms without a research staff, outside consultants or research firms may be used.

ESTIMATING THE POTENTIAL OF MARKET SEGMENTS

Once a market has been segmented, marketing managers seek to identify the level of demand that exists in each segment. This involves the use of market factors and the estimation of market potential for the segments.

Market Factors

Market factors are those realities of a market which cause demand for a product. For example, the market factor for baby beds is the number of babies born each year. Since a market is merely people with money and a motivation to buy, population figures and income figures are commonly used as market factors. However, it is usually possible to be much more specific in identifying market factors for a given company or product/service. The role of market factors is threefold: (1) identification of the factors that influence a product or service demand, (2) determination of the relationship between the factor and the product or service, and (3) forecasting that market factor for future years. Since many of the same market factors are used by different forecasters, much of that work may have already been completed and simply needs to be located. Population projections, for example, are available through many sources so there is usually no need to develop your own forecast of population.

Two basic techniques for selecting and determining the impact of market factors on a given product or service are arbitrary judgment and correlation analysis. Arbitrary judgment involves use of the decision maker's own experience and judgment in selecting factors and weighing them. (For new products/services this is a common technique since no sales history is available unless, of course, a test market is used.) For example, a drug manufacturer might determine from historical data that twelve dollars' worth of drugs are purchased for each person residing in a given market area. The number of consumers in a market area would be used to get information on the future size of that market area.

A more complex yet usually more reliable approach is to use correlation analysis to help identify factors and assign weights to them. Although it is beyond the scope of this book to discuss the details of this technique, a specific technique in correlation analysis called step-wise regression analysis not only weighs the various factors but also provides a measure of what the addition of each factor adds to an explanation of changes in sales. This method requires a sales history so it is limited mainly to existing products even though it could be used on test market data for new products.

Regardless of the technique used in analyzing market factors, the objectives include understanding the factors that influence demand for a product or service and the historical and future trend of that factor. This will be more evident in the discussion of using market factors to estimate market potential in the next section.

Market Potential

Once a market has been divided into various segments and characteristics of consumers and market factors have been analyzed, the next step is to estimate the *size* of the market. The term *market potential* is used to refer to the expected sales of a product or service for an entire market. Simply put, "If everybody that could buy would buy, how many units or dollars worth of sales would occur?" The answer to that question is the market potential. A market segment that does not have enough consumers spending enough dollars does not justify effort in that market unless a firm is seeking to accomplish some nonrevenue-related objective. You are not just seeking consumer markets but markets that can be served profitably by the firm attempting to meet its needs. Market potential is a quantitative measure of a market's capacity to consume a product in a given time period, which is a prerequisite to assessing profitability.

Estimating Potential for Existing Products or Services

Market potential can be measured in either absolute or relative terms. An absolute measure is one that can be expressed in units or dollars while a relative measure relates one part of a market to another and is expressed as a percent. Techniques for estimating absolute measures of potential are discussed as follows. These techniques are used when products and services are already on the market and the future size of the market is desired.

Sales index measure of relative potential. The sales index method provides a relative measure of potential for products that have reached the maturity stage of their product life cycle. This technique is useful in answering questions about the relative potential of various geographic market areas. Its use requires familiarity with the product in terms of stage and life cycle, penetration of distribution in various areas, and a sales history.

Market factor method. Normally, relative potential is not adequate and an absolute measure of potential is needed to provide estimates in units or dollars. One technique used to accomplish this is the market factor method. This involves identifying the factors that influence goods' or service's sales and relating the factors to sales in some way.

Regression analysis method. Another technique used to estimate potential is a statistical technique known as regression analysis. This technique relates market factors to sales in a more mathematically complex manner. Space does not permit a complete explanation of this technique; the purpose here is to show how it could be used in estimating potential. One result of regression analysis is an equation that relates market factors to sales. If more than one market factor is used, then multiple regression is needed. The resulting equation is then used to estimate potential. The approach still requires estimates of two market factors (independent variables) for the future time period for which the measure of potential is desired. This technique also permits calculation of a confidence interval for the estimate.

Estimating Potential for New Products or Services

When innovative new products or services are proposed, no industry sales are available as a point of reference for estimating potential. Under such circumstances, it is still important to identify market factors that are likely to influence the demand for the product or service. These factors can provide an upper limit to demand. For instance, knowing that there were 5 million men in a certain income and age category would be a useful reference point in beginning to analyze potential for a new product for males with these two characteristics. However, you would not expect each one of them to buy the product. Three techniques commonly used to refine estimates of potential from that upper limit are (1) judgmental estimates, (2) consumer surveys, and (3) the substitute method. A fourth technique combines several techniques and uses secondary data and consumer surveys to estimate potential.

Judgmental estimates. This technique involves the use of expert opinion of those knowledgeable about a market and product. This judgment can be used in a formalized approach such as the Delphi technique or it could involve pooled estimates and a reconciliation of differences between estimates given by different people.

Consumer surveys. Surveys of potential consumers can be used to estimate potential new products. This approach is especially useful for industrial products markets where the number of consumers is smaller and they can be more readily identified. For example, a part used in mud pumps for oil drilling rigs would involve only a few customers—manufacturers of mud pumps. They can be easily identified and their potential purchases can be estimated. This technique is more difficult to use in more diverse consumer markets but it can be adapted to consumer goods.

Substitute method. Most new products are substitutes for existing products on the market. If the size of these markets can be estimated, then the sales of the new product can be estimated based on its replacement potential. An acceptance rate would have to be estimated for the proportion of existing consumers who would switch to the new product when it was introduced on the market. This acceptance rate could be estimated through consumer research.

SUMMARY

A truly marketing-oriented organization seeks to understand the market, its competitors, and the financial implications of its possible actions before it begins to develop marketing plans. This chapter focused on the first of those activities—understanding markets—by discussing the rationale, benefits, and methods of market segmentation. Throughout, the marketing orientation philosophy of concentrating on understanding the market, rather than dictating to the market, was evident. Properly done, market segmentation is an extremely valuable first step in the process of identifying target markets and developing positioning strategies, which will be discussed in the chapters on marketing planning.

Chapter 3

Competitive Analysis

In this chapter we address the second element of what marketing managers must understand: competition (see Figure 3.1). After analyzing the needs of consumers or organizational buyers in specific market segments, the next step in the marketing analysis process is to analyze competition for each of the specific market segments. For new products that represent innovation, this analysis may be limited to potential competition rather than identifiable competitors. In most cases, however, an established market with clearly identified competitors must be evaluated for its strategies, strengths, and weaknesses.

This chapter presents the concepts and tools needed to analyze competition for existing markets. Especially useful is the marketing mix audit form, which permits evaluation of a competitor on all the basic strategy elements.

Societal marketing orientation

↓

Understanding
Customers (market segments): Chapter 2
Competition: Chapter 3
Financial implications: Chapter 4

↓

Planning

↓

Implementing

↓

Connecting with customers

FIGURE 3.1. The Effective Marketing Management Process

PURPOSE OF COMPETITIVE ANALYSIS

One fundamental question must be asked when undertaking competitive analysis: Which competitors are going after which market segments with what marketing strategies? The focus is on specific market segments that have been isolated through consumer analysis. At this point, managers should already know the size (potential) and the characteristics of each segment. The analysis begins to deal with competition on a segment-by-segment basis. Managers must uncover segments that are not currently being served, or segments that are not being served well by competition. In markets where competitors do not have clearly identifiable strategies and each seems to be using a strategy similar to the others, there are usually several segments that can be better served through strategies aimed directly at their needs. For example, the hair shampoo market was once characterized by only two broad categories of shampoo—dandruff and nondandruff. However, recognition of the different hair and scalp conditions of consumers led to the development of shampoos for dry, oily, and normal hair. This was an attempt to meet the needs of consumers more precisely than with what was previously marketed. The introduction of a shampoo specially designed for small children would represent an attempt to go after another market segment with different types of consumers and competitors.

IMPORTANCE OF UNDERSTANDING COMPETITION

Consider the example of a manufacturer of heart pacemakers that came up with a new line of products whose technology was better than anything else on the market. However, sales did not improve; in fact, in some territories they got worse. The company was puzzled, so it asked its sales representatives to investigate the tactics being used against them. Salespersons learned that competitors were plying physicians with cars, boats, and lavish junkets. The company claimed to be surprised to find that such promotions could sway cardiologists. They found that sales were deteriorating most where its competitors' giveaways were most aggressive. So, the company increased its educational support for doctors, began fielding many more service representatives, and actually matched some of the giveaways—not boats, but equipment related to pacemakers and their use. The effort helped make sales soar.[1]

Many companies fail to see available opportunities due to lack of attention to immediate zones and areas of interest. But some companies do a very good job. A famous example of this is when Gillette noticed that Bic, which had previously been a formidable competitor in the disposable lighter market, and pioneered disposable razors in Europe in 1975, then introduced the disposable razor in Canada. Thus, it became clear to Gillette that a major potential competitor was closing in on the U.S. market. Gillette responded by racing its Good News disposable razor into production and onto the national market that same year, which paved the way for its dominance of this market. By paying attention to its immediate zone and area of interest, Gillette capitalized on an opportunity it would have lost had it only focused on the U.S. market.[2]

Businesses have made increasing use of the Freedom of Information Act (FOIA) as an intelligence source. The experience of one company illustrates both the threats and opportunities provided by this act. When Air Cruisers Co. received Federal Aviation Administration (FAA) approval of its forty-two-person inflatable life raft designed for commercial aircraft it was the largest raft ever to gain FAA approval, and provided a substantial competitive advantage to the firm. Six months later, however, it learned that the FAA was about to release an eighteen-inch stack of confidential technical documents to a competitor, which had submitted an FOIA request. The list included results of performance tests and construction designs, which would enable the competitor to compress costly design, testing, and certification procedures. Although Air Cruisers was able to block the FAA from releasing all of the data, some documents were provided. This information helped the competitor design its own large raft with which it defeated Air Cruisers in a contest for an important European contract.[3]

A study by The Conference Board found that companies have beefed up their intelligence activities not only to identify major rivals but also to gain a competitive edge over them. Among executives surveyed in 315 companies covering a wide variety of industries, 59 percent of top management consider competitive monitoring to be "very important," while an even higher percentage (68 percent) of middle managers think it is "very important." A large majority (67 percent) of the executives surveyed believe competitive intelligence will grow even more in their companies in the future as they give greater attention and support to tracking and predicting competitive movements.

Unfortunately, many companies do not rate their current intelligence systems as being well developed. Only 3 percent characterized theirs as "fully developed," while over 33 percent said "fairly well developed"; but about 50 percent said only "loosely developed." Moreover, the programs are not perceived by respondents as achieving maximum effectiveness (only 9 percent rated theirs as "very effective" and 71 percent described them as "fairly effective").[4,5]

Competitive analysis in global markets can lead to new opportunities for companies. For example, the Cadillac Seville is a global vehicle from General Motors Corporation that has been called the best American car ever built. By making significant improvements to interior design, transmission, and systems, Seville has competed with the Mercedes-Benz E Class, BMW 5 Series, Nissan Infiniti Q45, and Lexus LS430.[6]

THE NATURE OF COMPETITION

To be complete, an analysis of competition must consider existing and potential competition. Trying to anticipate the moves of competitors can become the basis of choosing to go after a given segment and what strategy to use if the effort is made. This section begins with a discussion of the nature of competition and then develops basic tools for analyzing competitors.

Types of Competition

Marketers must understand some types of competitive conditions that they may face: pure competition, monopolistic competition, oligopolistic competition, and monopoly. Each of these situations calls for different marketing strategy decisions.

Pure Competition

One of the earliest types of competition identified by economists is called pure competition. Although all the characteristics of this type of competition are seldom found in the marketplace, it sometimes occurs in some market environments and serves as a useful concept in analysis. An industry or a local market which could be described as pure competition usually has the following characteristics: (1) a large number of relatively small competitors, (2) little or no differences between strategies, and (3) ease of entry by new competitors. The large number of small competitors means the actions of one competitor may be unnoticed by the others. Differences among strategies may be small, and good location may be of prime importance in attracting customers. The ease of entry may mean new competitors continually coming into the market or old ones leaving. Unless a well-financed competitor enters the market and alters the competitive environment, the market tends to be unorganized, even fragmented, with the number of customers and competitors within the geographic bounds of the firm determining both sales and strategies. Similarities in prices, products or services offered, distribution, and promotion are common.

Monopolistic Competition

In the market characterized by monopolistic competition, the individual images of the various firms begin to emerge in terms of more clearly differentiated strategies. Although there may still be many competitors and relative ease of entry, each firm has attempted to differentiate itself in some way from its competitors. It may be a market with much diversity of price, distribution, products and services, and promotional activities, or it can also be characterized by similarities among two or three variables in the marketing mix and variety in the other promotion, for example. In this competitive environment each competitor has more control over the marketing mix variables, and therefore a diversity of strategies is possible.

Oligopolistic Competition

In an oligopolistic, competitive environment, the number of competitors and ease of entry are both decreased. In this market, there are a few relatively large competitors, and perhaps a few smaller ones. The actions of one competitor are clearly recognized in both nature and impact by other competitors, and retaliation to competitive moves is anticipated. There is still a diversity of strategies in this type of environment, but it is most likely of the nonprice variety; price competition is not easily copied and must be responded to if customers readily substitute one firm's products for another. Price leadership may develop as one firm is allowed to set the pace for others.

Monopoly

A monopoly is a market environment characterized by one seller. There are usually legal restrictions to entry if it is considered a natural monopoly (e.g., electric utility company). Natural monopolies are regulated by government in terms of prices and distribution, and nonnatural monopolies, if successful, usually attract other competitors who are willing to overcome barriers to entry because of a potentially large return. Therefore, nonnatural monopolies are usually short-lived.

In global markets, competitors may be government-owned and operated, as in the oil industry. A government may support a company or group of companies' activity as a monopoly to compete in foreign markets. Japan has been especially successful in this approach to global competitors.

Levels of Competition

Competition must be understood at the level at which it is analyzed. At the manufacturing level, there may be only a few large producers (oligopoly) but many retailers reselling the products in highly competitive markets (monopolistic or purely competitive). Therefore, the planner must analyze the market in terms of where his or her own firm faces competition. If the marketing plan is being developed for a retail firm, the retail market is of prime consideration, whereas a manufacturer may be more concerned about competition at the manufacturing level.

In some instances it may be appropriate to look at competition vertically, with one channel system competing against another channel system, rather than only horizontally. This would be especially true where vertical integration is involved.

Table 3.1 provides a summary of the variation of several factors depending on the type of competitive environment. Instead of trying to define what is meant by "many" in the case of number of firms, and "ease of entry" in the case of how easy it is to enter a market, attention

TABLE 3.1. Effects of Competitive Environment

Factor	Competitive Environment			
	Pure competition	Monopolistic competition	Oligopolistic competition	Monopoly
Number of firms	Many	Many	Few	One
Entry and exit	Easy	Easy	Difficult	May be legally banned
Service	Undifferentiated	Differentiated	Differentiated	N/A
Fees	Undifferentiated	Undifferentiated if nonprice competition is emphasized	Undifferentiated if nonprice competition is emphasized	N/A
Access	Undifferentiated	Differentiated if nonprice competition is used by some competitors; undifferentiated if price competition is emphasized	Differentiated if nonprice competition is used by some competitors; undifferentiated if price competition is emphasized	N/A
Promotion	Undifferentiated	Differentiated if nonprice competition is used by some competitors; undifferentiated if price competition is used by some competitors	Differentiated if nonprice competition is used by some competitors; undifferentiated if price competition is used by some competitors	N/A
Competitive reaction	Little	Some, depending on type of action	A lot, especially related to prices	N/A

N/A = Not applicable

should be focused on the overall nature of the market as collectively described by the factors. Most economic reality lies somewhere between pure competition and monopoly. Identifying the nature of competition helps in understanding not only how firms compete in a market but also whether or not retaliatory actions can be expected.

Competitive Advantages

To understand the concept of competitive advantage and why it plays such a central role in marketing strategy, one must understand how marketers view competition. The most successful marketers do not wish to "beat the competition"; they wish to make competitors totally irrelevant to their customers. That is, marketers want to establish such a close, satisfying, long-term relationship with their customers that those customers have no interest in considering alternatives. The strength of the relationship makes movement to a competitor so inconvenient, risky, and unnecessary that the customer exercises a "willful suspension of choice" and continues to give the company his or her business. In a sense, marketers are trying to satisfy the customers so completely that the barriers to exit from the relationship are too high in their minds to justify seeking alternative means of addressing their needs. A marketer successful in establishing such a relationship with a customer has made competition irrelevant. Accomplishing this goal requires the identification and exploitation of a significant competitive advantage.

Effective competitive analysis will take into consideration the search for, and need for, competitive advantages. Competitive advantages are those factors in which a particular organization excels over competitors or has the potential to excel over them. Some strategic planners actually insist that the strategic planning process must identify some competitive advantage for the organization. This insistence is based upon the belief that until there is an answer to the question "Why would someone buy from us instead of someone else?" a strategy does not exist. Moreover, it is not enough for the firm's management to claim a competitive advantage exists. A competitive advantage is a wish instead of reality until the market acknowledges its existence. Several conditions must be met before a competitive advantage can be exploited. The advantage must be

- *real.* It must actually exist and not be just a wish.
- *substantial.* It must be great enough to make a difference in the market.
- *important.* It must translate into a benefit that the customer seeks and values.
- *specific.* It must explain "what" and "why" to avoid being perceived simply as puffery.
- *promotable.* It must be able to be communicated frequently enough in relevant language which is understandable and motivating to the customer.
- *sustainable.* It must be able to be maintained as changes occur in various facets of the environment.

Some examples of areas where competitive advantages may be found include the following:

Production: A superior ability to turn out a product is a critical competitive advantage that many companies have capitalized upon. The advantage may also be in a firm's ability to maintain superior production quality over competitors.

Technology: Initial innovative research and development, as well as properly managed scientific application, can establish and preserve competitive advantages.

Natural resources: Quite often, valuable or scarce resources are appropriate assets on which to base a strategy. Tremendous advantage can be given to organizations, cartels, and nations that control natural resources or that are located in favorable proximity to them.

Marketing: Market advantage usually refers to the advantage one firm has over another because it is more positively positioned in the minds of customers. Those firms having greater awareness, higher preference, or stronger loyalty have a distinct marketing advantage over their competitors.

Management: Management advantage comes in the form of positive personnel relations, effective planning and information systems, and overall managerial competence.

INDUSTRY ANALYSIS

Part of the competitive analysis process is to discover differential competitive advantages that will enhance the strategy of the firm. To discover these advantages one must understand how the particular industry functions. Four key questions are helpful in conducting an industry analysis:

How is the industry structured?
What is the industry's direction?
What are the industry economics?
What are the strategic issues within the industry?

Industry Structure

Analysis of an industry's structure involves ascertaining the number of competitors and each one's size relative to the total market, characterizing market leaders, analyzing distribution patterns, developing buyer profiles, and evaluating ease of entry and exit as well as other characteristics. One of the best approaches to this process is the guide to industry analysis suggested by Michael E. Porter.[7,8] Taken together, these elements are the key to forecasting a company's earning power.

The forces of competition greatly influence an organization's strategy formation and market opportunity decisions. Although each industry has its own unique characteristics, competitive pressures come from five main sources that represent the actual driving mechanisms of any given industry (see Figure 3.2).

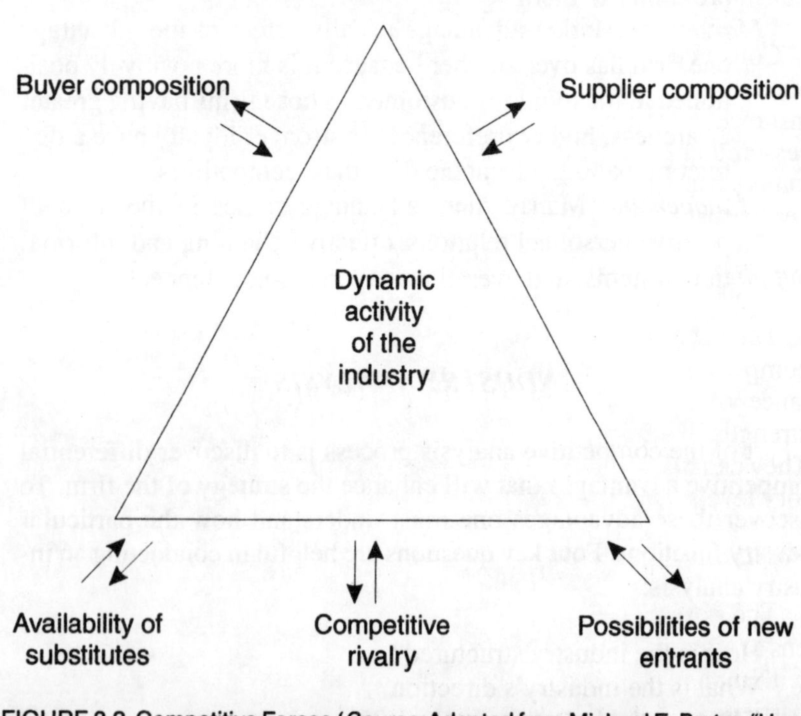

FIGURE 3.2. Competitive Forces (*Source:* Adapted from Michael E. Porter, "How Competitive Forces Shape Strategy," *Harvard Business Review,* 57(2), 1979, p. 141.)

Rivalry Among Existing Competitors

The rivalry among companies within an industry is constantly involved in dynamic interplay in an attempt to build a successful competitive edge over one another. The success of one organization's strategy in accomplishing this is based in large measure on the strategies of the other members. Constant monitoring of these interdependent strategic maneuvers is required to make the adjustments necessary to improve competitive position and achieve market success.

Sears, for example, has initiated a price strategy aimed at gaining back market share lost to rivals such as K-Mart and Wal-Mart. Competitive pricing can mean market share gains and can decrease the pressure on advertising to bring customers into the store. It can also mean retaliation from competitors who respond to such actions.

Consumer/Buyer Composition

Consumer/buyer composition can range from a few large-volume purchasers to a large number of low-volume purchasers. In the first instance, losing a few customers can be the difference between success and failure, the other extreme, losing that same number of customers has virtually no impact. Most firms try to minimize the number of customers that can exert an adverse effect on their business.

Supplier Composition

The supplier composition also has an important influence on the competing position of individual organizations. The relative importance of the goods and services they supply will determine the strength of their competitive influence over firms in the industry. They can have a positive or negative impact on profit margins, inventory levels, product quality, and prices.

Possibility of New Entrants

The possibility of new entrants into the market constantly threatens to alter market share, production capacity, and supply distribution within an industry. This threat can be minimal when there are strong barriers to entry, such as strong customer loyalty, large capital requirements, difficulty in establishing distribution channels, and strong response of existing firms. When entry barriers are weak or the expected response of existing firms is weak, then the possibility of entry is stronger. Hyundai Motor Company of Korea, for example, launched a new four-door sedan that was aimed at the midsized car market. The front-wheel drive Sonata was designed to sell for about $2,000 less than comparable cars made by Toyota or Honda.

Availability of Good Product Substitutes

The fifth force in this model is the availability of good product substitutes. A major threat to existing firms occurs when high-quality substitutes exist in ample quantity at competitive or comparable prices. Artificial sweeteners and sugar are examples of substitutable products.

Competitive strategy should take offensive or defensive action to strengthen a company's position in relation to the five competitive forces. The tasks of structural analysis, in the long run, are examining each competitive force, forecasting the magnitude of each underlying cause, and constructing a composite picture of the likely profit potential of the industry. Structural analysis is also useful in setting diversification strategy, since it provides a framework for answering the extremely difficult questions in diversification decisions.

Industry Direction

Once an industry's framework is understood the analysis turns toward determining the industry direction. Most industries go through an industry life cycle consisting of the development stage, the growth stage, the maturity stage, and the decline stage. However, this model of understanding and predicting industry direction is not always accurate. Some industries go through several cycles. Table 3.2 contains many of the variables that should be understood by the planner. Although only a summary of the range of possible factors, it highlights the key variables. Further in-depth research would be required to answer the question of where the industry is going and what is driving it that way.

Many other driving forces are not listed. Various industries will have different forces determining their direction, and the forces will have different magnitudes of importance from one industry to another.

TABLE 3.2. Industry Direction Checklist

Variable	Current trend		
Growth	☐ Slow	☐ Medium	☐ Fast
Customers	☐ Growing	☐ Declining	☐ No change
Technology	☐ Low	☐ Medium	☐ High
Product change	☐ Slow	☐ Medium	☐ Fast
Danger of obsolescence	☐ Low	☐ Medium	☐ High
Ease of entry	☐ Low	☐ Medium	☐ High
Quality of suppliers	☐ Low	☐ Medium	☐ High
Possibility of regulatory changes	☐ Low	☐ Medium	☐ High
Availability of raw materials/resources	☐ Low	☐ Medium	☐ High
Amount of capital required	☐ Low	☐ Medium	☐ High

Industry Economics

The third key question in accomplishing a competitive analysis is, "What are the underlying economics of the industry?" The answers to this question are capital investment requirements, break-even levels, cost structures, pricing structures, and other economic considerations. The key factors related to the economic characteristics are discussed in Chapter 4. However, the key success factors vary from industry to industry. An understanding of the economics of industry is necessary to take advantage of these factors. Whether it is transportation, distribution, promotion, technology, raw materials, location, or some other key element, an understanding of the underlying economic considerations increases the likelihood of selecting the key factors for success.

Strategic Issues

The fourth key question deals with identification of the strategic issues and problems facing the industry. These issues and problems vary from time to time and industry to industry. The following is a list of the most common issues and problems within an industry:

Does the industry have the ability to

- meet future needs?
- estimate changes in the demographic characteristics of consumers?
- deal with emerging opportunities and threats?
- trace the overall economy and estimate its impact on the industry?
- anticipate changes in government policies and regulatory controls?
- predict and respond to changes in supply, cost, competition, technology, growth, etc?

COMPETITOR ANALYSIS

Once a good understanding is established of how an industry functions, a specific competitor analysis should be done. Most firms in a given industry do not follow the same strategic approach regardless of the similarity of their understanding of the dynamics of the industry. Evaluating competitors' strategies allows a business entity to increase or reinforce its understanding of buyer behavior and identify the type of targeted customer. It is also useful in identifying strengths and weaknesses and, consequently, potential market opportunity. The analysis may assist the firm in evaluating whether to position itself as a *leader* competing head on with other competitors, as a *follower* with a "me too" strategy, or as a *niche* performer with a unique strategy tailored for specific strengths and weaknesses and specific market segments. Each major competitor should be studied separately. If this is not possible then the strategy of the closest competitors should be evaluated.

In evaluating different competitive approaches the following tasks need to be performed:

- Review current strategy.
- Review current performance.
- Determine strengths and weaknesses.
- Forecast future strategic possibilities.

Analyzing current competitor strategy involves determining how the competitor defines the industry in terms of market segments, product features, marketing mix, manufacturing policy, research and development commitment, growth policy, distribution, and promotion. This analysis can take several forms, but perhaps the most useful is the competitive marketing mix audit.

Who Are Our Competitors?

Major competitors are often easy to identify but some may be overlooked. One way of identifying competitors is to consider the product/market situation. All existing competitors should be identified based on the product/market they are satisfying. For example, a soft drink producer must specify all of the different choice options within the market under which his or her brand will be considered. This would comprise the bulk of the relevant set of competitors and indicates to the marketer that a variety of levels of competition may exist for a company. The most immediate level is *brand* and *item* competition. For example, the Palm IIIxe and the Handspring Visor Deluxe compete directly against each other in features and price points within the personal digital assistant (PDA) product category. At the next level—*industry* competition—a company competes with all other companies producing the same type of product. For example, Palm considers Brother, Casio, Compaq, Cybiko, Franklin, Handspring, IBM, Psion, Sharp, SONIC Blue, Sony, and Xircom as PDA industry competitors. At the *generic* level of competition are companies providing products serving the same basic need. For example, other computer companies (e.g., eMachines) could be considered to be PDA competitors since their products satisfy the same generic functions of data storage and processing, as would companies selling calculators and paper notebooks.

Another example of the threat of generic competition occurs with video games, movies, and television. The U.S. video game industry makes as much money as the U.S. film industry makes at the box office, and it steals viewers directly from the domestic television industry.[9] Yet these three industries would not generally perceive themselves as competitors.

We must also consider *new* and *existing* competition. For instance, if no consideration is given to new product possibilities, serving new markets, promoting in different ways, delivering by different channels with different prices, the marketer may fail to account for an important component in a changing competitive landscape.

Techniques to Identify Competition

Chapter 2 discussed market segmentation as a way to group buyers for purposes of developing a marketing plan or strategy. Market segmentation, then, defines characteristics of various segments in the marketplace and allocates marketing resources for those chosen segments. A product's *position* describes the place it occupies relative to competitors in a given market as perceived by the relevant group of target customers. Segmentation and positioning are tandem concepts. Positioning involves determining how markets perceive the company's product or service and then planning and implementing marketing strategies to achieve the desired market position. Companies may seek a specific position on the basis of such strategies as: product features, benefits to buyers, product usage, situation, user type, or competitors.

If the market for a product could be viewed as a multidimensional plane, all attributes of a product together make up its position. For simplicity, however, one or two key dimensions are usually chosen for analysis. For example, bath soaps might be positioned on the basis of moisturizing ability and deodorant protection—the primary attributes people consider when evaluating a soap brand. Because products can be perceived on many dimensions (such as price, quality, durability, safety, etc.), marketers analyze the most critical attributes to develop an understanding of how consumers distinguish between competing brands. Information is gathered by having consumers complete scaling questionnaires to indicate their perceptions of the various characteristics and similarities of competing brands. Perceptual "maps" are plotted displaying consumers' brand perceptions. An example of this idea is shown in Figure 3.3 using fictitious data on how consumers might perceive the automotive sport utility vehicle (SUV) market.

The *evoked set* concept also works well to identify competitive brands. Asking consumers what brands they would consider using may uncover the most immediate competition. Consumers will usually name a few select brands that they would potentially consider for purchase and consumption. *Inert* brand sets are those the consumer

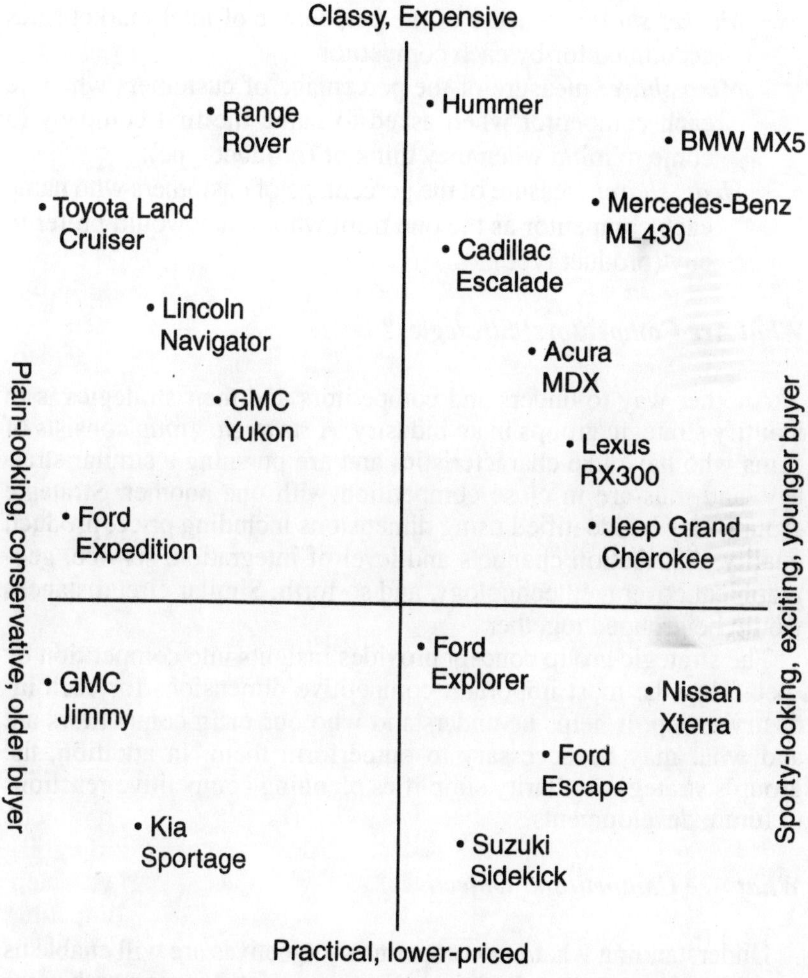

FIGURE 3.3. Speculative Perceptual Map of SUV Brands

fails to perceive any advantage in buying; that is, they are evaluated neither positively nor negatively. These brand sets have potential to change their position and become more relevant competitors.

Each of these competitive aspects should be tracked to uncover any shifts or trends in the market. Often, companies will measure the following factors to indicate their strongest competitors:

Market share: measure of the percentage of total market sales accounted for by each competitor.

Mind share: measure of the percentage of customers who cite each competitor when asked to name the first company to come to mind when they think of (product type).

Heart share: measure of the percentage of customers who name each competitor as the one from whom they would prefer to buy (product type).

What Are Competitors' Strategies?

Another way to understand competitors and their strategies is to identify strategic groups in an industry. A *strategic group* consists of firms who have like characteristics and are pursuing a similar strategy, and thus are in close competition with one another. Strategic groups may be identified using dimensions including price, product, quality, distribution channels and level of integration, service, geographical coverage, technology, and so forth. Similar circumstances would be grouped together.

The strategic group concept provides insights into competition by specifying the most important competitive dimensions for each industry group. It helps us understand who our main competitors are and what may be necessary to outperform them. In addition, the group's strategy similarity simplifies planning competitive reactions to future developments.

What Are Competitors' Objectives?

Understanding what our competitors' objectives are will enable us to predict their strategy direction. We must seek to learn what they are striving to accomplish in the market, and what motivates them. For example, it would be useful to know what competitors' short- and long-run financial objectives are, including profitability (maximum versus satisfactory), market share, sales, and cash flow. Analysis of these areas will help us to understand companies' directions and their potential reactions to our competitive strategy. Nonfinancial objectives are also important. For instance, competitors' plans for achieving technological or service superiority, market growth, or low-price aggression would help us plan our own programs.

What Are Competitors' Strengths and Weaknesses?

In order to evaluate whether competitors will be able to achieve their objectives through the strategies we have identified, we must understand their strengths and weaknesses. Knowing competitors' weaknesses allows us to focus on them with our strengths; similarly, we may avoid confronting their strengths or determine some way to counteract them.

Most of the information on competitors' strengths and weaknesses can be obtained from published data and personal reports. All will be helpful in interpreting the situation. The main areas for analysis of competitor strengths and weaknesses would include innovation, manufacturing, finance, management, marketing, and customer base.[10]

THE COMPETITIVE MARKETING AUDIT

The word *audit,* regardless of the business context in which it is used, refers to an unbiased appraisal of what is being done and how it is being done. Thus an accounting audit refers to an analysis of everything that is being done in the accounting area of a firm. In the same manner, a competitive marketing mix audit is one of the best ways of evaluating the marketing performance of a company and its competitors. An audit of this nature should be comprehensive, independent, and periodic. The audit should be based on specific objectives. Once the objectives and scope of the audit are established, a data-gathering effort should be initiated. This data collection effort can be accomplished by an objective outside consultant or by an in-house staff or task force. The results of the audit should be a clear comparison of the company and its competitors that shows relative strengths and weaknesses as well as opportunities and threats. Other possible outcomes include the detection of inappropriate objectives, obsolete strategy, ill-advised use of resources, and other needs for revising the direction of the company relative to competition.

The form shown in Figure 3.4 is a useful tool for performing such an audit for a retail company. Other audit forms with different comparison characteristics should be used for other industry categories. The audit involves the marketer in an appraisal of every aspect of a

	Our rank in comparison to:*		
	Comp. A – ? 0 +	Comp. B – ? 0 +	Comp. C – ? 0 +
Product or service			
1. Customer acceptance			
2. Customer satisfaction in use			
3. Product quality level(s)/innovations			
4. Adequacy of assortments			
5. Services provided			
Place			
1. Customer accessibility			
2. Suitability of site			
3. Customer traffic flow			
4. Appearance of facility			
5. Selling areas			
6. Parking facilities			
7. Drawing power of neighboring firms			
8. Customer image of facilities			
9. Store layout			
Price			
1. Comparative price level(s)			
2. Consumers' images of store's prices			
3. Number of price lines			
4. Consistency of price policies			
5. Credit policies and practices			
Promotion			
1. Promotional ability			
2. Amount and quality of promotional efforts			
3. Ethical standards			
4. Consistency of efforts			

*A minus sign (–) indicates that the business being evaluated ranks below the competitor on the specific factor; a question mark (?) indicates that the relative standing is unknown; a zero (0) indicates equal competitive standing; a plus sign (+) indicates that the business being evaluated ranks above the competition on the specific factor.

FIGURE 3.4. Competitive Marketing Mix Audit Form

firm's marketing mix (compared to that of its major competitors). Several steps are involved in using this form.

First, the form should reflect the nature of the marketing mix activities for the type of firms being analyzed. For example, if retail firms are being analyzed, the form must reflect the components important in retailing. Specifically, place would be analyzed in terms of appearance, layout, and traffic flows throughout the stores. This analysis would not be appropriate for a manufacturer since customers will not usually see the physical facility or move through it.

Second, the major competitors must be identified by name so that a realistic comparison can be made. This requirement forces the marketer to identify the specific competitors going after a market segment and permits the collection of data on those specific firms.

Third, sources of data must be identified to complete the audit. Some of the data may already be available from previous analyses or research and merely need updating. Or, data may have to be collected to complete the audit. For some types of comparisons, judgment must be used if research or other objective data are not available. Avoid the "halo effect" (being favorably biased toward one's own company) when comparing your company to competitors. One way to avoid bias is to use the judgment of several people rather than relying on that of one person.

Finally, some system must be developed to "grade" your own company's effort and your competitors' efforts on each aspect of the audit. For new firms anticipating entry into a market, competitors are compared with one another. The ranking system just described is one possibility. In this system, each competitor is assigned a ranking of "higher," "lower," "equal to," or "don't know" on each part of the audit. Or, you may prefer to rank competitors in order using 1 to indicate the best, 2 the second best, and so on.

Rather than a more general analysis of price levels, this audit would need to be completed for *each segment* analyzed. The planner is not particularly interested in the generalities here but rather the details about specific groups or segments in the market. Thoroughness is important in this type of analysis. Lack of digging into the details may even be misleading.

In a consumer study done for a restaurant, respondents were asked whether they thought their friends would eat at that particular restaurant. If the answer was no, they were then asked why. The most common response was that prices were "too high." Yet the competitive analysis shown in Table 3.3 tells a completely different story. The prices charged by the Holiday Restaurant were about the same as the other competitors for comparable menu items, which means respondents *thought* the prices were too high. This problem leads to a completely different type of strategy or tactics than if prices were in fact higher than those of competitors.

COMPETITIVE STRATEGIES AND RESOURCES

Several other factors should be analyzed for a more complete evaluation of competitors in a market. They include competitors' strategic tendencies and resources: marketing, financial, and production. These relate to long-run actions as opposed to short-run.

TABLE 3.3. Competitive Pricing—Restaurants

Restaurant	8-oz. rib eye $	Hamburger w/fries $	Breakfast $	Buffet $	Banquet $
Southern Inn	11.69	5.65	3.15	6.35	10.49
King's Inn	9.99	4.99	N/A	N/A	N/A
Charlie's Place	12.99	N/A	N/A	N/A	N/A
Tony's	10.99	5.29	2.89	N/A	8.49
Sandpiper	10.99	4.99	3.89	N/A	9.99
The Castle	12.75	5.75	4.99	N/A	On request
Ramble Inn	9.95	4.89	2.99	N/A	12.79
The Rib Joint	11.00	4.10	3.50	N/A	10.99-12.00
The Ice Box	11.50	5.45	N/A	N/A	10.45
Uncle Joe's	12.99	3.69	N/A	N/A	10.99
Captain Bill's	12.79	4.79	N/A	N/A	N/A
John's Diner	11.99	4.59	N/A	7.99	10.75
Holiday Restaurant	11.99	4.45	3.50	6.50-7.99	10.50

Source: Artificial data
N/A: not applicable, no similar offering

The first factor is concerned with competitors' willingness to change or react to competitive moves; the second deals with their ability to make strategic moves.

Assessing strategic tendencies involves deciding whether competitors' actions tend to be reactive or proactive. *Reactive* strategies are those which follow the lead of other firms in the market or simply settle into a niche. *Proactive* strategies involve market leadership or challenge to the market leaders. If market leaders and challengers can be identified, they are the competitors whose actions must be anticipated. The marketing mix audit of these firms helps identify the exact nature of their strategies in a short approach.

As discussed earlier in this chapter, an approach used by many firms in recent years is called *product positioning*—the placement of a product in terms of consumers' perceptions of it relative to other products. It is the answer to the question, "How do we want consumers to perceive our product relative to other products on the market?" The marketing mix is altered in an attempt to put that product in that position in the minds of consumers.

Assessing competitors' resources involves determining whether specific competitors have the marketing expertise to respond successfully to events in the marketplace, the productive capacity to respond in terms of both levels of demand and technology, and finally, the financial resources to respond to problems and opportunities that occur. Moreover, since most firms attempt to build on their strengths and nullify their weaknesses, analysis can help them forecast the type of response they are most likely to make. A firm that is strong financially with unused productive capacity but weaker in marketing skills is most likely to meet a challenge with lower prices or an increase in promotional expenditures than a firm with an opposite set of strengths and weaknesses.

As a market moves toward oligopolistic competition, the necessity of this type of analysis becomes more significant. Failure to expect and anticipate competitive reactions is to ignore the realities of market dynamics.

After completing the competitive analysis by market segment, it is important to develop summary statements about each segment with respect to competition.

EXPLOITING THE COMPANY'S COMPETITIVE ADVANTAGE

As each competitive firm's strategy, strengths, and weaknesses are analyzed for each market segment, the market analyst should look for those segments not being served or not being served well by existing competition. Successful entry and exploitation of a marketing opportunity is much easier if a firm builds upon its competitive advantage in the market. When this approach is used the analyst begins interpreting "holes in the market." Thus opportunities and abilities are matched.

Strategies by Market Position

Once you have adequately analyzed and assessed the competition, it is time to formulate the strategy, given a company's position in the market, based on the competitive analysis. Most companies will be either a market leader, a market challenger, a market follower, or a market nicher (see Table 3.4).[11]

Market leaders are the recognized leaders who have the largest market share of the relevant market. Although their position of dominance may be widely recognized, their success may be constantly challenged by other firms. The strategies used by market leaders focus on expanding their own control of the market while warding off or countering the activities of aggressive competitors. The leader's strategy becomes the pivot point around which other competitors adjust their own strategies.

Market challengers are the firms which are constantly trying to increase their market share in "head-on" competition with the leader, attacking the leader at its weak points or merging with smaller competitors. Market challengers are usually large firms in terms of revenues and profits, and may be even more profitable than the leader. The challenger usually tries to identify weaknesses in the leader's strategy and either confronts or goes around the leader or concentrates its efforts on taking over smaller firms. Pepsi's challenge to Coke's leadership position clearly demonstrates how the challenger's strategy can affect the strategies of other competitors. New Coke, which was closer in taste to that of Pepsi than Classic Coke, was clearly a competitive strategy response.

TABLE 3.4. Competitive Marketing Strategies

Market position	Possible strategies
Market leader (This is the firm acknowledged as the leader, and it has the largest market share and innovative marketing tactics.)	1. Expand total market: Develop new uses, new users, or more usage by existing customers. 2. Protect market share: Use the relevant market to retaliate against challengers.
Market challenger (This is the second, third, or fourth firm in market share; it may be quite large but smaller than the market leader.)	1. Direct attack strategy: Meet leader head-on with aggressive promotion and/or prices. 2. Backdoor strategy: Go around leader options through innovative strategy. 3. Guppy strategy: Increase market share by going after smaller firms.
Market follower (This is a firm which chooses not to challenge the leader but is content with imitation.)	1. Copy leader: Match as closely as possible leader's strategy without directly challenging. 2. Coping strategy: Adjust to strategies of both leader and challenger without direct confrontation.
Market nicher (Smaller firms that operate in a geographic or client niche without directly clashing with competitors. Specialization is unique key to their success.)	1. Geographic specialization: Specialize by offering quick response to customers. 2. Product specialization: Offer products which are unique to customers served.

Source: Adapted from Philip Kotler, *Marketing Management: Analysis, Planning, Implementation, and Control,* Eleventh Edition (Upper Saddle River, NJ: Prentice-Hall, Inc., 2003), pp. 254-272.

Market followers and *market nichers* adjust to the strategies of the market dominators without making challenges. Nichers usually try to specialize geographically or by products offered and basically avoid direct confrontation with other competitors. The followers simply copy the leader's strategy or adjust their strategy to cope with both the leader and the challenger's strategies, again without calling attention to their own activities. Rent-A-Wreck car rental service is an attempt to target the niche created by higher rental fees charged by most rental companies.

Successful strategizing, therefore, begins with an understanding of a company's market position in the competitive market as well as broad-based knowledge of its strengths, weaknesses, and capabilities. This allows the company to stake out a strategy that will lead to long-term growth. Often this will require making product innovations, creating positive relationships with key suppliers and customers, establishing consumer awareness, and developing internal efficiencies and competence.

How May Competitors React?

Competitors' reactions need to be systematically anticipated before taking initial proactive steps. In vigorous markets something is almost certain to happen in the competitive arena. Many firms simply wait to react to a rival's action; proactive innovators aim initially at serving markets excellently. A company must then count on reaction, which may possibly be strong.

If a company is making proactive strategic actions, it needs to anticipate the strength of market reactions. Thus, the marketing strategist needs to ask several questions to determine the likelihood of strong competitive reactions:

- *Is this product central to the competitor's business strategy?* If we challenge the very core of a business, they will likely respond very aggressively.
- *Should we rock the boat?* We may be content to "live and let live," feeling that any significant move to achieve an advantage could be matched or wiped out by rivals. It could also make us vulnerable in our own core areas.
- *Are we in the cross fire?* If our brand is between two other leaders, we may be brought into the fray because of their competitive actions (e.g., aggressive couponing, advertising, pricing).
- *What is the competitor's fighting tradition?* Some firms scrupulously avoid proactive moves, waiting instead to study innovators' mistakes and then hit with a counterpunch.[12]

Various actions may be necessary to answer those questions:

- *Obtain competitive intelligence.* All firms should review and improve their intelligence procedures. This subject will be discussed later in this chapter.
- *Play war games.* Play internal war games, with staff members playing the roles of rival managers.
- *Develop competitive response models.* Make an empirical analysis of competitive responses to develop models that may yield insights.
- *Be subtle.* Some firms that make advances do so quietly in order to lessen the chance of retaliation. Be aware that conspicuous success on a powerful rival's "sacred turf" will be countered, regardless of the rival's profit, or even loss.
- *Get ready for the next stage.* If you win round one, remember round two, in which massive and effective reaction on another front may be forthcoming.
- *Change time horizons.* Long-term competitive advantage may be impossible; instead, make good short-run gains and then get out quickly as the powerful competition pours in.[13]

GATHERING COMPETITOR INTELLIGENCE

Competitor intelligence (CI) techniques are being used with increasing frequency to gain and hold market share. A number of factors contribute to the growing interest in CI. The speed of business is increasing all the time. This faster pace requires frequently updated knowledge of competitors. The rapid rate of technology change also can bring about quick and drastic changes in the competitive landscape. Political and legal changes can alter the competitive makeup. Consider the federal government's attempt to break up Microsoft and decisions on deregulation in the electric utility industry, as examples of significant changes in the competitive situation. Increased global competition as well as more aggressive domestic competition can also contribute to a greater need for CI.

Several advantages result from collecting and analyzing CI. Clearly, there should be fewer surprises from competitors when a company has a well-developed "early warning system." Having enough of the right type of competitive information at an early point in time also allows a company to more effectively react to threats and opportunities. Effective CI is a valuable foundation for strategic and tactical planning efforts. Without a clear view of the competitive situation a company will be unable to chart a course to accomplish its goals.

In spite of an obvious need, according to the Society of Competitive Intelligence Professionals (SCIP), only 7 percent of large U.S. companies and about 5 percent of small companies have a full-scale, formalized, competitive intelligence system.[14] Why are so few companies committed to the function of CI? First, many businesspeople believe they already know about everything that is going on in their industry. (Besides, if it is not happening in their company, industry, or country it is not important.) Second, CI may be perceived as too expensive and a cost rather than profit center. Third, businesspeople typically have not been trained in CI and therefore do not know how to perform it. Finally, CI may be perceived as "spying" and "unethical."[15]

Building a competitive intelligence system involves more than simply gathering information. CI system development should include the following steps:

1. Designate a CI director and give the position organizational clout.
2. Determine who needs what type of CI for which decisions.
3. Conduct a CI audit to determine what data exist, where they are held, and in what format.
4. Design an information infrastructure to share CI within the company.
5. Develop ethical and legal guidelines for CI.[16]

Where does CI come from? Ninety percent of it can be obtained by talking to colleagues, accessing annual reports, press releases, newsletters, speeches, government filings, and commercial databases. The remaining 10 percent can be obtained through sound deductive reasoning. Respondents to one survey thought that the most valuable competitive information dealt with pricing, strategy, and sales. The survey also reported that organizations rate their own sales forces as the most important agents in gathering intelligence, with customers ranked second, followed by trade and industry periodicals.[17,18]

CI gathering has sometimes been abused by those who are unscrupulous and believe it is okay to hack into computer systems, steal trade secrets, or sift through competitors' garbage. Thus, a company should establish guidelines that encourage ethical practice and advise employees not to do anything illegal or that would embarrass or endanger the company.

Managers of small- and medium-sized organizations frequently believe that their limited financial resources prevent them from developing a CI program. In fact, some CI activities cost nothing; some require only very modest expenditure, and some others cannot be done at any price.

When gathering CI companies can take the following simple but important steps at a minimal cost:

- Buy competitors' products, tear them down, and evaluate them.
- Require field sales personnel to provide feedback on customers, suppliers, distributors, and competitors.
- Assign key officers to spend several days a year talking to customers.
- Study internal security to ensure that competitors cannot gain access to company secrets.
- Stay abreast of what foreign competitors are doing.
- Be familiar with competitive information available under the Freedom of Information Act—trade secrets and IRS submissions are protected. (All states have their own version of the FOIA.)
- Cultivate relationships with securities analysts and stockbrokers who keep tabs on competitors.
- Play or have a subordinate play customer to find out how competitors market their products.
- Use a small market research firm to provide continuous data on a competitor for an annual fee.
- Use computerized information services or databases.
- Subscribe to a clipping service that scans newspapers, financial journals, and business publications for articles on competitors (often these publishers are not on any database).
- Purchase shares of a competitor's common stock.
- Check industry associations for information.
- Search U.S. and international patent databases, as well as databases containing information about patent court cases involving infringement.[19,20]

Difficulties arise when the competition is privately held. Some financial information may be obtained from state offices, but most information is impossible to obtain ethically. CI programs in small or moderate-sized companies are usually best directed by the president or vice president of marketing.

A CUSTOMER OR COMPETITOR ORIENTATION?[21]

For almost four decades marketers have stressed a customer orientation as their guiding philosophy. Satisfying customer needs was viewed as the best way to achieve a company's objectives of growth and profit. Although marketers have preached a customer orientation for many years, they have not always practiced it. Most companies probably know much less than they should about customer needs and ways of satisfying buyers.

Typically, given even less weight is a competitor orientation in which competitive conditions are factored carefully into marketing plans. Those taking a competitive orientation argue that sales, profit, and growth goals must usually be reached at rivals' expense and that customer satisfaction is merely one way of reaching them.

Differences in the two orientations are best understood in the context of a situation analysis to discover marketing problems and opportunities. A *competitor orientation* would lead a company to focus on conditions in individual (local) markets, because of widely differing competitive conditions. A *customer orientation* would lead a company to treat its entire geographic market as a unit.

The application of a customer orientation requires answers to the following kinds of questions:

- Who are our main customers? What strategies are we using that they like? How satisfied are they? What strategies turn away other segments?
- In what segments are we growing fastest; where are we losing the most customers; and what accounts for these changes? Are dissatisfied segments likely to switch?
- What are the most important benefits our buyers are seeking? What problems or complaints do they have? How best can we design our offerings to match these needs? What are potential buyers willing to pay for those benefits?

In contrast, the application of a competitor orientation would address the following kinds of questions:

- Which rivals are vulnerable and what are their weaknesses? Can we capitalize on them to gain market segments?
- What are our vulnerabilities and how can we correct or minimize them? Can we defend our market segments sufficiently?
- From which rivals are we gaining the most customers? How can we continue this trend? To which are we losing the most customers? How can we minimize this problem?

Because different questions are asked, different conclusions will typically be reached about a firm's marketing problems and opportunities, leading to different marketing action programs. Competitor-oriented firms look for vulnerabilities or weaknesses in rivals, such as those related to the following:

- Customers (complaints about quality, price, etc.)
- Resellers (dissatisfaction about margins, price protection, deliveries, etc.)
- Employees and management (morale, turnover, absenteeism, etc.)
- Fiscal affairs (cash flow, interest expense, etc.)
- Suppliers (service, stocks, etc.)
- Costs (labor, materials, technology, etc.)

Both a customer orientation and a competitor orientation are necessary in order for the marketer to focus appropriately on the marketing challenge.

SUMMARY

At this point in the analysis, the marketer should begin to see several clear-cut problems and opportunities. Not only have general and specific characteristics of the market been analyzed but also the responses of competitive firms that are pursuing these markets.

For new firms in a market, the competitive analysis has another advantage. Because other firms have already adjusted to market conditions with their own strategies, their own approaches to the market are suggestive of successful and unsuccessful ways to enter and compete in it. Their trials and errors should become a guide to avoiding mistakes already made and activities already proven unsuccessful either by their nature or by the way they were carried out by existing firms.

Chapter 4

Financial Analysis for Marketing Decisions

In this chapter we address the third element of what marketing managers must understand: the financial implications of marketing decisions (see Figure 4.1).

FINANCIAL ASSESSMENT

After the analyses described in the previous chapters have been completed, financial assessment should be undertaken. The financial assessment usually covers at least four different areas: (1) revenue

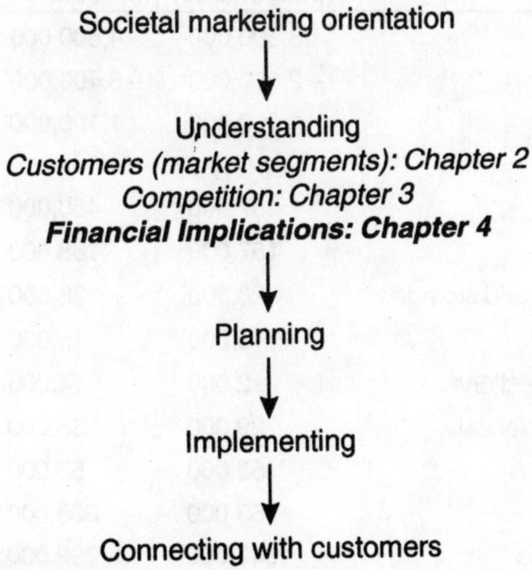

FIGURE 4.1. The Effective Marketing Management Process

analysis, (2) cost analysis, (3) cash-flow analysis, and (4) analysis of return on investment (ROI).

One of the most beneficial ways to combine these four types of analyses is to utilize a pro forma income statement. It is the basic document to be generated by the financial analyses. A pro forma income statement is a projected income statement for a specific future time period using estimates of the revenues and costs associated with that time period. It provides an estimate of future cash flows to be produced by a given market segment which can be discounted to determine the present value of these cash flows. This, in turn, is used in calculating the rate of return anticipated as achievable from a given segment.

A pro forma income statement for a proposed opportunity is shown in Table 4.1. The approach used for this venture was to develop three alternate pro forma statements, each based on a different assumption about revenues generated by the new venture. This approach permits identifying the "optimistic," "pessimistic," and "most likely" scenar-

TABLE 4.1. Pro Forma Income Statement

	Low (pessimistic)	**Medium (most likely)**	**High (optimistic)**
Sales	3,500,000	4,500,000	5,500,000
Cost of sales	– 2,500,000	– 3,400,000	– 4,300,000
Gross margin	1,000,000	1,100,000	1,200,000
Expenses			
Direct selling	457,000	480,000	512,000
Advertising	157,000	168,000	180,000
Transportation and storage	28,000	38,000	48,000
Depreciation	15,000	15,000	15,000
Credit and collections	12,000	14,000	16,000
Financial and clerical	29,000	38,000	47,000
Administrative	55,000	55,000	55,000
Total	753,000	808,000	873,000
Profit before taxes	247,000	292,000	327,000
Net profit after taxes (NPAT)	128,440	151,840	170,040
Cash flow (NPAT + depreciation)	143,440	166,840	185,040

ios of a given situation. It is also in line with a more realistic approach to demand forecasting which produces a range of sales volume for new products. When products or services have already been on the market for several years, industry sales history is available to use in projecting sales.

Revenue and costs can change radically over the course of a product's life cycle. For example, high investments in promotion and building a distribution network produce losses in early years; while, on the other hand, reduced variable costs achieved by increasing production efficiency and technological improvement may produce high profit levels in later years. Consequently, any realistic financial analysis must take into consideration an adequate time frame and associated changes in cost structures.

Since the financial analysis of a given opportunity is usually long run in nature, either the pro forma must be estimated for each year for some assumed length of time, or an "average" year can be used which represents three to five years into the future. Then the discounted cash flow from this year is used as an average for the venture's anticipated life to calculate the ROI or break-even point of the project.

If subjective probabilities are assigned to each alternative, then decision tree analysis can be used to calculate an expected value for the cash flow from the project. Subjective probabilities are assigned by the analyst based on judgment rather than chance processes. When the alternatives are evaluated in a "tree" diagram, a schematic chart of the decision problem showing each alternative and the likelihood of each alternative is developed. Otherwise, the ROI can be calculated for each alternative and then compared with a predetermined rate to evaluate the financial impact of each alternative.

Developing a pro forma income statement requires a forecast of both expected revenues and operating expenses. The procedures for developing each of these estimates are discussed later in this chapter. Thus, the revenue analysis produces an estimate of revenues, the cost analysis produces an estimate of the costs associated with those revenues, and the analysis of ROI or break-even point relates those returns to the investment to be made in the venture. This, in turn, provides the answer to the basic question posed in financial analysis: What is the projected financial impact of pursuing this particular market opportunity?

Not-for-Profit Financial Analysis

Many not-for-profit organizations fail to apply opportunity assessment to their decision making. A large hospital, for example, decided to build a new wing for geriatric outpatients to provide rehabilitation services for those suffering from major traumas such as strokes or heart attacks. The facility was built to accommodate twenty-five patients. However, when it opened, only two patients showed up to take advantage of the new facility. An analysis of demand for such services prior to their provision would have avoided such a costly mistake.

Although the analysis of returns from a decision made by a not-for-profit organization uses different criteria, such an evaluation should be made nonetheless. This type of analysis is simply an application of a basic management concept—evaluate the impact of a decision *before* you make it. This principle applies to not-for-profit as well as for-profit organizations. One type of analysis especially suited for not-for-profit organizations is benefit-cost analysis which is discussed later in this chapter.

REVENUE ANALYSIS

Once the size of the total market has been estimated and the competition analyzed, the next step in the market opportunity assessment process is to estimate the sales revenue the opportunity can be expected to generate on an annual basis. The point is not trying to determine how many consumers will buy a product or service, but how many will buy *your* offering of that product or service.

Forecasting Market Share

For established markets, forecasting involves estimating market share. The question is, "What share of total sales can we reasonably expect to attain?" The percent is then converted to a dollar amount—the sales revenue expected in a given time period. The key element in the estimate at this point is judgment. (If a test market is used later in the development process, this estimate can be reevaluated for soundness.)

This judgment is based on an analysis of your offering versus competitive offerings. If four competitors are in the market and your product is expected to compete on an equal footing with other offerings, then a 20 percent market share should be used as an initial estimate of market share. This basic estimate would then be raised or lowered to reflect competitive strengths and weaknesses in the market.

For new products and services not currently on the market, an acceptance rate must be estimated. The acceptance rate is the proportion of the segment that will buy your product or use your service. Two approaches can be used to estimate the acceptance rate. These are described next.

Judgment Estimates

One way to estimate the acceptance rate is to use judgment. After careful analysis of the market, the person preparing the feasibility study sets the rate, in conjunction with other people who are knowledgeable about the market. Such an "educated guess" can be effective if people who are knowledgeable about a market—retailers, wholesalers, industrial users—are consulted. This estimate also reflects what the company can bring to the market in terms of marketing skills and innovation, brand equity, and the like.

Consumer Surveys

Another approach to estimating the proportion of consumers who would buy a new offering is a survey of potential consumers. Data obtained in this way have been referred to as "iffy" data, e.g.,"I would buy your product *if* it were offered on the market and *if* I were in the market at that time, and *if* . . ." Although purchase intent statements in survey research cannot be taken completely at face value, various methods of discounting stated purchase intent are available to reflect realistic estimates of actual purchase behavior that can be expected in the marketplace. For industrial users, however, surveys with purchase decision makers can be highly effective since they are in a position to evaluate the use of a product in a more judicious manner than many individual consumers.

These two approaches are often combined to provide a sales forecast. A set of assumptions—about market acceptance, competitive reactions, economic conditions, degree of distribution, and promotion—must also be developed as a basis for the forecast. These assumptions must precede the actual dollar forecast used in the pro forma income statement.

An example of how these approaches can be combined to estimate sales revenue is shown in Table 4.2. This table shows the estimates of attendance at a proposed themed water park. Assumptions were made about the penetration or acceptance rates by the market segment and

TABLE 4.2. Attendance Projections

Facts/assumptions attendance/penetration	Alternative attendance forecasts		
	Low	**Most likely**	**High**
(a) Local market population	520,000	520,000	520,000
(1) Target market (ages 10-25)	120,000	120,000	120,000
penetration	× .65	× .70	× .85
attendance	78,000	84,000	102,000
(2) Local market (other age groups)	110,000	110,000	110,000
penetration	× .03	× .05	× .07
attendance	3,300	5,500	7,700
(b) Regional market population	100,000	100,000	100,000
penetration	× .10	× .15	× .20
attendance	10,000	15,000	20,000
(c) Tourist market population	250,000	250,000	250,000
penetration	× .03	× .05	× .07
attendance	7,500	12,500	17,500
(d) Group sales market attendance	18,000	20,500	25,000
(e) Repeat business attendance	72,000	78,000	95,000
Total attendance (a+b+c+d+e)	188,800	215,500	267,200

the number of repeat visitors that could be expected. The admission charge was anticipated to be fifteen dollars per person given the following alternative sales forecasts:

Low forecast	\$2,832,000	(188,800 x \$15)
Most likely	\$3,232,500	(215,500 x \$15)
High forecast	\$4,008,000	(267,200 x \$15)

A sales range of about \$2,832,000 to \$4,008,000 was estimated. To derive a figure for the pro forma income statement, the following probabilities were assigned to each forecast:

Low forecast	.25
Most likely	.50
High forecast	.25

The *expected value of sales revenue* (EVSR) was then computed by multiplying the expected sales revenue by its associated probability as follows:

$$\text{EVSR} = [(\$2{,}832{,}000)\,(.25)] + [(\$3{,}232{,}500)\,(.50)] + [(\$4{,}008{,}000)\,(.25)] \quad (4.1)$$

$$\text{EVSR} = \$3{,}326{,}250$$

This final value, \$3,326,250, was used as the estimated sales revenue to be generated from attendance in the pro forma income statement.

COST ANALYSIS

The bottom line of any operation or project is significantly affected by the underlying cost structure. Consequently, cost analysis is closely allied with revenue analysis. Once revenue estimates have been made, cost analysis must be carefully considered. This section will discuss various cost concepts, cost information sources, cost sensitivity analysis, technical analysis, and cost forecasting.

Cost Concepts

Accounting for the costs of conducting business operations is complex. This is also true of analyzing costs for market opportunity assessment. As a business functions, assets lose their original identity. The business operation converts the assets into some other form. For example, raw materials of many kinds may go into a final manufactured product and many of these raw materials may be unrecognizable in the end product. Costs, however, are traced through the business operations as the assets and resources are converted into goods and services. Since the profits and losses of a business are measured as the difference between the *revenue* received from customers and the *costs* associated with the delivery of the products or services, a project cannot be judged as feasible or profitable without dependable cost estimates.

Types of Costs

Because there are many different types of costs, they must be selectively chosen to match the purpose for which they are used. Care must be taken to understand the specific application of a cost under consideration. Costs can be divided into several major categories, some of which will be very instrumental in developing the project cost summary discussed later in the chapter.

Period costs. Period costs are associated with and measured according to time intervals rather than goods or services. For example, equipment rental may be at the rate of $1,200 a month. Regardless of the amount of business or product supported by the equipment, the rental cost of the equipment remains $1,200 each month. This expense amount is allocated against revenue according to the time interval without regard to the amount of business transacted. Equipment expense for the year will show $14,400 on the income statement. Generally speaking, selling and administrative costs are designated as period costs.

Product costs. In some cases it is inappropriate to classify costs as period costs. Some situations in the income determination process call for costs to be offset as expenses against the activity, good, or service that produced the revenue. Under this concept of income determination, the period in which the benefit is received is the period in which the costs should be expressed and deducted as expenses. Following our equipment rental example, the equipment rental for a certain period should not be charged off as rent expense for that period if the goods produced by the equipment are not sold until a later period. If costs of this type are handled as product costs, they are matched against the revenue generated from their sale in the period of that sale. In most cases, manufacturing costs are treated as product costs rather than period costs and are included in the cost of goods sold.

Fixed costs. Costs that can be expected to remain constant over a period of time regardless of activity levels are called fixed costs. Examples of this type of cost are executive salaries, interest charges, rent, insurance, equipment leases, depreciation, engineering and technical support, and product development expense. Obviously, a fixed cost, like any other cost, can be increased or decreased, particularly in an inflationary period. These variations, however, are caused by other external factors and not caused by the firm's output or activity.

Fixed costs can be broken down further as committed fixed costs and discretionary fixed costs. Various management decisions may commit the company to a course of action that will require the company to conform to a certain payment schedule for a number of years in the future. Costs incurred in this way are committed fixed costs. The costs related to acquiring a new building are examples of committed costs. On the other hand, discretionary fixed costs are established as a part of a budget that can be altered by management action on a monthly, quarterly, or yearly basis. These costs are much more easily altered, and have a high degree of flexibility. Examples of discretionary fixed costs are the research and development budget or supervisory salaries that are set by management action.

Variable and semivariable costs. Costs that vary closely with production are considered variable costs. In the strictest sense of the term, variable costs should vary in direct proportion to changes in production levels. Direct material cost and direct labor costs are good examples of variable costs. Most costs, however, are semivariable. Semivariable costs tend to fluctuate with volume, but not in a direct relationship to production. Market research expense, advertising and sales promotion expense, supplies expense, and maintenance expenses are all examples of semivariable expenses. In some cases, semivariable costs can be broken down into fixed and variable components to make application for decision making possible.

Direct and indirect costs. Direct costs are those identifiable with a particular product, activity, or department. Indirect costs are not directly identifiable with any particular product, activity, or department. Often, the distinction between direct and indirect costs depends upon the unit under consideration. A cost of specific supplies used may be identified directly as a cost of a particular department but may not be a direct cost of the product manufactured. When a cost can be directly identified to the unit under consideration, it is considered a direct cost relative to that unit. When a cost is associated with a unit only through allocation, it is an indirect cost.

Controllable and noncontrollable costs. Like direct and indirect costs, a reference point is required to classify costs as controllable or noncontrollable. Obviously, at some point in the organizational structure, all costs are controllable. Top management can dispose of property, eliminate personnel, terminate research projects, or whatever is necessary to control costs. At middle and lower levels of management, however, costs can be termed as noncontrollable. If a specific level of management can authorize certain costs, then these costs are considered controllable at that level. A plant manager, for example, may have control over the supplies used by his or plant, but he or she may have no control of promotional costs established by central headquarters.

Sunk costs. A sunk cost is usually a cost that was spent in the past and is irrelevant to a decision under consideration. Sunk costs may be variable or fixed.

Differential costs. The purpose of cost analysis is to provide management with the data necessary to compare alternatives and make a choice. In order to simplify the comparison of alternatives, any costs that remain the same regardless of the alternative will be disregarded in the analysis. A difference in cost between one course of action and another is referred to as a differential cost. In most cases the decision will result in an increased cost. This increased differential cost is often specifically referred to as an incremental cost. Differential costs are often referred to as marginal costs when the differential cost is the additional cost required to produce one more unit of a product.

Opportunity costs. Ordinarily, costs are viewed as outlays or expenditures that must be made to obtain goods and services. The concept of opportunity costs extends this to include sacrifices that are made by foregoing benefits or returns. An opportunity cost takes into consideration the fact that choosing one of several alternatives precludes receiving the benefits of the rejected alternatives. The sacrifice of a return from a rejected alternative is referred to as the opportunity cost of the chosen alternative. Many of the costs mentioned are overlapping in nature. Thus fixed cost may also be a sunk cost, noncontrollable cost, or a period cost. Judgment must be used in identifying specific costs in the development of cost estimates for a specific opportunity or business venture.

Data Sources

Many sources of data are found in a company's historical records. These records can provide cost information to establish reasonable cost estimates. Many other sources of data provide information to form the basis of a reliable cost forecast. Some of these are listed next:

- *Trade publications*—provide comparative financial ratios, cost-of-goods-sold information, gross margin data, and other information.
- *Time studies*—establish standards for estimating labor cost.
- *Experiments*—test processes in terms of time, material, labor, and other resources necessary to complete production processes.
- *Pilot plant or process activities*—involves the intermittent or continuous operation of a new plant activity or process to perfect engineering specifications and to establish cost standards.
- *Historical cost data*—these can include past material cost, labor cost, overhead expense, administrative costs, utility expense, and many other categories of expense.
- *Interviews*—correspondence include personal, telephone, and mail designed to gather data that provide primary cost information unavailable from other sources.

Cost Behavior, Sensitivity Analysis, and Risk Analysis

Before moving on to the actual development of detailed cost forecasts, a discussion of sensitivity analysis is in order.

Sensitivity Analysis

Sensitivity analysis is a technique that illustrates how the costs of an operation or activity will be affected by changes in variables or by errors in the input data. Sensitivity analysis is sometimes called "what if" analysis because it asks and answers questions such as, "What if labor costs increase an average of $1.75/hour?" and "What if sales fall to 350,000 units?"

Other questions that can be answered by sensitivity analysis include the following: "What happens to profits if we change the selling price?" "What happens to profits if we buy more efficient equipment, change our formulation and accompanying cost structure, or increase or decrease personnel?" The starting point for sensitivity analysis is to establish a base case or most likely situation. Once the base case or most likely forecast elements are established for items such as unit sales, sales price, fixed costs, and variable costs, the analyst will selectively change key variables to determine their impact on the base case results. The analyst can ask all the "what if" questions necessary to see the effect of changes in variables such as product price, raw material costs, and operating costs on the overall results of a project. The analyst can determine which variable has the most negative or positive effect on the project's profitability. Given the possible range of a variable, such as material costs, the range of effects on the outcome can be calculated and charted. The more sensitive the outcome is to the tested variable, the more serious an error in estimating the variable would be. The purpose of sensitivity analysis is to identify the variables that have the stronger impact on the outcome of a project. Sensitivity analysis is effective in determining the consequences of a change in a variable.

Break-even analysis. To construct a break-even analysis, one must have estimates of fixed costs, variable costs per unit, volume of production, and price per unit. As discussed earlier, fixed costs do not change with the level of production. Variable costs are directly related to units of production and change with the level of production. The following list illustrates different costs attributable to fixed costs and variable costs.

Fixed costs	**Variable costs**
Depreciation	Factory labor
Plant equipment	Material costs
Fixed utilities	Commissions
Office expense	Freight in and out
Insurance	Variable factory expense
Rentals	Utilities (other than fixed)
Debt interest	Cost of goods sold
Salaries (executive and office)	Sales expense

The elements and relationships of break-even analysis are illustrated next:

$$\text{Break-even (BE) } Q = \frac{FC}{P - VC}$$

Where:
- FC = Fixed costs
- P = Sales price per unit
- Q = Quantity of production in units
- VC = Variable cost per unit
- P – VC = Contribution margin

Expressed another way:

$$\text{Total revenue} = \text{Total cost at the break-even point} \quad (4.2)$$

$$TR = TC$$

or

$$TR - TC = 0 \text{ (at break-even point)}$$

$$TR = PQ = \text{Total revenue}$$

$$TC = FC + VQ = \text{Total cost}$$

Substituting:

$$PQ = FC + VQ$$

Solving for Q will derive break-even quantity.

In a situation in which a new production line is being considered, the following data might be indicated by market analysis:

Production line capacity	=	2,200 units		
Potential selling price	=	\$220/unit	=	P
Fixed costs	=	\$60,000	=	FC
Variable costs	=	\$170/unit	=	VC

When TR = FC, the break-even point is 1,200 units.

PQ	=	FC + VQ
\$220 (Q)	=	\$60,000 + \$170 (Q)
\$220 (Q) – \$170 (Q)	=	\$60,000
\$50 (Q)	=	\$60,000
(Q)	=	1,200 Units

Solved another way:

$$BE = \frac{FC}{P - VC} = \frac{\$60{,}000}{\$220 - 170} = \frac{\$60{,}000}{\$50}$$

Break-even point by quantity

$$BE = 1{,}200 \text{ units}$$

To apply sensitivity analysis, the analyst might use various values of volume, price, variable cost, and fixed cost to measure their relative effect on profit.

Table 4.3 illustrates changes in volume of production (and sales) of 100 unit increments above and below the break-even point. The table also shows the impact of these changes in production on profits and that changes in the volume of production and sales near the break-even point result in large variations in profits and losses.

Using the same basic formula shown in equation 4.2, an analyst can test the sensitivity of price and profits (see Table 4.4).

Equation 4.2 shows a production capacity of 2,200 units and a break-even point of 1,200 units. If market analysis shows a market potential in the range of 1,400 to 1,700 units, then the project can be

TABLE 4.3. Sensitivity Analysis of Production and Profits

Volume	Profit (loss)	Incremental percent change
700	(25,000)	25
800	(20,000)	33
900	(15,000)	50
1,000	(10,000)	100
1,100	(5,000)	
1,200	0	
1,300	5,000	
1,400	10,000	100
1,500	15,000	50
1,600	20,000	33
1,700	25,000	25

TABLE 4.4. Sensitivity Analysis of Price and Profits (Volume Set at 1,200 Units)

Price	Profit	Incremental percent change
180	(48,000)	
190	(36,000)	33
200	(24,000)	50
210	(12,000)	100
220	0	
230	12,000	
240	24,000	100
250	36,000	50
260	48,000	33

considered a viable proposition. Further calculations can be made to estimate a range of profits based on previous cost assumptions.

Profit = $220 (1,700) – $60,000 – $170 (1,700)
Profit = $374,000 – $60,000 – $289,000
Profit = $25,000
Profit = $220 (1,400) – $60,000 – $170 (1,400)
Profit = $308,000 – $60,000 – $238,000
Profit = $10,000

The analyst can use the same calculation method to compute a minimum sales price for any level of volume. Other variations can be used to determine the effect of changes on profit and loss. Break-even analysis, used in this way, provides managers with a profit or loss estimate at different levels of sales and at different cost estimates. It can also approximate the effect of a change in selling prices on the company.

Sensitivity analysis can be applied to other techniques of analysis as well. It may be used in the capital budgeting decision using discounted cash flows. Changes in the required rate of a return can be quickly converted into changes in the project's net present value, which represents the potential increase in wealth the project offers. The discounted cash flow method of making capital budgeting decisions will be discussed more fully later in this chapter.

Other uses of sensitivity analysis include testing price change impact on sales plans, testing changes in the productive life of equipment, and testing the changes in demand on profitability.

Risk Analysis

Sensitivity analysis is appropriate for asking "what if" questions and for determining the consequences of various changes in relevant variables. Sensitivity analysis, however, cannot identify the likelihood that a change in a variable will occur. Risk analysis is the process used to identify and assign a degree of likelihood to changes in important variables that may be essential in determining the feasibility of a project or venture.

The process of cost forecasting. The use of cost estimates for planning purposes is very important in developing the project cost summary. The firm's chief accounting officer should be instrumental in assembling the cost data used as a basis for a company's new venture activities.

As demand analysis estimates the market potential of the new project, product, or services, cost analysis is the basis for determining the actual financial and technical feasibility of the proposed activity.

Cost estimates must be provided for the following categories:

1. Fixed investments such as land, buildings, fixtures, and other equipment
2. Manufacturing costs such as direct material cost, direct labor cost, and manufacturing overhead
3. Start-up expenses such as training costs, increased overtime, scrap expense, consulting fees, and legal fees
4. Marketing expenses such as warehousing, distribution, promotion, and selling costs

A broad series of assumptions and decisions must be made to provide the framework for developing these cost estimates. A detailed step-by-step forecasting checklist must be followed to establish accurate cost estimates. An example of this type of checklist is illustrated in Figure 4.2.

Yes	No	
____	____	Are the objectives of the study clearly defined?
____	____	Are the various alternatives clearly identified?
____	____	Are reliable cost estimates available for fixed investment, manufacturing costs, and other related start-up costs?
____	____	Are the likely changes in material costs identified?
____	____	Are the likely changes in labor costs identified?
____	____	Are the changes in unit factory overhead rates caused by the proposed production identified?
____	____	Has the demand analysis provided a realistic forecast of sales?
____	____	Have the production personnel provided estimated overhead costs for the new project based on the sales forecast?
____	____	Have all appropriate departments submitted budget estimates (general and administrative departments, warehousing and distribution, selling and advertising, research and development, and so forth)?
____	____	Has a final project cost summary been completed?

FIGURE 4.2. Cost Forecast Checklist

Accurate cost estimates require a solid analysis of the technical requirements of projects. This type of analysis will vary in depth with each project. Technological complexity, the amount of resources required to accomplish the project, and the number of viable alternatives will influence the amount of attention given to the technical analysis. Most new ventures have enough "unknown" characteristics to require close attention to the specific aspects of the project. The project cost summary provides the information necessary for a projected statement of the cost of goods sold. This summary, coupled with information from the market analysis, provides the basis for the pro forma income statement, which estimates the profitability of the project. Additional aids can now be produced to assist the planner such as pro forma balance sheets, cash flow projections, and detailed cost summaries.

Forecasting procedures. Cost forecasting can utilize many of the tools described in forecasting sales. Developing cost forecasts of totally new ventures for which there are no historical cost figures is more difficult and subject to greater error than forecasts for projects that have cost histories.

The correct procedure to forecast costs varies from project to project. The objective of cost forecasting is to approximate the real expenses involved in an undertaking so that profitability can be projected. The actual procedure for forecasting cost may be determined by an examination of the objectives and resources of the principals to the venture.

The following forecasting techniques can be used to estimate costs.

Judgment techniques—The various experiences of key personnel have led to heuristics or "rules of thumb" that can, in some cases, determine certain types of costs. These techniques are subjective in nature and should not be the sole basis for cost analysis.

Survey techniques—Just as market information can be acquired through consumer surveys, so can cost information. One-on-one or telephone interviews with persons who have experience in the appropriate field are commonly used. Such surveys of expert opinion can generate helpful cost data.

Historical data techniques—When historical data are available, cost forecasting can be accomplished by making certain subjective assumptions and then projecting historical cost elements into the future.

Trend analysis—Programmable hand calculators can project past points of costs to specific future dates. A simple technique of plotting the past cost history of a certain cost element can be helpful. The scatter diagram technique charts cost data for a number of periods. However, many costs are distinct entities and cannot be projected in the same way that sales can.

Multiple regression—Multiple regression is a more sophisticated approach to forecasting. In simple regression, a cost is assumed to be the function of only one variable. In multiple regression, the cost or dependent variable is dependent on a number of variables.

Percent of sales—Many costs can be adequately expressed in a percent of sales format. Sales commissions, for example, are calculated as a percentage of sales. A good sales forecast is an essential foundation for this method of estimating costs. The percent of sales method implies a linear relationship between sales and the expense item being calculated. Not only can certain expense items be forecast as a percentage of sales, but balance sheet items and external financing requirements can be developed by this method as well. Table 4.5 illustrates some important costs expressed as a percent of sales.

PROFITABILITY ANALYSIS

The final and perhaps the overriding consideration in defining the exact nature of an opportunity is the potential profitability it represents. Previous sections have dealt with the analysis of demand and the forecasting of costs associated with assessing market and business opportunities. This section focuses on the analytical techniques that can be used to ensure profitable investment decisions.

One of the major objectives of all the time, energy, and resources put into a project is to generate a "good" profit. A "good" profit, how-

TABLE 4.5. Variable Cost As a Percent of Sales

Cost category	Fixed cost	Variable cost	Variable cost as a percent of sales (sales = $70,000)
Raw materials	–	3,100	4.4
Direct labor	–	27,500	39.3
Indirect labor	200	150	0.2
Factory maintenance	100	100	0.1
Utilities	500	400	0.6
Property tax	300	–	–
Depreciation	900	–	–
Sales commissions	–	5,250	7.5
Advertising	–	1,200	1.7
Sales expense	2,200	800	1.1
Administrative salaries	25,000	–	–
Depreciation (office)	750	–	–
Bad debt expense	1,200		
Totals	$31,150	$38,500	55.0%

ever, may be a matter of personal judgment. A company should establish certain acceptable levels of return on investment before choosing among project alternatives.

Return on Investment

Simply stated, return on investment (ROI) is how much an investment returns on an annual basis. ROI is the most meaningful and popular measure of economic success. This term is widely understood by accountants, financial analysts, bankers, managers, and investors. ROI analysis is very helpful in determining the health of a project. ROI itself, however, does not measure the safety of an investment, only its performance expressed as a percentage.

Return on investment can be calculated by dividing net profit by the total investment required to generate the profit. The following formula illustrates the calculation of ROI:

$$\text{Return on investment (ROI)} = \frac{\text{Net profit}}{\text{Total investment}} \qquad (4.3)$$

$$\text{ROI} = 20.5\% = \frac{\$37{,}500}{\$182{,}000}$$

ROI can be calculated for a wide range of investments including savings accounts, profit centers, divisions, and entire companies. Return on investment can also be expressed as a combination of the profit margin on sales and the turnover activity ratio of an investment:

Net profits divided by sales equals the profit margin:

$$\frac{\text{Net profit}}{\text{Sales}} = \text{Profit margin}$$

Sales divided by investment = Turnover of assets

$$\frac{\text{Sales}}{\text{Investment}} = \text{Turnover}$$

Return on investment is equal to turnover × profit margin

$$\frac{\text{Net profit}}{\text{Sales}} \times \frac{\text{Sales}}{\text{Investment}} = \text{ROI}$$

This second approach to determining return on investment brings together the profitability margin on sales and the activity ratio of asset (investment) turnover. This approach to ROI takes into consideration the combination of the efficient use of assets (investments) and the profit margin on sales. This method, known as the DuPont system of financial analysis, has been widely accepted in American industry.

Financial Analysis Process

Financial analysis and capital budgeting consist of the process of selecting among alternative investments in land, buildings, productive equipment, or other assets for future gain. Since decisions of this type usually commit the firm to a long-term course of action, careful analysis is required to identify the potential return.

Capital budgeting is conceptually very simple. Simply list all the investment opportunities available, rank them according to profitability, and accept all investments up to the point at which marginal benefits equal marginal costs. However, in reality, the complexity of revolving planning horizons makes the choice of capital outlays more difficult. Different project length, start-up time, and payout time make meaningful comparisons among investment alternatives problematic.

The depth of the economic analysis needed depends on the type of project, its urgency, and the objectives of the firm. For example, a burned-out generator in a power plant must be replaced. The decision is not replacement versus nonreplacement; the decision concerns only which particular generator is most productive, least costly, or most readily available.

Before discussing in detail the analytical techniques for determining profitability and for making capital decisions, a framework for the decision process should be established.

Step one: Define problem.
Step two: Identify alternatives.
Step three: Identify relevant costs and revenues that will change because of the action taken.
Step four: Determine the alternative that has the most beneficial result.

Step One: Define Problem

The first step appears obvious; however, even though it is elementary, it is often overlooked. Many times a statement of a problem such as "We need more trucks" is not a problem statement at all but, rather, a suggested alternative solution. Too often, decision makers jump prematurely to step two without clearly articulating the problem. The importance of proper problem definition cannot be overemphasized. Replacement of a worn-out piece of equipment, development of a new product, and the construction of a new plant all create uniquely complex problems to overcome. Each of these examples generally produces several alternatives, which must be clearly identified and evaluated.

Step Two: Identify Alternatives

Alternative actions can range from doing nothing to going out of business to replacing with the same type of equipment, replacing with different equipment, replacing with larger or smaller equipment, and so on. From this wide range of alternatives, only the appropriate alternatives should be selected for further analysis.

Step Three: Identify Relevant Costs and Revenues

The next step is to identify the relevant costs and revenues that will change as a result of the action taken. Many aspects of technical analysis and cost forecasting also apply to this step in the capital budgeting process. Do not assume that past operating costs will apply to new ventures. Although it is tempting simply to project historical costs into the future, it is very hazardous to do so. Methods of dealing with the uncertainty surrounding the cost and revenue flows involved in capital budgeting must be incorporated to realistically identify and estimate costs and revenues. These methods will be discussed later.

The basic question asked in step three is, "What are the changes in costs and revenues that will occur because of an action taken?" Other questions to be addressed follow:

What additional revenues will be generated?
What revenues will be lost?
What is the net impact of the action on revenue?
What additional costs will be generated?
What costs will be eliminated?
What is the net impact of the action on costs?

The preceding questions lead to the economic principle of incremental changes in cash flow. Once an after-tax cash flow change has been determined, we are ready for step four.

Step Four: Determine the Alternative with the Most Beneficial Result

The capital budgeting decision alternative with the most positive return on investment is generally considered the superior one. The specific method of analysis used to calculate which alternative has the most sufficient economic returns over the life of the investment must in some way take into account the trade-off of current cash outlay and future cash inflow.

Methods of Analyzing Investments

Many methods are available to evaluate investment alternatives prior to making the capital budgeting decision. Some of the more common methods will be discussed as follows. The focus of capital budgeting is to make decisions that maximize the value of a firm's investment. Choose a method that will answer most appropriately the question, "Which is the most profitable alternative?" The most common criteria for choosing among alternatives may be identified as nontime value methods and time value methods.

1. Nontime methods
   a. Payback period
   b. Simple return on investment
   c. Average return on investment
2. Time value methods
   a. Net present value
   b. Internal rate of return
   c. Present value index

Each of these methods has advantages and disadvantages which will be discussed along with a description of each method.

Nontime Methods

Payback period. The payback period method is simply an estimate of how long it will take for the investment to pay for itself. No interest factors are included in the calculations. Once the payback period is determined, it is usually compared with a rule-of-thumb or standard period. If it is determined that the investment will pay for itself in less time than the standard period, the investment would be made. In deciding between mutually exclusive alternatives, the one with the shortest payback period is generally chosen.

The payback period can be calculated in several ways. The most common method uses this formula:

$$\text{Payback} = \frac{\text{Net investment outlay}}{\text{Net annual cash flow benefits}} \tag{4.4}$$

When annual cash flow benefits are irregular or investment outlay comes in various time frames, the approach shown in Table 4.6 can be used to determine the payback period. In this case the payback period is four years. The payback period method is widely used because of its ease of calculation. Because it does not take into consideration the time value of money, however, it has serious flaws of logic.

Advantages	**Disadvantages**
1. The calculations are easy.	1. The method completely ignores all cash flows beyond the payback period.
2. Choosing the project with shortest payback period has the more favorable short-run effect on earnings per share.	2. It does not adjust for risk related to uncertainty.
3. The method is easily understood.	3. It ignores the time value of money.

TABLE 4.6. Calculating the Payback Period

Year	Investment outlay $	Annual cash flow benefits $	Cumulative cash flow $
1	150,000	40,000	(110,000)
2	10,000	40,000	(80,000)
3	0	40,000	(40,000)
4	0	40,000	0
5	0	40,000	40,000
6	0	20,000	60,000
7	0	20,000	80,000

Some firms are beginning to use the payback method in combination with one or more of the time-value methods described as follows. When this is done, the payback method is used as a risk measurement while the time value method is used as an indicator of profitability.

Simple return on investment. The simple return on investment method is an outgrowth of the logic of the payback method. This method can be represented by manipulating the payback formula. This method is an attempt to express the desirability of an investment in terms of a percentage return on the original investment outlay.

$$\text{Return on investment} = \frac{\text{Net annual cash flow benefits}}{\text{Net investment outlay}} \tag{4.5}$$

The simple ROI method has all the drawbacks and disadvantages of the payback method. No reference at all is made to the project's economic life. An investment of $40,000 with an average annual benefit of $8,000 will yield a 20 percent return regardless of whether the length of the project is one, five, or ten years.

Another example follows:

$$\text{ROI} = \frac{\$5{,}000}{\$50{,}000} = 10\%$$

Average return on investment. The expected average rate of return is a measure of the estimated profitability of an investment. This calculation differs from the simple return on investment by using the average net investment.

$$\text{Average return on investment} = \frac{\text{Net annual cash flow benefits}}{\text{Average net investment outlay}} \tag{4.6}$$

Assuming straight-line depreciation and no residual value at the end of its life, an average investment would be equal to one-half of the original investment. Using the previous example, a net annual cash flow of $8,000 on an original expenditure of $40,000 would be 40 percent, not 20 percent.

$$\text{Average ROI} = \frac{\$5{,}000}{\$25{,}000} = 20\%$$

Time-Value Methods

Investment decision value involves the trade-off between current dollar outlays and future benefits over a period of time. As a result, it is not prudent to ignore the timing of the benefits of investment alternatives. In this regard, the quicker the return the better. Money has value directly related to the timing of its receipt or disbursement. The delay of receiving money means an opportunity cost in terms of lost income. Thus, it is obviously preferable to receive benefits quickly and defer expenditures.

Net present value method. The basic idea of the net present value (NPV) method is to overcome the disadvantage of nontime value methods. The NPV method provides a balance or trade-off between investment outlays and future benefits in terms of time-adjusted dollars. The present value of discounted cash flows is an amount at present that is equivalent to a project's cash flow for a particular interest rate. Generally, the interest rate used to discount future cash flows is a company's cost of capital rate. The net present value method involves the following:

- Determining the present value of the net investment cost outlay
- Estimating the future cash flow benefits
- Discounting the future cash flows to present value at the appropriate cost of capital
- Subtracting the present value of the costs from the present value of the benefits

If the amount derived from the fourth step is positive, then the investment is considered to be profitable since the time-adjusted internal rate of return of the investment is greater than the cost of capital. Conversely, a negative figure indicates that the project is earning a rate of return less than the cost of capital chosen by the firm as a standard of decision.

Net present value (NPV) can be calculated by the following formula:

$$NPV = \frac{R^1}{(1+i)^1} + \frac{R^2}{(1+i)^2} + \ldots + \frac{R^n}{(1+i)^n} - IC \qquad (4.7)$$

Where:

NPV = The net present value of the investment
R = The expected dollar returns or cash flows each year
i = The appropriate interest rate (cost of capital)
IC = The present value of the investment cost
n = The project's expected life

The net present values of two alternative projects are illustrated in Table 4.7.

Project one has the highest return, even though the payback period is identical. The greatest benefit will be provided by selecting project one. If the two projects are not mutually exclusive and funds are available, both investment opportunities should be accepted.

TABLE 4.7. Value Comparison

Year	Net return or cash flow $		Interest factor (1 + i)n		PV of cash flow $	
Project 1						
1	400	×	0.91	=	364	
2	500	×	0.83	=	415	
3	600	×	0.75	=	450	
4	800	×	0.68	=	544	
					1,773	PV of inflows
					–1,500	Less PV of cost
					$273	Net present value
Project 2						
1	800	×	0.91	=	728	
2	300	×	0.83	=	249	
3	400	×	0.75	=	300	
4	400	×	0.68	=	272	
					1,549	PV of inflows
					–1,500	Less PV of cost
					$49	Net present value

The present value method has several advantages which make it more suitable than the payback methods as a basis of comparing investments.

Advantages	Disadvantages
1. Considers the time value of money.	1. Assumes benefits and costs can be estimated for the lifetime of the project.
2. Concentrates the values of costs and benefits in a comparable time frame.	2. Requires equal time periods for comparison of several investment alternatives.
3. Fairly simple to understand and calculate.	3. Sensitive to changes in the interest rate used to discount the values.

Internal rate of return. The internal rate of return (IRR) is simply the yield of a project. The IRR is defined as the interest rate that discounts the future cash flows, or receipts, and makes them equal to the initial cost outlay. The time value of money is taken into consideration. The formula used for net present value can also be used for calculating the IRR with one slight variation. Instead of solving for net present value, the present value of the cost is made equal to the present value of the benefits. In other words, the internal rate of return of a project is the discount interest rate that generates a net present value of zero. Below is the NPV formula and the change necessary to create the IRR formula.

NPV formula:

$$NPV = \frac{R^1}{(1+i)^1} + \frac{R^2}{(1+i)^2} + \ldots + \frac{R^n}{(1+i)^n} - IC \qquad (4.7)$$

IRR formula:

$$\frac{R^1}{(1+i)^1} + \frac{R^2}{(1+i)^2} + \ldots + \frac{R^n}{(1+i)^n} = IC \qquad (4.8)$$

or

$$0 = \frac{R^1}{(1+i)^1} + \frac{R^2}{(1+i)^2} + \ldots + \frac{R^n}{(1+i)^n} - IC$$

Solve for i, and i = IRR.

In the new formula for IRR, i represents the interest rate that equates the present values of the benefits and the costs of a project. In the NPV formula, i represents the firm's cost of capital. If the cost of capital is used in the formula and NPV = 0, then the internal rate of return is equal to the cost of capital. When NPV is positive, the IRR is greater than the cost of capital; when NPV is negative, the IRR is less than the cost of capital. If the IRR is greater than the firm's cost of capital, the investment is a positive one. The IRR can be found by trial and error. The IRR method is widely accepted as a ranking device. The yield is reasonably accurate and much superior to the simple payback and simple return on investment methods.

Advantages	Disadvantages
1. Because the IRR method is closely related to the NPV method, it is familiar to many business practitioners and thus more readily accepted.	1. The internal rate of return does not do a good job of comparing investments with large differences in magnitude. For example, a $20,000 investment with an IRR of 42 percent cannot be compared with an investment of $100,000 with an IRR of 30 percent. It may be far better to direct all resources toward the $100,000 investment even though the IRR is lower than the other investment.
2. Calculation of the firm's cost of capital is not required as it is with the NPV method.	2. In the same manner, length of the life of the investment is also important. It may be more advantageous to invest funds at a lower IRR for a longer term than to invest short-term for a slightly higher IRR. The pertinent criticism of the IRR method is that it assumes reinvestment can be made at the IRR, which may not be true.
3. The method time values money.	

Present value index. This method is similar to the present value method. A ratio is determined between the present value of the cash flow benefits and the present values of the net investment outlays or costs. The present value index is sometimes referred to as the benefit/cost ratio of discounted cash flows. Several alternative projects may have similar NPVs but require widely different investment amounts. To choose an alternative based simply on the size of NPV would ignore the relative different sizes of the projects. Equal NPV's coming from different sized investments will have different IRRs. A formal way of expressing this difference is to compare the projects on a benefits/costs basis.

$$\text{Present value index} = \frac{\text{Present value}}{\text{Present value of net investment outlay}} \tag{4.9}$$

The higher the index, the better the project. However, any present value index over 1.0 beats the minimum standard built into the calculation of present value and should be funded. Most projects, however, are competing for limited funds. Table 4.8 compares the PV index and the NPV ranking methods. Slightly different results are shown. Alternatives 1 and 3 have the same NPV, but alternative 1 has the higher PV index and is, therefore, more favorable. The advantages and disadvantages of the PV index method are similar to those listed for the net present value method.

TABLE 4.8. Present Value Index

Alternative	Present value of benefits	–	Present value of costs	=	Net present value	PV index
1	$10,500		$8,500		$2,000	1.24
2	16,000		13,000		3,000	1.23
3	15,000		13,000		2,000	1.15
4	17,500		18,500		–1,000	.95
5	20,000		16,000		4,000	1.25

METHODS OF ANALYZING RISK

The riskiness of an asset is measured by the probability that the future returns will fall below expected levels. This is often measured by the standard deviation or the coefficient of variation of expected returns. In the earlier discussion of the various methods of making capital budget decisions, the only treatment for risk was the informal aspect of making judgments concerning estimates of economic life and cash flow amounts. Some situations, however, call for a more formal assessment of risk and the effect of uncertainty. Sensitivity analysis can be used to calculate a project's NPV under alternative assumptions.

Projects for which the variability in expected returns is very large require an even more formal approach to evaluating risk. Risk analysis attempts to identify the likelihood that events will occur. Risk results from lack of experience, misinterpretation of data, bias in forecasting, errors in analysis, and changes in economic conditions. In the process of project feasibility analysis and assessment, a number of variables are usually in question.

More than seven out of ten companies report that they employ some type of risk assessment in project analysis. Some of the most common risk evaluation techniques are risk-adjusted discount rate or rate of return, risk-adjusted cash flows, and risk-adjusted payback periods.

Risk-Adjusted Discount Rate

One of the most frequently used methods in risk assessment is the risk-adjusted discount rate method. The basic objective of this method is to increase the applied discount rate when dealing with risky projects. (If the simple rate of return method is being used, the cut-off rate is raised to allow for a greater "cushion" for risky projects.) The increase in the discount rate (cost of capital) is a risk premium that protects the firm from the uncertainty of future cash flows of investments.

As mentioned earlier, the variability of the probability distributions of expected returns can be estimated. In some cases, the probability distribution can be estimated objectively with statistical techniques. In many situations, the estimates must be determined by subjective probability distributions. Once the probability distribution has been determined, the variability of the distribution can be measured using standard deviation or coefficient of variation. The project with the larger deviation represents the greatest risk and is assigned the higher discount rate.

The higher discount rate reduces the present value of the future benefits and makes it more difficult for a risky investment to achieve a positive net present value. Consequently, marginal projects that are more risky will be rejected.

The risk-adjusted discount rate method is easy to apply but it has some disadvantages. Usually, the adjusted rate applies to all costs and revenues, even those that can be estimated with relative certainty. The lack of discrimination among the cost and revenue estimates is the major criticism of this method.

Risk-Adjusted Cash Flows

As forecasts are being made to develop the point estimate or most likely estimate, the analyst will incorporate perceived risk into the estimate. Then, the analyst defines the degree of uncertainty in terms of probability of occurrence. For example, an "optimistic," "most likely," and "pessimistic" estimate is made taking historical data, environmental analysis, and expected trends into consideration. This three-level method of forecasting was exhibited earlier in Table 4.2.

Consider the following calculation of the expected value of cash flows from two projects shown in Table 4.9. Table 4.10 shows the calculation of expected value based on the data of Table 4.9.

The expected value of the cash flow of project 1 is $640 instead of the $700 point estimate (the highest probability of occurrence), while the expected value of the cash flow of project 2 is $670 rather than $900. The expected value gives forecasters and decision makers a better idea of the risk involved in the decision.

The risk-adjusted cash flow is generally lower than the best estimate cash flow. The effect of using a risk-adjusted cash flow in the net present value method of capital budgeting is a lower net present value than would have been obtained by using the best estimate cash flow. The result is that marginal projects with risky potential benefit are more readily discarded.

TABLE 4.9. Probability

State of economy	Probability	Project 1 cash flow $	Project 2 cash flow $
Recession	.2	850	350
Normal	.5	700	900
Boom	.3	400	500
	1.0		

TABLE 4.10. Expected Value of Cash Flows

Cash flow $	Probability of economic condition	Expected value $
Project 1		
850	.2 Recession	170
700	.5 Normal	350
400	.3 Boom	120
	1.0	640
Project 2		
350	.2 Recession	70
900	.5 Normal	450
500	.3 Boom	150
	1.0	670

SIMULATION MODELS

Computer simulation can be used to extend probability concepts in decision making. This allows decision makers to estimate, for each of a dozen or so variables of major products, ranges of possible outcomes and the probability distributions for these ranges. The focus might be placed on sales volume, prices, key cost elements, salvage values, interest rate fluctuations, or cash flows. A series of outcomes for the project is then developed using the computer simulation. The computer output allows statements to be made, such as, "There is a 65 percent likelihood that the net present value of the project will be $200,000" or "There is a one in ten chance that the project will lose

$210,000." The sophistication of this type of analysis and the limitless number of variables places obvious limitations on its use.

NOT-FOR-PROFIT COST ANALYSIS

Cost analysis for not-for-profit organizations is difficult. When a nonprofit organization is choosing between alternative programs that fall within the scope of its objectives, benefit/cost analysis can be helpful. Benefit/cost analysis is a formalized attempt to obtain the maximum benefits from a given level of funding. For example, a community wants the best possible police protection, a university wants the best faculty, the Red Cross wants the most effective blood donor recruiting program that the given level of funding can support. Benefit/cost analysis allows nonprofit organizations to evaluate various alternatives.

In this analysis, each program can be evaluated based on a comparison of benefit/cost ratios. For example, a public library may be considering the addition of a new business section, a film rental library, or an arts library. These alternatives are illustrated in Table 4.11. Alternative one and two have a positive net benefit, and a benefit/cost ratio greater than one. Alternative two has the most favorable benefit/cost ratio. However, if the library has approximately $80,000 available, it should embark on both alternatives. Alternative three fails both the net benefit test and the benefit/cost ratio test. Unless other overriding nonfinancial considerations exist, alternative three should be rejected. The basic disadvantage of this type of analysis is the difficulty of estimating both costs and benefits. Costs are perhaps the easiest part of the equation. Cost of construction, equipment, supplies, salaries, and so forth, can usually be accurately estimated. Social costs are more difficult to appraise. On the other hand, benefit analysis poses many difficult problems. As we attempt to identify

TABLE 4.11. Benefit/Cost Ratio Analysis

Alternative	Benefits $	Costs $	Net benefit $	Benefits/costs ratio
1	32,500	28,400	4,100	1.14
2	48,000	40,000	8,000	1.20
3	17,700	22,800	(5,100)	.78

each type of benefit, we run into some social, aesthetic, and non-monetary benefits. How these are assigned dollar values radically influences the benefit/cost analysis.

When difficulty occurs in comparing alternatives on the benefit/cost basis, cost effectiveness analysis may be appropriate. Cost effectiveness analysis deals with the effect of variations in cost on benefit. The focus of this analysis is to determine effectiveness of operations rather than trying to see how much more benefit there is than cost.

SUMMARY

Accurately estimating the financial impact of a decision is extremely difficult. There are many unknowns and contingencies which cause forecasts to vary from actual revenues. Nonetheless, the revenue forecast is a basic prerequisite to complete financial analysis. Overly optimistic forecasts produce unrealistic expectations, whereas overly pessimistic predictions may lead a firm to pass up a good opportunity.

Accurate cost estimation is also extremely important to opportunity assessment. Cost overruns are common and often disastrous to the principals involved in a venture. Consequently, every attempt should be made to identify and estimate accurately all costs associated with a specific opportunity. This is best accomplished by a thorough technical study and an accompanying cost forecast. The results of the forecasting process should yield a project cost summary that can be used in determining return on investment.

The final consideration of the overall financial analysis is "How profitable will the project be?" The concept of return on investment is essential to answering this question. Hopefully, the analysis will lead to a clear "yes" or "no." In some cases, however, an "I don't know" will be the response.

To answer the question "yes" implies that the market exists, costs are identifiable and controllable, the process or service works, the financial returns on the investment are satisfactory, and the uncertainty is tolerable. In other words, the overall opportunity assessment has determined that the project is both feasible and profitable.

Chapter 5

Marketing Planning: Strategic Perspectives

Chapter 5 begins the two-chapter sequence addressing the next stage of the effective marketing management process: planning (see Figure 5.1).

Marketing managers who begin with adoption of a societal marketing orientation (SMO) feel it is important to understand *before* they plan. An integral part of the SMO is the desire to serve the short- and long-term needs of customers and society at a profit, and accomplish this objective better than competitors. Thus, we seek to first understand the market (i.e., consumers, competitors, and the financial implications of what we do) and then use that understanding to develop plans of how we can create mutually beneficial exchange rela-

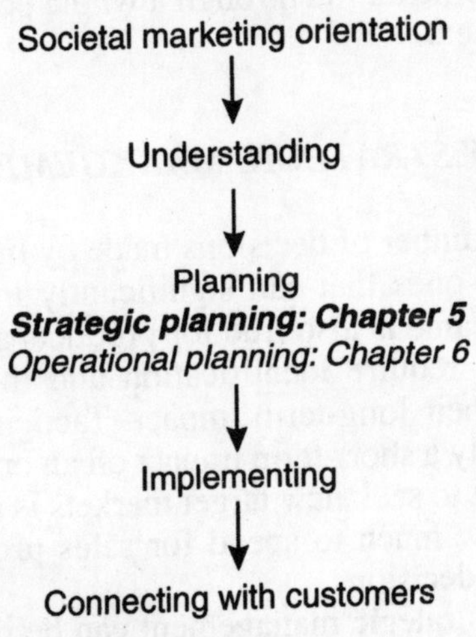

FIGURE 5.1. The Effective Marketing Management Process

tionships. This planning process occurs at two levels—a corporate level, which is referred to as strategic planning, and a product/market level, which is referred to as operational or marketing planning. This chapter addresses broader, strategic planning issues.

Many of today's most successful companies evolved out of an era in which they introduced a good product or service into a market which was ready to accept the product. Geographic growth was achieved by expanding to new markets and later by adding new products to build a complete line of products rather than concentrating on one. In many companies, growth just appeared to happen with little or no formal thought about the management processes that went into it.

However, with significant shifts in economic, environmental, and competitive forces, most managers have now realized that for survival and growth to occur they must be much more aware of the impact of the decisions they are making and the management processes used to make these decisions. Two characteristics differentiate successful from less successful firms: (1) good management and (2) the development of a competitive advantage. Managers of successful firms tend to be action-oriented "strategic thinkers" who focus their attention on customers, markets, and competitors as well as internally on operations. They seem to be able to blend strategy development with strategy implementation through a whole process referred to as strategic management.

WHY STRATEGIC MANAGEMENT?

Out of a large number of decisions made by managers there are a handful of critical ones that can significantly impact an organization's future. The same is also true for products and services. These strategic decisions require identification and thoughtful consideration because of their long-term impact. Tacticial decisions, while important, have only a short-term impact on an organization. For example, the decision to seek new target markets is a strategic decision while deciding how much to spend for sales promotion in a given month is a tactical decision.

Perspectives of strategic management can be illustrated with this question: Who are the two most important persons responsible for the success of an airplane's flight? Would you say it is the pilot and the navigator, the pilot and the maintenance supervisor, the pilot and the air traffic controller, or the pilot and the flight engineer? All of these responses recognize the day-to-day hands-on importance of the pilot. They all introduce one of several other important support or auxiliary functionaries to the answer. However, each of these suggested responses ignores the one person who is perhaps the single most important individual to the ultimate success of the airplane—the designer. Perhaps the pilot and the designer are the two most important individuals to the success of an airplane. The pilot because of his or her day-to-day responsibilities in commanding the craft and the designer because of his or her ability to create a concept that can be economically constructed, easily operated by competent flight crew, and maintained safely by the ground crew. Most modern executives perceive themselves as the "pilots" of their organizations; taking off, landing, conferring with the navigator, and communicating with the air traffic controller. They generally view themselves as the chief hands-on operational managers. However, what has been most lacking in American industry in the past few years has been an appreciation for the long-run strategic viewpoint. There is a need for more emphasis on the "designer" approach to operating an organization. A well-conceived strategic management system can facilitate this emphasis.

THE STRATEGIC MANAGEMENT PROCESS

The strategic management process is illustrated in Figure 5.2. This process consists of (l) defining the purpose or mission of the business, (2) developing a set of corporate objectives, (3) formulating a corporate strategy, (4) implementing the strategy, and (5) evaluating and monitoring the strategy to determine if changes are needed in any of the preceding steps. The first three steps are referred to as strategic planning. When these three steps are completed, an organization can prepare its strategic plan, which is the written document that contains the results of these three stages.

Once the overall corporate- or business-level strategies are developed, the marketing objectives and strategies should be developed. Marketing objectives and strategies must be consistent with the overall corporate objectives and strategies to ensure coordination of plans throughout the organization. A corporate objective of a 20 percent return on investment, for example, would lead to marketing objectives

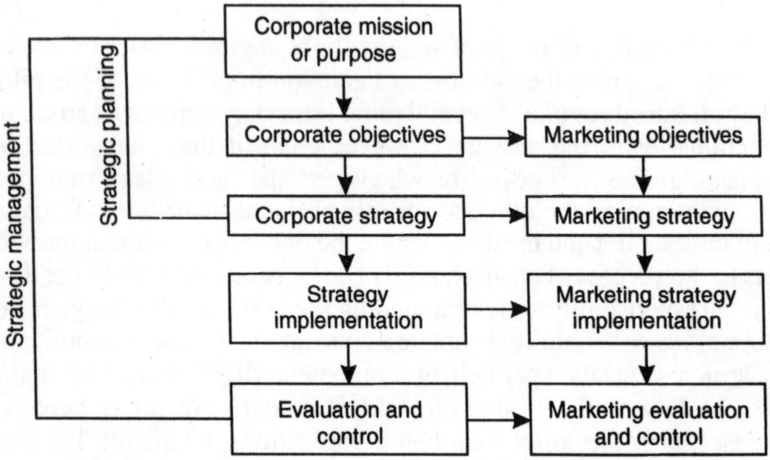

FIGURE 5.2. The Strategic Management Process

that are also profitability oriented. A corporate strategy that positions a firm as the low-cost producer in an industry may lead to greater emphasis on price in a firm's marketing strategy.

Before discussing marketing planning in more detail, the strategic planning process will be discussed from the standpoint of the whole organization. This will put marketing planning in perspective.

Corporate Purpose or Mission

Peter Drucker has referred to an organization's purpose as its mission or reason for being. To define a business's purpose is to ask,

> What is our business and more importantly, what should it be? Only a clear definition of the mission and purpose of the business makes possible clear and realistic business objectives. It is the foundation for priorities, strategies, plans, and work assignments. It is the starting point for the design of managerial jobs and above all for the design of managerial structure.[1]

One aspect of every firm's purpose should be to meet a need in the marketplace. However, a statement of purpose needs to be a formal written statement that spells out in some detail the uniqueness which has led to the creation of the business enterprise. Such a statement becomes a reference point for subsequent managerial action. In effect, it becomes the reference point on which all operating areas in a firm must reflect as a part of their decision-making processes. Typical questions faced by most firms are: Do we enter a particular market? or, Should we introduce a particular product? Answers should be based on how these decisions relate to accomplishing the stated purpose of the organization. If it does not help the organization accomplish its stated purpose, it should not be undertaken, no matter how profitable or otherwise successful it appears to be. A firm's purpose can be altered over time to reflect changing environmental conditions or changing managerial philosophies, but at any given point there must be a standard of relevance for managerial thought and action.

A clear understanding of company purpose is needed to ensure alignment of strategies with the way the firm has defined its mission. Otherwise, strategies will be at cross-purposes with the organizational mission or, there will be a failure to attempt strategies beneficial to fulfillment of purpose. Common vision and unity can be achieved only by common purpose.

The statement of purpose shown in Box 5.1 was prepared by an energy resource company's management and illustrates the type of statement that can be developed to provide unity and guidance in decision making.

A few of the implications of this statement for strategy development will help show how a company's statement of mission or purpose is related to the strategies a firm can pursue. Paragraph one of this mission statement, for example, states that the company will produce at an optimum rate that provides orderly community growth, protects the environment, and so on. This means that the strategies must not be based on rapid expansion of sales volume, which would cause a large increase in productive capacity and would involve both rapid community growth and less environmentally compatible production techniques. Another restraint can be derived from the third paragraph—"quality product." This stipulation limits strategies aimed at lower-product-quality markets to reach more cost-oriented customers or customers actually wanting a lower-quality product.

BOX 5.1. Sample Mission Statement

The primary purpose of the Company is to operate at a profit for the benefit of owners, employees, and the community. We will produce coal resources at optimum rates that will provide orderly community growth, protect the environment, and contribute to alleviating our nation's energy needs.

The Company is committed to adhering to its approved mining plan by following laws, rules, and applications with a minimum disturbance to the environment, and timely restoration to disturbed areas.

Our purpose is to produce a quality product and to provide superior services to customers. We will provide a work environment for employees that allows them, through training and other means, to achieve personal growth while helping the Company to achieve its stated objectives.

An equal opportunity employer, the Company makes every effort to provide safe, healthy working conditions for employees as it seeks to operate within the tenets of the free enterprise system.

Finally, the Company is committed to conducting its business relationships in such a manner as to be a credit to its partners, employees and their families, customers, and the community. The Company is proud to be a leader in the mining industry of our country.

Source: Adapted from Colowyo Coal Company, *Colowyo Magazine,* 1(1)(1980), p. 1.

These examples illustrate the impact of statements of purpose on strategy development. To be effective, strategies must be consistent with overall purpose.

Corporate Objectives

Corporate objectives vary so widely in their nature, content, and specificity that it is difficult to describe a common "state of the art" of what corporate objectives should be. Even the terms used to describe objectives vary widely: *policy, goals, values,* and *objectives,* are often used interchangeably even within the same company. The definition used in this book is a generally accepted view of what is meant by objectives.

Basically, an objective is an end result desired, a statement of what is to be accomplished by an organization. Achievement of objectives is the way the organization fulfills its purpose.

The following three objectives are basic to any business organization:

1. Do something that is both economically and socially useful.
2. Maintain and/or survive as a business entity.
3. Grow in size and/or excellence of operations—whether measured in sales, profits, number of employees, or some other growth or effectiveness criterion.

These objectives are almost inherent to a business even though many firms do not formally state them. However, to provide more specific guidance to the organization as both a statement of end results sought and as a tool for evaluating performance, objectives need to be more explicit in defining what is to be accomplished.

Peter Drucker points out the importance of objectives being more than abstractions: "If objectives are only good intentions they are worthless. They must degenerate into work. And work is always specific, always has—or should have—unambiguous measurable results, a deadline and a specific assignment of accountability."[2]

Box 5.2 shows an example of corporate financial objectives from a major food company. Notice the differences in the degree of specificity of the objectives. Some companies state their objectives in a more quantifiable format while others do not. When objectives are quantified, they can be evaluated on an absolute quantitative basis. Otherwise, they must be analyzed on the basis of what was accomplished on a relative basis—relative to other years and perhaps other companies.

Corporate Strategies

The final stage in the strategic planning process is the development of the overall corporate strategies that will be used to accomplish objectives. The strategy development process can be viewed as a matching process. The organization attempts to match its capabilities and skills with the key requirements of the market to take advantage of an opportunity that has opened up. Opportunities are created or opened

BOX 5.2. Sample Goals and Objectives

Our financial goals and objectives are based upon measures of superior competitive performance. Management believes these standards are appropriate guides for development of plans and evaluation of performance over time.

These goals include:

1. to earn the highest possible return on shareholders' equity consistent with responsible business practices;
2. to ensure repetitive, predictable, and steadily growing per-share profits and dividends as the yield from an ample stream of reinvestments; and
3. to perform consistently better than the industry in every market where our products and services compete.

These goals translate into the following financial objectives:

1. Annual earnings per share growth of 12 to 15 percent.
2. Pretax return on average invested capital of 25 percent.
3. After-tax return on average stockholders' equity of 18 percent.
4. A strong "A" credit rating on senior debt of the parent company.

by changes in the environment. However, opportunities also close—like a window. This concept has been referred to as the *strategic window.*[3] In other words, the opportunity that matches what the firm can do well with the needs of the market exists for only a specific and often a short period of time. The timing of a strategy becomes a key element of success. The strategic planner attempts to develop the right strategy at the right time.

SWOT Analysis

Many organizations evaluate opportunities utilizing an analysis framework referred to as a SWOT. SWOT is an acronym for strengths, weakness, opportunities, and threats. The ultimate goal of a SWOT analysis includes, on one hand, the matching of vital operational strengths with major environmental opportunities. On the other hand, it provides a basis for improving weaknesses or at least minimizing them and avoiding or managing environmental threats to operations. Ideally, a SWOT study helps identify a *distinctive competence,* something the organization does exceptionally well. Table 5.1 illustrates one format for evaluating internal strengths and weaknesses in light

TABLE 5.1. Analysis of Strengths and Weaknesses

Factor	Opportunity implication
Marketing resources	
Strengths:	
Established facilities	New service could use the same facilities
Weaknesses:	
No in-house advertising and dependence on agency relationship	Service needs strong advertising effort—must use ad agency
Financial resources	
Strengths:	
Good cash position and strong earning records	Offer customers payment plans
Weaknesses:	
Higher than average debt/equity ratio	Must fund through internal resources
Productive capacity	
Strengths:	
High-quality production	Go for quality end of market
Weaknesses:	
Low labor availability	Must offer limited quantities
Managerial resources	
Strengths:	
Strong research and development staff	Cost effectiveness in operation
Weaknesses:	
No experience with new product	Hire new manager

of external opportunities by considering the application of major organizational resources. Each factor—capacity, personnel, marketing, finance, and management—is rated in relation to an opportunity on a quantitative basis.

This approach is used to analyze resources as strengths or weaknesses in relation to opportunities in the organization's environment. For each strength and weakness identified, strategy implications are drawn. Analysis of strengths and weaknesses flows logically from the identification of the resources relative to the opportunity.

Strategy Development

Designing strategies is a process that involves (1) identifying strategic options, (2) assessing options, and (3) selecting the most appropriate strategy or strategies. Since most companies include growth as a basic objective, one area of strategy development revolves around the question of how growth will be obtained. Two possible alternative growth strategies are:

1. Product/market expansion strategies
2. Integrative strategies

Several strategic alternatives can be illustrated in a 2 × 2 matrix called a product/market growth matrix. This type of matrix is shown in Figure 5.3.

Product/Market Expansion Strategies

Product/market expansion strategies involve growth through (1) penetration of existing markets with existing products, (2) development of new products aimed at existing markets, (3) development of new markets for existing products, and/or (4) development of new products aimed at new markets.

Market penetration is a strategy of growth aimed at increasing sales of existing products in existing markets. This expansion of sales can occur by (1) altering purchase patterns of existing customers—getting them to buy more when they purchase or to purchase more frequently, (2) attracting nonusers to purchase the product, and (3) enticing purchasers of competitors' products to switch, thereby increasing market share. Alternatives 1 and 2 involve increasing the total size of the market; alternative 3 involves increasing market share.

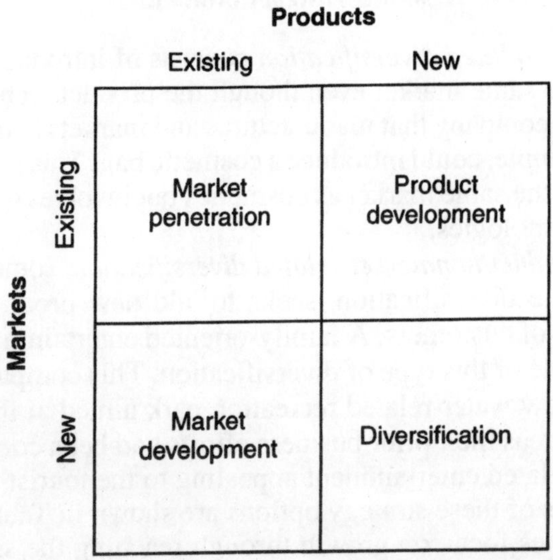

FIGURE 5.3. Product/Market Growth Matrix

Product development is a strategy aimed at increasing sales through the introduction of new products to existing markets. Product development may involve altering existing products by (1) adding new features, (2) offering different quality levels, or (3) offering different sizes of the product.

Market development is a strategy which entails offering existing products to new markets. These markets can be (1) new geographical markets such as foreign countries, or (2) new market segments not currently using the product.

Diversification is a strategic alternative aimed at growth. Diversification entails introducing new products into new markets or acquiring other firms that are already in these new product/market situations. Diversification strategies can take various forms. The most common are (1) product/technology-related, (2) market-related, and (3) nonproduct/nonmarket-related.

1. *Product/technology diversification* consists of adding products that are technologically related to existing products even though they are aimed at different markets. A company that manufactures electronic watches and develops a line of industrial gauges using the same electronic technology would be an example of this type of diversification.

2. *Market-related diversification* consists of introducing products aimed at the same market even though the product technologies are different. A company that manufactures and markets a line of cosmetics, for example, could introduce a cosmetic bag. This product would be aimed at the same market as cosmetics but involves quite different product technologies.

3. *Nonproduct/nonmarket-related diversification,* sometimes called conglomerate diversification, seeks to add new products aimed at new classes of customers. A family-oriented entertainment company is an example of this type of diversification. This company might introduce a new water-related recreation park aimed at the nontourist market whereas their prior business efforts had been concentrated on nonwater-related entertainment appealing to the tourist market.

Examples of these strategy options are shown in Table 5.2. These four strategies focus on growth through reaching the same markets with new products, reaching new segments, gaining increasing usage from existing segments, or pursuing new segments with new products. Each of these strategic options carries with it advantages and risks as far as management is concerned. In a market penetration strategy, management has the advantage of both product knowledge and knowledge of existing markets. The obvious disadvantage is the fact that the products will eventually pass through various product life-cycle stages ending with sales decline and extinction.

In a product development strategy, the advantage is knowledge of the relevant market since the products are aimed at existing markets. The disadvantage is lack of product knowledge.

When a market development strategy is used, product knowledge is the advantage, while market knowledge is the disadvantage. When a diversification strategy is used, management is under the most strain. Management has neither product knowledge nor market knowledge as an advantage so it must quickly acquire it or rely on acquiring managers or companies who already possess it.

Integrative Strategies

As a strategic alternative a company can choose growth through integration of activities within its current industry. Three alternatives are suggested for this type of growth: (1) forward integration, (2) backward integration, and (3) horizontal integration.

TABLE 5.2. Strategy Examples in the Product/Market Matrix

Market	Products: Existing	Products: New
Existing	*Market penetration strategy examples:* 1. Ford uses rebates to stimulate prospective buyers. 2. Charmin uses larger package sizes for heavy users. 3. Northwest Airlines provides WorldPerks miles and benefits to frequent flyers. 4. Aleve uses comparative ads to induce brand switching. 5. AOL offers free service for limited time periods.	*Product development strategy examples:* 1. Microsoft launches Windows XP to improve previous Windows versions. 2. Kimberly-Clark adds ridges and softness to Scott Towels. 3. Jeep redesigns the Cherokee and renames it Liberty. 4. State Farm adds long-term care insurance to its line of home, life, and auto coverage.
New	*Market development strategy examples:* 1. GM launches the Saturn auto in Japan. 2. Arm & Hammer baking soda is promoted as a carpet deodorizer. 3. Kodak and Fuji targets the children's photographer market with promotions and special programs. 4. Tuna is promoted as a calcium additive for the diet. 5. McDonald's opens outlets in Wal-Mart, airports, zoos, casinos, etc. 6. Lipton provides dip recipes for its dry soup mixes.	*Diversification strategy examples:* 1. Starbucks moves into grocery stores with Starbucks Frappuccino bottled drinks, and Tazo Tea. 2. Coleman adds air compressors for the building contractor market. 3. Coca-Cola acquires Mad River Traders to gain entrance into premium teas, sodas, and juice drinks. 4. Philip Morris adds foods and beers to its cigarette core.

Forward integration means the company looks "down" the channel of distribution to the next channel members who currently represent a customer type. For example, a manufacturer who "looks down the channel" generally sees either wholesalers or retailers as the next channel member. Thus, forward integration takes the form of expanding—either internally or through acquisitions—through taking over wholesaling or retailing functions.

Backward integration seeks growth through ownership of companies "up the channel," in other words, suppliers of products or raw materials. A manufacturer of automotive tires that builds its own plant to produce synthetic fibers used in tire production would be growing through backward integration.

Organizations that do not want to acquire other organizations through forward or backward integration can accomplish some of the benefits of vertical integration through a concept called supply-chain (also called value chain) management. This involves managing the relationships among the entire sequence or chain of suppliers that are involved in the creation or delivering of a product. This process affects relationships with upstream suppliers and downstream users. Effective suppiy-chain management can create a competitive advantage for a marketer by increasing innovation, decreasing costs, improving cooperation, and helping resolve conflict among chain members.

Horizontal integration seeks growth through ownership of competitors. This strategy involves identifying and acquiring firms that are in competition with the firm seeking growth. Another approach to horizontal growth can come through strategic alliances. A strategic alliance is a partnership with other companies to create a competitive advantage. These relationships are created to improve each partner's ability to create or enhance its competitive stance in today's fast-changing market.

One example of this strategy is combining a service station/convenience store with a fast-food operation and/or a donut shop. This creates traffic flow to a location from which all partners can benefit.

Factors Influencing Strategy Selection

Many factors must be evaluated before selecting a particular strategy. The most important factors and the attendant changes that may occur with each strategy option are shown in Table 5.3. Note that the diversification strategy alternative results in the most changes in operations and therefore has potentially more risks. Many companies pursuing diversification strategies have later divested of these products/companies and moved back to their original product/market positions.

TABLE 5.3. Factors Influencing Strategy Selection

Strategy position	Competition	Product	Distribution	Market knowledge
Market penetration	Well known and well established	Often at maturity stage of life cycle with no anticipated changes	Existing relationships unchanged	Extensive and based on considerable experience
Market development	Often new due to move into new markets	Product has potential but none in present market	May require new channels of distribution, new relationships	Sometimes minimal due to move into new markets
Product development	Usually well known and well established	New product developed for an existing market	Usually can maintain existing channel relationships	Extensive and based on considerable experience
Diversification	May be totally new because of new product and new market	Often totally new and in early stages of life cycle, but might not be if product introduced into an established program	May require completely different channels, new relationships	Often very minimal due to new products in new markets

Source: Adapted from David W. Cravens, "Marketing Strategy Positioning," *Business Horizons*, December 18, 1975, pp. 53-61.

PLANNING LEVELS

Many companies have discovered that new organizational concepts are needed for more effective strategic planning. One concept that is extremely useful in this process is the strategic business unit.

A strategic business unit (SBU) meets the following criteria:

1. It has a clearly defined market.
2. It faces identifiable competitors in an external market (as opposed to being an internal supplier).
3. As a separate, distinct, and identifiable unit whose assets do not depend on the existence of another SBU, its manager has control over planning and decision areas that determine success of the business.

In large, multiproduct line companies planning typically occurs at three levels:

1. *Corporate-level planning:* generates a strategic plan
2. *Strategic-business-unit-level planning:* generates a strategic marketing plan
3. *Product-market-level planning:* referred to as an operating marketing plan

Table 5.4 shows the typical questions and outcomes addressed at each of these levels. In moderate-sized businesses with a single SBU, the strategic marketing and operating marketing planning may be conducted as a single process, with longer-term strategic planning being conducted at the corporate level. In smaller organizations the planning process incorporates all three levels simultaneously.

For example, PepsiCo is the parent company for Pepsi Cola Bottling, Inc., Taco Bell, Inc., Kentucky Fried Chicken, Inc., and Pizza Hut, Inc. At the corporate level, PepsiCo acts as a holding company with a portfolio of investments in several companies. Management of PepsiCo must decide what types of businesses to add or delete from this portfolio to fulfill its corporate mission and objectives.

At the SBU level, Pepsi Cola Bottling, Inc.'s management is focused on the overall marketing plan to position Pepsi products in world markets to create and sustain a competitive advantage versus other beverage companies. This plan would focus on creating the operating marketing plan for a specific product line within the Pepsi SBU, detailing product introductions, promotional campaigns, pricing, and distribution strategies to achieve annual objectives relating to market share, sales, profits, etc.

TABLE 5.4. Levels of Planning

Level	Name	Question	Output
Corporate	Strategic planning	What is our business? What should it be?	Mission, objectives, SBU portfolio
SBU	Strategic marketing	Where should we be going?	Marketing strategy to gain a sustainable competitive advantage
Product/market	Market management	How do we get there?	Marketing plan

In this chapter we focus our attention on planning at the corporate and SBU levels. Planning at the operational or product/market level will be the focus of Chapter 6.

STRATEGIES FOR EXISTING STRATEGIC BUSINESS UNITS

Once an organization's SBUs are identified, strategic planning can be carried out for each. However, care must be exercised to ensure that the activities of each SBU are interrelated to the corporate level objectives and purpose.

Growth-Share Matrix

The Boston Consulting Group (BCG), a well-known consulting organization, has developed an approach to strategic planning that permits classifying SBUs on the basis of their relative market share and market growth rate. This approach, depicted in Figure 5.4, permits development of strategies for each SBU based on its classification within the matrix.

The vertical axis shows annualized market growth rates for each SBU in its respective market. The division of high-low rates at 10 percent represents the midpoint of the range of growth rates for SBUs under consideration.

The horizontal axis shows the market share of each SBU in relation to the industry leaders. Thus it is relative market share and not absolute market share. If relative market share for an SBU is 1.5, that SBU is the market leader and its share is one and a half times greater than the next closest competitor. A relative market share of .8 would indicate that the SBU's market share was 80 percent of the market leader's share. Relative market share places each SBU in relation to the leader and provides more information about market position than absolute market share. The 1.0x division is the generally accepted point for separating SBUs into high-low relative market shares.

The size of each circle in the figure represents the proportional dollar contribution of each SBU to total company sales. The larger the circle, the larger the SBU's contribution to total company sales.

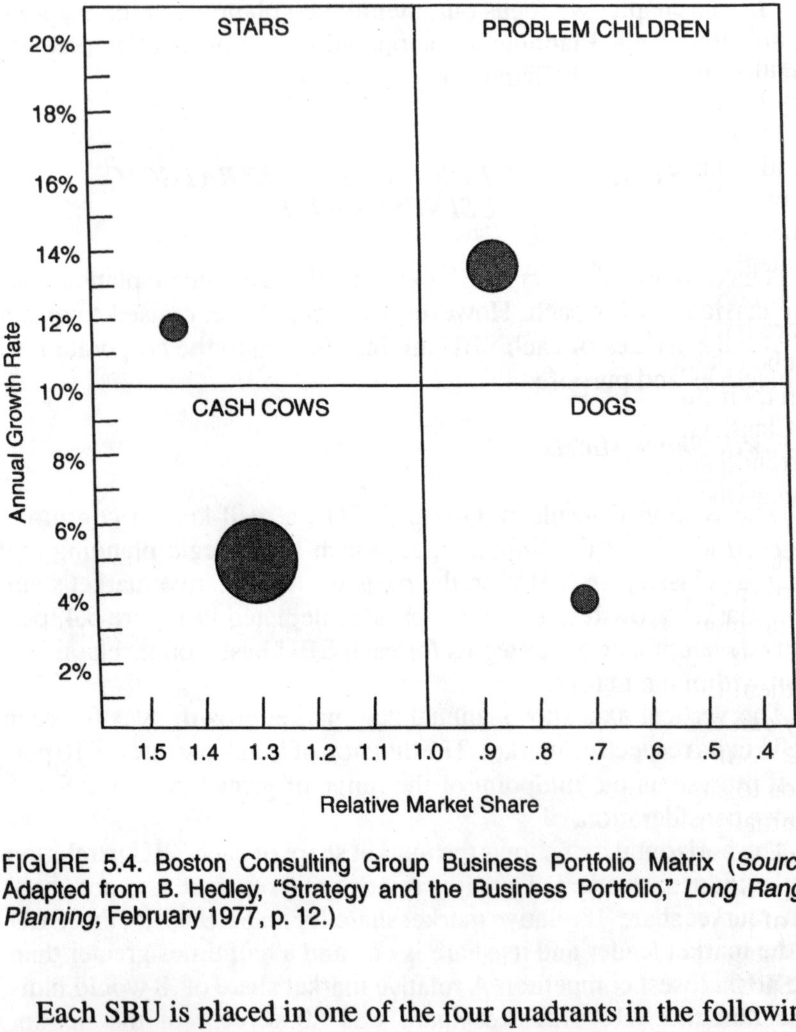

FIGURE 5.4. Boston Consulting Group Business Portfolio Matrix (*Source:* Adapted from B. Hedley, "Strategy and the Business Portfolio," *Long Range Planning,* February 1977, p. 12.)

Each SBU is placed in one of the four quadrants in the following four classifications:

1. *Cash cows*—A cash cow is an SBU with a high relative market share compared to other competitors in the market, but it is in an industry that has a low annual growth rate. These SBUs generate more than enough cash to cover operating expenses, and their growth rate does not warrant large investments in that industry. The cash generated can therefore be used to support other SBUs which offer more potential for growth.

2. *Stars*—Stars are SBUs that have a high relative market share and are also in an industry with expected high rates of growth. Stars usually have a high demand for cash to finance their growth.

3. *Problem children*—Problem children are SBUs that have a low relative market share but are in industries with a high annual rate of growth. The potential exists for them to become stars but their low relative share represents a major challenge to management to create strategies capable of increasing relative market share.

4. *Dogs*—Dogs are SBUs that not only have low relative market share but also are in industries with low growth potential. They may not be operating at a loss but they generate only enough cash to maintain their operations and market share.

Classifying a company's SBUs into such a matrix helps define the current position of each SBU and also suggests strategic options for management to improve performance. Although the position of an SBU will change over time because of changes in growth rates or market composition, the following four strategic actions are implied for the four cells: (1) "milk" the cows, (2) "shine" the stars, (3) "solve" the problems, and (4) "divest" the dogs.

1. *"Milk" the cows*—The strategy for cash cows is to spend enough on them to maintain their market share and "keep them healthy" so they can continue to generate cash.

2. *"Shine" the stars*—The strategy for stars is to continue to invest funds to support their growth rate and high market shares. They will eventually slow in growth and become cash cows and help generate funds for new stars.

3. *"Solve" the problems*—The strategy for these SBUs involves one of two options: (a) develop and test strategies for improving market share, or (b) divest and use the cash to support other more promising SBUs.

4. *"Divest" the dogs*—Dogs SBUs with low share and low growth potential are prime prospects for divestiture. Cash generated by divesting these SBUs can be reinvested into other SBUs with more potential.

Utilizing the Growth-Share Matrix

The BCG portfolio approach treats investments in SBUs like an individual investor's portfolio of stocks and bonds. Managers can invest or divest to improve the overall performance of the portfolio. This approach provides general strategy implications for each SBU and is a useful tool for analyzing multiline business companies. However, there are several limitations to this approach:

1. The identification of the midpoints on the axis is arbitrary. What is a high-growth industry? Is a 10 percent increase in annual sales volume too high or too low to be classified as a growth industry? Should it be 16 percent?
2. Not all business units will fall neatly into the four quadrants. Strategy implications are quite different for SBUs that appear to be falling into the problem child and dog categories.
3. An SBU might be classified as a star or cash cow at any given point but the trend in market share or industry growth could mean the SBU is gaining or losing share.
4. An SBU classified as a dog may still be profitable for years to come even though it never gains market share. It could be in a market niche that will sustain its position for years. Should it be divested or harvested?

These limitations of the BCG portfolio led to the development of other approaches to the same set of strategic questions. One of these approaches is referred to as the business screen.

The Business Screen

An alternative matrix approach has been developed by General Electric with the help of the consulting firm of McKinsey & Company. This matrix is based on two dimensions: long-term industry attractiveness and the business strength/competitive position of the firm in the industry. This matrix is shown in Figure 5.5. The "red, yellow, and green" areas each represent different combinations of industry attractiveness and company strength/position. The "red" zone represents SBUs of low to medium industry attractiveness and average to weak business strength/position. These are prime candidates for harvesting or divestment unless some type of turnaround strategy is developed. The "yellow" zone consists of the three diagonal cells stretching from the lower left to the upper right. These SBUs warrant

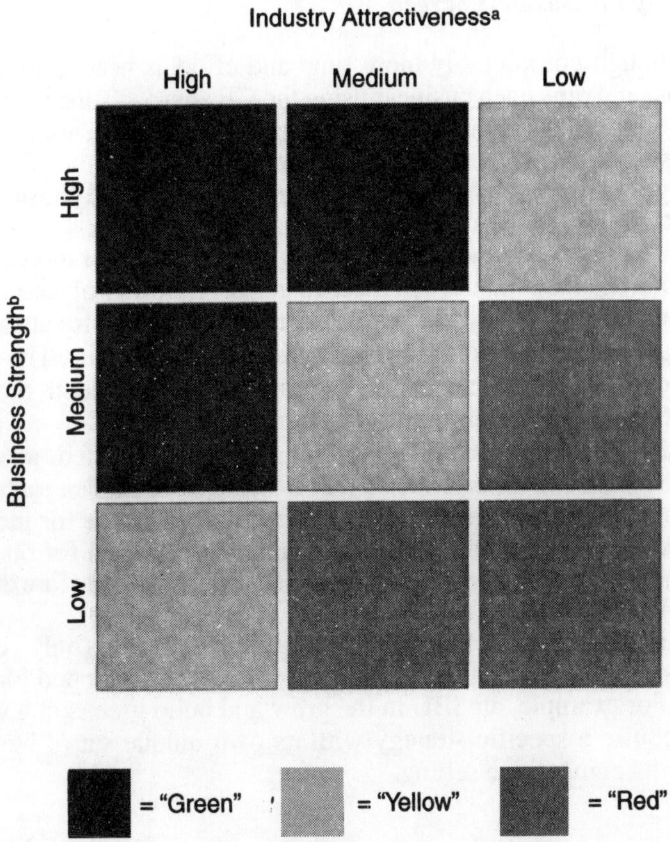

FIGURE 5.5. The Business Screen (*Source:* Adapted from M. G. Allen, "Strategic Problems Facing Today's Corporate Planner," speech given at the Academy of Management, 36th Annual Meeting, Kansas City, Missouri, 1976.)
[a]Industry attractiveness is determined by market size, market growth, pricing, competitive structure, profitability, technology role, social, environment, legal, etc.; [b]Business strength is determined by company size, market share and growth rate, brand position, profitability margins, technology position, product quality, image, etc.

only a medium investment allocation and the strategy is usually "hold and maintain." The "green" zone represents SBUs that are in the most attractive industries where the company has relatively favorable strength/position. These SBUs are in the highest investment priority. The strategy for these SBUs is "grow and build."

Utilizing the Business Screen

Although considerably more time and effort is needed to collect the data and rank each business using the GE approach, the results are much more detailed in terms of strategy implications. This approach allows for intermediate rankings of firms on the two dimensions and clearly identifies the SBUs which should be built and those which should be harvested or divested.

One advantage of the GE approach is that it allows for more classifications of SBUs including a medium range. It also involves analysis of many factors to evaluate business strength and industry attractiveness and not just market share and industry growth rates. The detail and richness of this type of analysis provide a more in-depth perspective of an SBU's current position.

Each industry attractiveness factor must be identified, a weight must be assigned to the importance of the factor, and then each must be evaluated on a rating scale to create an overall value for industry attractiveness. The same procedures must be followed for business strength/competitive position to create an overall value before the position of the SBU can be plotted.

This matrix approach, like all such approaches, yields only general strategy implications. Detailed strategies must be developed for each SBU. For example, an SBU in the grow and build green zone would still require a specific strategy with its own unique set of business strengths/competitive setting.

CORPORATE PLANNING AND MARKETING PLANNING

The strategic planning process described thus far has concentrated on corporate level and business unit planning. These two levels of planning precede development of the strategic marketing plan and the annual or operating marketing plan. The strategic marketing plan contains the overall approaches to marketing within a business unit and the annual marketing plan details what is to be done on a day-to-day, week-to-week, and month-to-month basis to translate the major strategies into specific actions, responsibilities, and time schedules.

Both strategic and operational marketing plans must be consistent with corporate strategic plans. Although marketing plans are more detailed and cover only the marketing functions, the marketing planning process involves steps similar to the strategic planning process at the corporate level. Steps usually include a detailed analysis of the company's situation, setting specific objectives, developing strategy, implementing strategy, and evaluating and controlling strategy. The details of the marketing planning process are discussed in Chapter 6.

The relationships between the corporate strategic plan, the strategic marketing plan, and the annual operating marketing plan are demonstrated in Figure 5.6. This approach to planning ensures a consis-

FIGURE 5.6. Relating Marketing Plans to Corporate Plans

tency between what is done on a weekly or monthly basis and the overall marketing strategy. The strategic marketing plan is devised from and, in turn, supports the corporate plan.

STRATEGIC PLANNING IN GLOBAL ORGANIZATIONS

Many organizations have adopted a global perspective to strategic planning. International markets have been sought as a means of growth under a strategy of market development discussed earlier. Some companies, such as Singer, Massey Ferguson, and Weyerhaeuser, have increasingly turned to international markets for new opportunities. Massey Ferguson, a U.S. farm equipment producer, has about 70 percent of its sales outside the United States.

Global competition is prevalent in many industries: oil, televisions, motorcycles, automobiles, aircraft, and sewing machines. To be successful, companies in these industries must take a global view of strategic marketing.

Following are three basic strategy options for competing on a global basis:

1. Competing worldwide with an entire product line in all markets where the same, basically unchanged products can be successfully sold.
2. A global focus concentrating on marketing the same basic products in a few countries.
3. A country-by-country focus strategy in which differences in each country are recognized and the products are customized to match market conditions.

Each of these strategies must be evaluated in terms of consistency with overall corporate objectives and strategies to make sure the global marketing strategies match the firm's resources and skills. The third approach, a country-by-country strategy, requires detailed knowledge of the consumers in each market. Then the marketing strategy elements of product, price, promotion, and distribution are adjusted to each situation. This requires more resources and marketing management skills than the first two approaches.

Market Entry

Once a firm has identified the basic strategic approach it wants to adopt in international marketing, the next step is to decide exactly how to enter the market. Several options are available, and each of these should be evaluated carefully because each requires a different level of commitment of resources and also different levels of risk. Each of these alternatives will be discussed next.

Exporting

The lowest level of commitment and risk in multinational marketing is exporting. Exporting involves marketing products that are domestically produced in another country. A company can market its products directly to customers in a country, sell to retailers, or use an independent exporting intermediary.

The most common approach is to sell to an export firm, called an export merchant. The export merchant sells the products to its customers around the world and assumes all risks associated with the sales.

Another type of intermediary is called an export agent or broker. They serve essentially the same task as agents and brokers in domestic distribution. Export agents may reside in a foreign country and represent the domestic company to foreign customers or they may reside in the domestic producer's country and represent foreign customers. These agents may also arrange for financing and distribution of the products.

Licensing

Licensing is a process in which one company agrees to license a company in another country to manufacture or brand products for sale in other countries. This is a legal arrangement that specifies what can be done, in what location, and the conditions of sales.

The licensor must carefully monitor the activities of the licensee to ensure that quality, pricing, distribution, and promotion levels are consistent with the contract levels. If the licensee decides to violate the contract, the licensor may not be in a position to control such actions. International law is often ineffective in dealing with such contractual arrangements.

Joint Ventures

A joint venture combines a domestic firm and a foreign firm for a specific business venture. The domestic firm supplies capital and sometimes managerial resources to a foreign company and receives part ownership in that venture. The arrangement is for a specific venture and does not commit the firms to other activities.

Many countries' governments promote joint ventures to aid the economic development of their own country. Resources flow from one country into the economy of another and yet production, marketing, and employment are enhanced and controlled locally.

Contract Manufacturing

Contract manufacturing enables a multinational company to enter a market without building a plant by having a firm located in the foreign market manufacture the product and affix the multinational's brand name. If the sales of the product continue to grow, the company can then build its own manufacturing plants.

Under contract manufacturing, the local manufacturer performs only the manufacturing function for the multinational firm. Marketing would continue to be controlled by the brand's owner.

Direct Investment

The highest level of commitment and risk is associated with direct investment. Direct investment means a company operates a wholly owned manufacturing and marketing operation in another country. Although substantial returns can be experienced with this option through savings in transportation and/or manufacturing costs, risks are also high. Unstable political and social conditions can lead to governmental overthrows, wars, and expropriation of company assets by foreign governments.

Some countries discourage direct investment in favor of joint ventures while others encourage direct investments. A country's tax structure can be altered to reward or punish companies making direct investments.

SUMMARY

In this chapter we presented the basic concepts used in strategic planning for whole organizations as well as for the marketing function. Strategic issues were dealt with rather than tactical or operating issues. Strategic decisions are of critical importance to an organization because of their long-term impact on what the company is and does for its customers.

Strategic management is a process that involves defining the business, setting objectives, formulating strategy, implementing strategy, and evaluating and controlling strategy. Strategic marketing plans are developed after the corporate-level plan and must be consistent with them.

Several tools were introduced to aid plan development. The product market matrix was used to show growth alternatives while the Boston Consulting Group Matrix and the business screen were presented as aids in diagnosing existing SBUs.

This chapter concluded with a discussion of global strategic planning. Three basic strategies for entering the international realm were identified.

Chapter 6

Marketing Planning: Operational Perspectives

In Chapter 5 we learned that marketing managers must first adopt a strategic perspective for marketing planning, then translate that perspective into an operational marketing plan. In this chapter we learn how to do planning at the operational level (see Figure 6.1).

The strategic planning process described in Chapter 5 concentrated on corporate-level and strategic-business-unit planning. These two levels of planning precede development of the strategic marketing plan and the annual operating marketing plan. The strategic marketing plan contains the overall strategic approaches to marketing within a business unit. The annual plan spells out the details of what

Societal marketing orientation

↓

Understanding

↓

Planning
Strategic planning: Chapter 5
Operational planning: Chapter 6

↓

Implementing

↓

Connecting with customers

FIGURE 6.1. The Effective Marketing Management Process

is to be done on a day-to-day, week-to-week, and month-to-month basis to translate the strategic marketing plan into specific actions, responsibilities, and time schedules.

Strategic marketing plans are derived from corporate strategic plans. Although they are more detailed and cover only the marketing function, strategic marketing planning involves steps similar to strategic planning at the corporate level. The steps usually include a detailed analysis of a company's situation, setting specific objectives, developing strategy, implementing strategy, and evaluating and controlling strategy.

The operating marketing plan is a detailed tactical statement explaining what must be done, when, and how. In other words, the strategic marketing plan deals with what is to be accomplished in the long run, while the operating marketing plan deals with what is to be done in a given time period, usually a year.

The operating marketing plan focuses on the tactical decisions needed to carry out the strategic marketing plan. The time frame for the operating marketing plan is usually a year and normally coincides with an organization's fiscal year. The situation analysis deals only with the current operating environment and details only important events that influence changes in marketing activities. The strategy portion contains the detailed tactical decisions that spell out changes in such areas as advertising themes, new products, etc.

One of the most important aspects of this type of planning process is the perspective managers must have to use it properly. Managers must study the entire marketing process from the customer's vantage point, which creates new patterns for administrative development and organization. An understanding of the planning process provides a framework for organized thought patterns for the variety of marketing activities that take place in an organization.

Because of the scope and importance of a new product, it may require a separate plan. There are three reasons for this practice: (l) the approval procedure for a new product plan may differ from that for regular product plans; (2) there may be seasonal differences between the new product introduction and existing product plans; and (3) timing patterns may be different for new and existing products. The actual new product plan will often contain many of the elements that are in the plans for established products.

The short-term plan for the new product introduction should include results, targets, actions, responsibilities, schedules, and dates. The plan should indicate details and deadlines, production plans, market introduction program, advertising and merchandising actions, employee training, and other information necessary to launching the product. The plan should answer a series of questions—what, when, where, who, how, and why—for each objective to be accomplished during the short-term planning period. With enhanced understanding of consumers comes the ability to develop more tailored marketing programs. The need to target selected segments and position products effectively is increasingly being recognized by marketing managers. For instance, a recent survey of top marketing executives showed that developing target-market-segmentation strategies was one of the key pressure points they had to deal with in a recent year.

THE OPERATING MARKETING PLAN FORMAT

An outline of a format for a marketing plan is provided in Figure 6.2. The marketing plan is a written document that contains four basic ele-

I. Situation analysis
   A. Product/market analysis
   B. Customer analysis
   C. Competitive analysis
   D. Opportunity analysis
   E. Current strategy assessment

II. Objectives
   A. Sales objectives
   B. Profitability objectives
   C. Customer objectives

III. Strategy
   A. Overall strategy
   B. Marketing mix variables
   C. Financial impact statement

IV. Monitoring and control
   A. Performance analysis
   B. Customer data feedback

FIGURE 6.2. Outline of a Marketing Plan

ments. It is premised on the fact that a company must (1) determine where it is now (develop a summary of the situation analysis, including general developments, consumer analysis, competitive analysis, and opportunity analysis), (2) decide where it wants to go (provide a set of objectives), (3) decide how it is going to get there (provide a detailed strategy statement of how the marketing variables will be combined to achieve those objectives as well as the financial impact), and (4) decide what feedback is needed to stay on course (suggest a set of procedures for monitoring and controlling the plan through feedback about results). A complete marketing plan provides the specifics to all these areas.

Situation Analysis

Successful marketing planning is very much a process of "if-then" reasoning: *If* the analysis reveals certain specific characteristics of the market, *then* our best strategy would be one selected to respond to this particular situation. In other words, there is a direct translation of our understanding into our planning. What do we need to focus on in our situation analysis? The situation analysis should include (1) the product/market definition, (2) customer analysis, (3) key competitor analysis, (4) opportunity analysis, and possibly (5) current marketing strategy assessment.

Product/Market Analysis

The product/market, properly defined, should contain all products or services that satisfy a set of related generic needs. The first tasks include estimating demand, determining end-user characteristics, learning about industry practices and trends, and identifying key competitors for the end-user groups being considered as possible market targets for a specific product.

Some competitors may offer the same product, and others may offer a different product that will meet the same set of needs. For example, Remington electric shavers compete with brands such as Norelco and Panasonic, as well as safety razor brands such as Gillette.

As was pointed out in Chapter 2, analysis of the product/market involves determining the size of the total market, identifying the factors that are influencing the growth, stability, or decline of the market, and market share. Understanding the factors that are causing the market to evolve helps determine what short- and long-term adjustments must be made in the marketing mix to be successful. For example, new technologies create the need for strategic and operational changes in marketing activities. The new satellite television technology with eighteen-inch dishes and hundreds of channels has created the need for cable companies to evaluate their corporate strategies. However, they must also adjust their operational strategy to respond to new forms of competition while the strategic actions are being evaluated.

Regardless of the techniques used in analyzing market factors, the basic information sought involves understanding the factors that influence demand for a product or service and their historical and future trend. This information helps develop the basis from which objectives and strategies are developed.

Customer Analysis

Nothing is more central to marketing than customer analysis. Customers' needs are the pivotal point around which objectives and strategies are developed. Estimates of demand, descriptive profiles, and criteria important in the purchase decision are useful in strategy design. Firms should also include market segment identification and analysis to precisely define target markets.

As the process of customer analysis continues, a profile of the consumers in each segment emerges. This profile should be as complete as possible for each segment and should include socioeconomic, behavioral, and psychological characteristics. The results of the analysis can be used in subsequent time periods so they should be easily accessible. In fact, if this type of analysis has already been completed, it can be updated or expanded.

The results of the analysis may be summarized as shown in Table 6.1. This approach allows a comparison of the characteristics for each segment.

The target market decision is the focal point of marketing strategy; it serves as the basis for setting objectives and developing strategy (more on target marketing will be presented later in this chapter). The decision to use a strategy is based on revenue-cost analysis and assessment of competitive position.

TABLE 6.1. Consumer Characteristics by Segment

Characteristics	Segment 1	Segment 2	Segment 3
Socioeconomic			
Age	26-40	41-65	Over 65
Sex	Male	Male	Male
Income	Upper	Middle	Lower
Location	Southwest	Southeast	Southwest
Behavioral			
Shopping behavior	Specialty stores	Department stores	Discount stores
Purchase rate	High	Moderate	Low
Psychological			
Options	Fashion oriented	Comfort oriented	Economy oriented
Awareness	High brand name awareness	Some brand name awareness	Low brand name awareness

Analysis of Key Competitors

Evaluation of competitors' strategies, strengths, limitations, and plans is a key aspect of the situation analysis. Both existing and potential competitors must be identified. Typically, a subset of firms in the industry will comprise the strategic competitor group.

Two fundamental questions are answered through the competitive analysis: What is the nature of the forces that shape competition in this market? and, Which competitors are going after which market segments with what marketing strategies? The first question focuses on overall competition and the forces that influence the nature of competition in a given product/market situation.

The second question focuses on specific market segments that have been isolated through consumer analysis. After analyzing the size (potential) and the characteristics of each segment, the analysis begins to deal with competition on a segment-by-segment basis. The focus is on uncovering segments that are not currently being served or segments where competitors do not have clearly identifiable strategies but each seems to be using a strategy similar to the others. Usually, several segments can be better served through strategies aimed directly at their needs. This creates the opportunity to gain a competitive advantage or edge over competition in specific market segments.

Several other factors should be analyzed for a more complete evaluation of competitors. They include competitors' strategic tendencies and resources (marketing, financial, and personnel). The first factor is concerned with competitors' willingness to change or react to competitive moves; the second deals with their ability to make strategic moves.

Assessing strategic tendencies involves evaluating whether competitors' actions tend to be reactive or proactive. Reactive strategies are those that follow the lead of other firms in the market or simply settle into a niche. Proactive strategies involve market leadership or challenge to the market leader. If market leaders and challengers can be identified, they are the competitors whose actions must be anticipated. In Japan's "beer wars," for example, Asahi Breweries, Ltd. took on the competitive position of the initiator of change in the industry because of the success of its dry beer. A marketing mix audit helps identify the exact nature of competitors' strategies.

After completing the competitive analysis by market segment, develop summary statements about each segment with respect to competition. This provides an overview of the competitive forces at work in each segment.

Opportunity Analysis

Opportunity analysis should identify future environmental changes that may alter market opportunities, competition, and a firm's marketing strategy. The major forces that may influence market opportunities and strategies include technological advancements, demographic and social trends, governmental and political constraints, economic conditions, and the physical environment.

To evaluate opportunities successfully, you must combine the external analysis with internal analysis, which directly influences a firm's willingness and ability to respond to opportunities. Internal factors include purpose or mission statements and company resources.

If the opportunity is consistent with purpose, a firm's resources must be analyzed to determine the company's ability to respond to an opportunity. At least four types of resources must be analyzed: marketing, production, financial, and managerial.

Other factors should also be analyzed when choosing opportunities. The importance of economic conditions, technology, political/legal, and cultural/social conditions will vary by opportunity and should not be overlooked. In a technologically driven industry, such as personal computers, the inability to develop new technologies or to incorporate new technologies into products can severely limit or even prohibit a company's entrance into a market. On the other hand, new and better technologic breakthroughs can become the means by which market entrance is achieved.

Current Marketing Strategy Assessment

An evaluation of the effectiveness of a firm's current marketing strategy should identify important strategy issues, strengths, and limitations. Management should evaluate the firm's strategic situation and the appropriateness of the marketing strategy being used for that situation.

The process of reviewing internal operations for strengths and weaknesses and scanning the organization's external environment for opportunities is called a SWOT analysis (see Chapter 5).

The ultimate goal of a SWOT analysis, on one hand, is to match vital operational strengths with major environmental opportunities. On the other hand, a SWOT analysis provides a basis for improving weaknesses or at least minimizing them and avoiding or managing environmental threats to operations. Ideally, a SWOT study helps identify a distinctive competence that can be used to tap an important opportunity in the environment. This type of SWOT analysis is similar to the one at the corporate level (Chapter 5), but here it is being conducted at the product/market level.

Setting Objectives

After completion of the product/market, consumer, competitive, and opportunity analyses, the next step in the development of a marketing plan is to set objectives. The basis for setting the specific objectives is the qualitative and quantitative data gathered from previous analyses. The objectives, in turn, become the basis for the development of the marketing strategy. Realistic objectives cannot be established without consideration of the operating environment and the specific consumer segments to which the marketing effort is to be targeted.

Some companies prefer to set objectives that apply to the total marketing strategy for all targeted markets. Overall strategy objectives represent a composite of specific objectives for each market target.

Marketing contributes to sales, market share, and profit objectives. Firms also need various operating objectives or subobjectives to provide performance guidelines for each marketing mix component. These also contribute to sales, market share, and profit contribution objectives. For example, suppose that one objective of a company's advertising strategy is to increase target customers' awareness of a particular brand by some amount during a specific time. Management believes that increasing brand awareness will have an effect on sales. In the case of operating objectives (e.g., increasing awareness), establishing a direct cause-and-effect relationship to sales is often difficult. Management may be convinced that increasing awareness will increase sales but is often unable to predict that an X percent change in awareness will cause a Y percent increase in sales. Even though this is a problem, management should still formulate operating objectives or it will have no basis to gauge progress.

Marketing Strategy Selection

After setting objectives, the next step is the development of the marketing strategy. This step involves deciding on the specific ways to combine the marketing variables to satisfy the needs of the market's targets and accomplish the objectives of the organization. In some situations, the corporate strategic plan may dictate the marketing strategy. For example, if the corporate strategy involves positioning the firm as the low-cost producer in an industry and emphasizes volume in the corporate objectives, the marketing mix would have to reflect this. The marketing mix would probably emphasize low price to generate sales volume. This would also be the major focus in promotional messages.

If the corporate strategy is not oriented in this way, then marketing managers have much more autonomy in strategy selection. A firm may, for example, decide at the corporate level to hold and grow a specific SBU. It then becomes the responsibility of marketing management to come up with a creative strategy to produce growth.

Like management itself, marketing strategy development is both a science and an art and is a product of both logic and creativity. The scientific aspect deals with assembling and allocating the resources necessary to achieve a company's marketing objectives with emphasis on opportunities, costs, and time. The art of strategy is mainly concerned with the utilization of resources, including motivation of the workforce, sensitivity to the environment, and ability to readjust to counter strategies of competitors.

Marketing strategies provide direction to marketing efforts. Alternate courses of action are evaluated by management before commitment is made to a specific strategy outlined in the marketing plan. Thus, strategy is the link between objectives and results. It is the answer to one of the basic questions posed in a marketing plan: How are we going to get there?

The marketing strategy is the result of the blending together of various marketing elements. These elements consist of (1) the *product* to be offered to buyers; (2) the distribution of products to various outlets—referred to as *place;* (3) the *promotion* or communications to prospective customers using various techniques; and (4) the *price* charged for the product. The term *marketing mix* has been used to describe these various elements. Therefore, marketing strategy may be viewed as a mix aimed at satisfying the needs of selected market segments and accomplishing specific marketing objectives.

When you evaluate the various strategies that can be used in marketing, you are asking what combination of these variables could be used to satisfy customer needs and accomplish the plan's objectives. Once a strategy is chosen it may be followed for several years, being altered only in response to counterstrategies of competitors or changes in other relevant environments. For example, if you are working with an established product, the question of strategy is: Do we need to change our strategy to respond to new conditions in the environment, and if so, in what ways?

Plan Monitoring and Control

The final stage in preparing the marketing plan is to establish the evaluation and control procedures that will be used to track the progress of the marketing effort. Decisions should be made about the specific data needed for tracking, how and when the data are to be collected, and who is to receive what type of reports. Such data become the basis for the decisions to alter the plan and to focus on the objectives-results relationship. Alterations in the operational plan should be made to "fine-tune" it or the way it is being implemented. Many companies fail to understand the importance of establishing procedures to monitor and control the planning process, a failing that leads to less than optimal performance. Control should be a natural follow-through in developing a plan. No plan should be considered complete until controls are identified and the procedures for recording and transmitting information to managers are established.

Many problems can be avoided when a sound control system is established. Failure to establish control is analogous to looking once at a map before a long trip and never looking at road signs, markers, or check-points.

The planning process results in a specific course for a product or service. This plan is implemented (marketing activities are performed in the manner described in the plan) and results are produced. These results are sales revenues, costs, profits, and accompanying consumer attitudes, preferences, and behaviors. Information on these results is given to managers who compare them with objectives to evaluate performance. This performance evaluation identifies the areas where decisions must be made. The actual decision making controls the plan by altering it to accomplish stated objectives, and a new cycle begins. The information flows are the key to a good control system. Deciding what information is provided to which managers in what time periods is the essence of a control system. Controlling the marketing process is discussed in detail in Chapter 8.

PREPARING THE PLAN AND BUDGET

The selection of a marketing strategy and evaluation procedures moves the planning process to preparation of the actual plan and its supporting sales forecast and budget. Preparing the plan involves several activities and considerations, including selecting the planning cycle and frequency, deciding the nature and use of the annual plan, choosing a format for the plan, and forecasting revenues and estimating expenses.

Developing the overall marketing budget involves developing the sales budget, promotion budget, distribution budget, and administrative budget. After the budgets are prepared and approved, the next step is to implement the marketing plan. This will be discussed in Chapter 7.

TARGET MARKETING AND MARKETING STRATEGY DEVELOPMENT

Selection of a target market is a decision of strategic scope. At the three levels of planning (see Chapter 5) the issue of scope requires answers to these questions:

Corporate level: Which business should we be in?
SBU level: Which product/markets should we be in within this business?
Operational level: Which customer group(s) should we target?

The selection of the group(s) or segment(s) of customers toward which an organization will direct its marketing efforts is addressed at the operational level. Adoption of a market orientation is an implicit acceptance of a philosophy that has deliverance of customer satisfaction at its core. This requires understanding customers first, before making decisions that affect ability to deliver satisfaction (how else can we know what is "satisfying"?). Usually, not all customers can be satisfied with the same market offering. Those who can be satisfied similarly are called a market segment. Most markets consist of multiple segments of consumers who are similar to other people in the same segment, but different from people in another segment in some way, which affects their response to a marketing appeal. When we make targeting decisions we are selecting those segments where we believe we can gain a competitive advantage in delivering satisfaction. The question then becomes, How do you select which segment(s) to target?

Target Market Selection

What determines a segment's attractiveness? No universal criteria exist which define attractiveness, but three categories might capture what most organizations would find of interest:[1]

Market opportunity: What could be gained from targeting a segment?

Competitive environment: Are competitors capable of preventing us from gaining it?

Market access: How difficult will it be to capture the opportunity?

Market Opportunity

Factors that define the extent of a market opportunity vary by industry and company, but market size, growth rate, and potential, and the bargaining power of buyers are factors most managers consider as measures of market opportunity.

An ideal segment would be large, growing, and offer good potential for future growth. Also, the customers occupying the segment would not possess bargaining strength, which puts the seller at a disadvantage. Buyers who can easily switch between sellers, or who can drive down prices because of their relative size make such segments less attractive.

Competitive Environment

The second major category of market attractiveness concerns the level and nature of competition for segment customers. The intensity of competition could be influenced by the number of competitors, the ease with which they can enter a market, the degree to which you can differentiate your product from competitors' products, the number of substitute products, and the degree to which competitors have satisfied the needs of the market segments. Other factors related to competitive environment may be more or less important, depending on the particular product/market in question (e.g., existence of exit barriers, level of competitor commitment to the market, feistiness of management, etc.).

Market Access

Although market opportunity considers factors that influence the extent of the gain which could be derived in targeting a market segment, competitive environment and market access consider the costs or obstacles which must be incurred in achieving that gain. Access to the market will be affected by the degree of difficulty in achieving access to customers, the synergies available within the company in offering the product to the market (e.g., the use of an existing channel of distribution versus establishing and maintaining another channel), the degree to which a product/market is regulated, and the source and extent of competitive advantage. For example, access to buying patterns of its card holders allows American Express to efficiently target promotions for trips, and other products and services to very small target markets.

Market Attractiveness Index

Development of a set of attractiveness criteria delivers more value to a firm when those factors can be combined to generate an overall measure of attractiveness. This permits comparison of attractiveness scores by market segments and between product/markets, allowing for more objective selection of segments as target markets. Because the units of measure vary by factor (e.g., market size may be in dollar sales, market growth rate in percentages), it is necessary to establish a standard unit of "attractiveness" that allows direct comparison of market segments. An index of attractiveness standardizes the units of measure and establishes different values or weights for the factors (e.g., one manager may think size of a market is twice as important as buyer power). See Table 6.2 for an example of the development of an attractiveness index.

The index shown for this segment would be compared to the index of others to evaluate the relative attractiveness of each segment or a target market. The overall index computation provides a measure of attractiveness on a 100-point scale, with fifty as average. This is useful in giving a broader perspective on market attractiveness. For example, if five segments are evaluated and the highest total market attractiveness score of the five is 800, we can say only that that segment is relatively more attractive than the other few segments. We are still left wondering if it is attractive enough to justify targeting. The overall index score gives us the context in which to view that score. Over time, companies can establish threshold points of the overall index which can be used in making targeting decisions. For example, experience may show that an overall index score of 60 is the threshold for go/no-go decisions (over sixty is the target market; below sixty is not

TABLE 6.2. Development of a Market Attractiveness Index

Market attractiveness factors	Relative importance	Unattractive to very attractive: 0	1	2	3	4	5	6	Attractiveness score (RI × Score) × 100
Market opportunity									
Market size	.40							X	240
Growth rate	.30			X					60
Buyer power	.20			X					40
Market potential	.10				X				30
	1.00								370
Competitive environment									
Number of companies	.30				X				90
Differentiation	.30			X					60
Ease of entry	.20						X		100
Substitutes	.20					X			80
	1.00								330
Market access									
Customer access	.20							X	120
Company synergies	.40						X		200
Sources of advantage	.30					X			120
Regulation	.10							X	60
	1.00								500

Total Attractiveness Score

Major attractiveness market forces	Relative weight	Factor index	Weighted index	Maximum index	Overall index*
Market opportunity	.30	370	111	180	62
Competitive environment	.40	330	132	240	55
Market access	.30	500	150	180	83
	1.00		393	600	66

Source: Adapted from Roger J. Best, *Market Based Management* (Upper Saddle River, NJ: Prentice-Hall, 1997), p.125.

$$\text{*Overall index} = \frac{\text{Weighted index}}{\text{Maximum index}} \times 100$$

targeted). Other considerations such as cost of serving segments and revenue generated by segment members can be used in making targeting decisions.

Once the target market decision is made, the following information is often needed in building the plan: (1) size and growth rate of the target market; (2) description of end users in the target group; and (3) information about competitors that will be helpful in selecting a positioning strategy.

In Chapter 2, Worthington Foods segmented the vegetarian and meat-restricting markets for their line of meat-alternative products. How did they choose which of these segments to target? They used a slightly less sophisticated method than the one previously described to compute a market attractiveness index for each of the segments identified in their research study of 2,000 consumers. Table 6.3 shows how the index was constructed.

Three categories of consumer information were measured: behaviors, attitudes, and intentions. Six behaviors, three intentions, and one attitude were measured (an average score of agreement for sixteen item statements in the survey). Of the ten measures, 60 percent were behaviors, 30 percent intentions, and 10 percent attitudes. These provide the "weights" used to construct the attractiveness index (see previous discussion). The units of measure for these components are different (e.g., a behavior measured as the number of times per week consumption takes place versus an attitude measured as the amount of agreement with an item statement in the questionnaire).

Therefore, all ten parts of the attractiveness scale must be standardized. We do that by indexing—making the segment with the highest level of each of the ten measures equal to 100 percent and then calculating the other segments' performance on that measure as a percentage of that number. For example, if the Alternative Advocates state that they eat meat alternatives 5.6 times/week, and Convenience-Driven segment members eat them 5.1 times/week, then Alternative Advocates have a 100 score (i.e., their 5.6/week is the highest consumption rate of all segments and is recorded as 100 percent), and the Convenience-Driven segment receives an index score of 91 (5.1 ÷ 5.6 = 91 percent).

Totaling up the index scores for all ten measures results in a single number (out of a possible 1,000 index points) that represents the attractiveness of each market segment as a potential target market. A

TABLE 6.3. Worthington Foods Segment Attractiveness Index

	Vegetarian segments					Meat-restricting segments			
	AA	**CD**	**RV**	**AL**	**AO**	**AF**	**TS**	**ML**	**NN**
Behavioral measures									
A. MSF users as a % of total	100	91	41	45	14	91	45	14	9
B. MSF users as a % of segment	100	100	43	39	17	48	26	9	4
C. MFPF % users × usage rate	59	100	30	34	13	30	26	5	1
D. MA % users × usage rate	100	86	16	76	4	33	4	1	12
E. MSF % users × usage rate	100	83	39	20	5	24	16	7	2
F. HOFPF users × usage rate	74	79	100	19	30	83	97	41	30
Intent measures									
A. % definitely purchase + one-half of % probably purchase	100	81	76	40	25	80	47	26	23
B. % trial interest × intend rate	86	81	100	52	34	88	71	46	51
C. # products "50% +" trial interest	100	42	21	26	5	16	5	5	5
Attitude measures									
Average agreement for 16 statements	100	70	61	47	16	75	36	24	11
Total index score (1,000 possible)	919	813	527	398	163	568	373	178	148

Ratio of highest to lowest = 6.2:1

Key: MSF = Morningstar Farms (a MA brand of Worthington Foods); MA = Meat Alternative (the type of product); MFPF = Meatless Frozen Prepared Foods; HOFPF = Health-Oriented Frozen Prepared Foods; AA = Alternative Advocates; CD = Convenience Driven; RV = Reluctant Vegetarians; AL= Animal Lovers; AO = Alternative Opponents; AF = Alternative Fans; TS = Time Savers; ML = Meat Lovers; NN = Natural Nuts

large range of scores among the segments indicates that the segmentation process was very useful in differentiating the most attractive groups from the least attractive. In the example, the highest scoring segment, the Alternative Advocates, is 6.2 times more attractive than the lowest-scoring segment, the meat-restricting Natural Nuts. A small variation in scores would indicate a mass market rather than a market with segments that should influence marketing strategy development.

In this case, as in the Mobil case, the market is not a mass of consumers all motivated and behaving very similarly. Rather, it is comprised of very different groups of people with different attitudes, behaviors, etc. Also, just as in the Mobil case, not all segments will be targeted (to be discussed in the Positioning section of this chapter). Sales improve when strategies are developed to better serve the needs of the fraction of the total market that comprises the targeted segments. The Worthington Foods case is a clear example of the "if-then" approach to planning discussed at the beginning of the chapter.

Targeting Strategies

Organizations may choose to target none, or one or more market segments based on target market attractiveness and profitability. Choosing how many segments to target is also a strategic decision. Possible target selection strategies are illustrated in Figure 6.3.

The mass marketing approach was common after World War II when pent-up consumer demand and lack of foreign competition meant firms could sell almost anything "to the masses." As markets

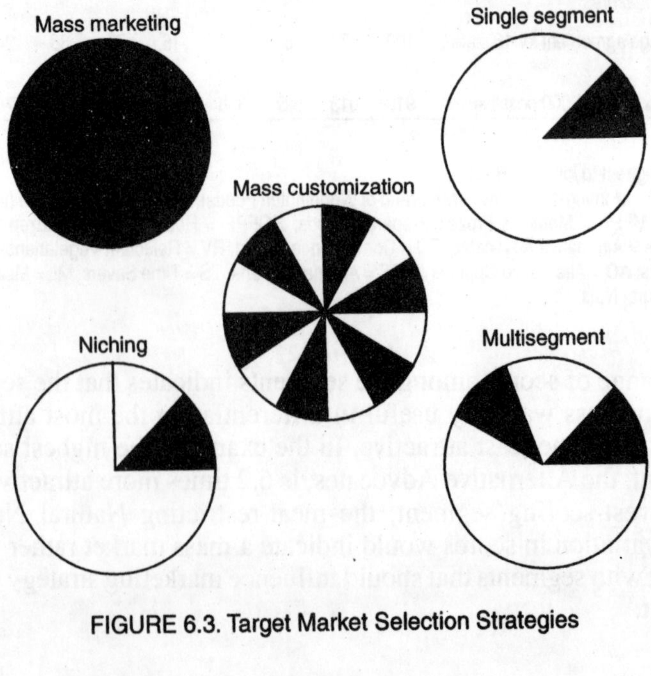

FIGURE 6.3. Target Market Selection Strategies

have splintered into smaller segments with different expressed needs and harder-to-satisfy customers, mass marketing approaches have lost the ability to attract consumers. However, many small business without the resources or know-how to do target marketing are, in essence, practicing mass marketing strategies when they determine what they want to offer to the market and broadcast their appeal, hoping that someone, somewhere, will respond. Even if they possess a product that is desirable to some customers, the inefficiencies of such a strategy can mean the demise of such operations.

Single Segment

Single-segment strategies consist of marketing a product or line of products to a single segment. For instance, Mercedes-Benz traditionally pursued a single-segment strategy by marketing a line of luxury automobiles to affluent customers. In the late 1990s they broadened their target market to less affluent consumers with the C-Class cars, the SLK-Class sports cars, and an SUV targeted to compete with the top end of the "luxury" SUV market. Single-segment strategies are pursued by many companies who have extensive knowledge of customers within that segment and can specialize their production, distribution, and promotion. The danger in this strategy is that the single segment may face declining membership or increased competition, which places severe pressure on profits without revenues being generated from serving other markets.

Niche Targeting

Niches are narrowly defined customer groups that are usually a subsegment with a distinctive set of traits searching for specialized benefits. For example, Ferrari serves the needs of a niche within the luxury sports car segment. According to Kotler, an attractive niche is characterized as follows:

- Niche customers have distinct needs and will pay a premium to have them satisfied.
- The "nicher" has the skills to serve the niche well and gains certain economies through specialization.
- The niche is not likely to attract other competitors.
- The niche has sufficient size, profit, and growth potential.[2]

Niche marketing will be more prevalent among large companies in the future. Small companies and start-up firms quite often use niche marketing strategies to avoid confronting larger competition in highly attractive market segments.

Multisegment

In multisegment marketing a company may choose to target several segments at once. If there is little or no synergy among the segments but each scores high on the market attractiveness index, the firm is using a selective specialization approach. This strategy diversifies a company's market risk, allowing for exiting a market which becomes unattractive without impact to the other targeted segments. Product/market specialization is producing different, but related products for slightly different segments in a market. For example, Intuit sells software for personal finance and for small businesses. This strategy builds a strong reputation for expertise with the product category, but makes product specialization firms vulnerable to changes in technology, unless they lead the change. Serving market segments with different products is referred to as market specialization. Some consulting firms specialize in serving different segments of the educational market (high schools, primary schools, public universities, small private colleges, etc.) with computer system design, recruitment, accreditation help, etc. Companies with a market specialization strategy can build a strong reputation for having an expertise in addressing market needs, allowing for easier expansion of services. The risk is that all segments of the market may suffer from budgeting or environmental impact simultaneously.

Finally, some multisegment strategies can be characterized as sequential targeting approaches, whereby a firm pursues targeting a series of market segments over time. This strategy makes sense when limited resources prevent targeting all desired segments at once. Each successive targeted segment generates resources which can be used to penetrate newly targeted segments. Toyota's success in the U.S. market is an example of such an approach. The original low-cost/ high-quality brand, which was targeted at the low-price end of the market, gave Toyota the financial support and reputation to penetrate increasingly more expensive car, truck, SUV, and luxury car segments. Such a multisegment strategy was not possible when they entered the American market in the 1960s.

Mass Customization

Mass customization is the ability to prepare on a mass basis individually designed products and communications to meet each customer's requirements. Before the industrial revolution, this was the only way products were marketed. Database marketing and computer-aided manufacturing make mass customization cost effective today. For example, a swimwear manufacturer has a computer/camera system in several stores that can be used to digitize an image of a customer wearing an off-the-rack swimsuit; the system then adjusts to create a perfect-fit suit. The customer selects from more than 150 patterns and styles and the computerized measurements are transmitted to the factory computer for production. The suit is mailed to the customer within days. Levi Strauss sells custom jeans in some of its retail locations using a similar system. Extensive databases of customer purchasing patterns and other vital information permit direct marketing of products and services to fit the needs of individual customers. This is niche marketing taken to the extreme and may not be that effective for all companies.[3]

Target Marketing Under Different Market Conditions

Target market selection and strategy may vary under different market conditions. Several of these market conditions are described next with implications for targeting strategy.[4]

Emerging Markets

When a new market begins to emerge, consumer needs and wants are not sharply defined. Hence, segments may not yet be formed because consumers are searching for the same basic benefits from new technologies or services. The interaction of consumers with the new products will more clearly define consumer wants and distinguish one segment of consumers from another. In emerging markets, targeting is directed at the common "center" of the market until segments begin to acquire an identity. The entry of new competitors with differentiable product features will cause consumers to reveal emerging segments.

Growth Stage

When markets enter the growth stage segments of consumers begin to emerge. Segments based on usage rates (low, medium, high) and other characteristics related to interest in the product and product usage can be identified. During growth, other competitors begin to enter the market and target specific segments. Segments not served by larger firms may be the target of smaller competitors seeking to gain a competitive advantage by focusing on single-segment needs. Marketing efforts change from building awareness and knowledge of the product category to emphasizing product differentiation.

Mature and Declining Markets

The search for and exploitation of a competitive advantage is at its greatest during the maturing stage of a market's life cycle. Markets fragment into many segments, so firms must actively analyze them for opportunities arising out of new segment formation and threats from new competitors. Market nichers are also at their most active during the maturity stage, which can erode market potential in older segments. Buyers in mature markets are typically very demanding and difficult to satisfy, making databases of customer purchasing patterns, preferences, attitudes, etc., particularly valuable as a means of identifying and addressing buyer demands. Pressure to increase profits may mean dropping some marginal segments as targets, while concentrating on more profitable products and customer groups. Strategies for mature markets include market modification, product modification, and marketing-mix modification.

1. *Market modification*—Companies may try to increase sales by either expanding the number of brand users by converting nonusers, entering new market segments, or winning competitor customers, or by increasing the rate of usage by current users by encouraging more frequent usage, more usage per occasion, or discovering new and more varied uses.

2. *Product modification*—Companies operating in mature markets may seek to stimulate sales through modifying products. They may improve quality of performance along the lines that customers value,

add new features that deliver new benefits, or change style to increase aesthetic appeal.

3. *Marketing-mix modification*—Marketing managers might make changes in one or more parts of the marketing mix (product, place, price, promotion) to adjust to a maturing market. No accepted rule of thumb dictates which of the parts of the mix is most effectively modified at this stage to generate increased sales. Managers must evaluate each maturing market separately to determine what would be most effective in each circumstance.

When markets reach the decline stage of their life cycle, competition typically lessens as firms either abandon the market or substantially reduce marketing expenditures. Consequently, the targeting decision may consist of appealing to broad market segments, similar to those decisions in emerging markets, or in dropping the products that are now incapable of generating acceptable levels of profit.

PRODUCT POSITIONING

Effective product positioning is a key ingredient of successful marketing. This section discusses the importance of positioning as it relates to target market strategy and several approaches to the process.

The Interrelationship of Market Targeting and Product Positioning

Target marketing essentially accommodates different consumer groups in a marketing plan or strategy. Various consumers react differently to products, promotions, prices, and channels. Therefore, the marketer cannot consider simply the overall population's response, but rather the reaction among different market segments. In this process, the marketer is both defining the characteristics of various attractive segments and allocating marketing resources among these segments. Product positioning is closely linked with this. A product's "position" is the place that it occupies relative to competitors in a given market as *perceived* by the relevant group of target customers. Positioning involves determining consumers' perceptions of a product and also implementing marketing strategies to achieve a desired position. Product, price, distribution, and promotional ingredients are all potential tools for positioning a company and its offerings. Targeting and positioning work in tandem. The process may start either by selecting a target-market segment and then trying to develop a suitable position, or by selecting an attractive product position and then identifying an appropriate market segment. Positioning is a key ingredient for achieving successful market results.

Because positioning decisions have not always been made consciously or successfully by businesses, a systematic approach to the decision is needed. The next section will discuss various strategies and techniques used in positioning.

Strategies to Position Products

Many strategies exist for positioning a product or service or even an organization. The following examples illustrate some of these approaches. Combinations of these approaches are also possible.

A product may be positioned on the basis of its features or benefits. For example, an advertisement may attempt to position the product by reference to its specific features. Although this may be a successful way to indicate product superiority, consumers are generally more interested in what such features mean to them, that is, how they can benefit from the product. Toothpaste advertising often features the benefit approach, as the examples of Crest (decay prevention), Close-Up (sex appeal through white teeth and fresh breath), and Aquafresh (a combination of these benefits) illustrate. The difference between a benefit approach and the features approach is illustrated by the adage, "Don't sell the steak, sell the sizzle."

Many products are sold on the basis of their consumer usage situation. A company may broaden its brand's association with a particular usage or situation. For many years Campbell's Soup was positioned for use at lunchtime and advertised extensively over noontime radio. It now stresses a variety of uses for soup (recipes are on labels) and a broader time for consumption, with the more general theme "Soup is good food." Gatorade was originally a summer beverage for athletes who needed to replace body fluids, but it has also tried to develop a positioning strategy during the cold and flu season as the beverage to drink when the doctor recommends consuming plenty of fluids. Arm & Hammer very successfully added a position to its baking soda—as an odor-destroying agent in refrigerators—and sales jumped tremendously.

Another approach associates the product with a user or a class of users. For example, some cosmetics companies seek successful, highly visible models as their spokespersons. Other brands may pick lesser-known models to portray a certain lifestyle. The Nissan Xterra is positioned as the SUV for young, active, extreme-sports enthusiasts. A company may change its positioning as it changes market targets. Volkswagen did this when it changed from being targeted as an economy car to its position as a "fun" car for "twenty-somethings" buying their first new car. Because users and usage situations are related, they may often be linked in an ad.

Finally, a company may look for weak points in the positions of its competitors and then launch marketing attacks against them. In this approach, the marketer may either directly or indirectly make comparisons with competing products. An example is KFC's positioning as a more attractive fast-food alternative to hamburgers.

In Table 6.4 Worthington Foods positions its line of meat alternative products in the two vegetarian and two meat-restricting segments that had the highest attractiveness scores (see Table 6.3). It focused on the unique selling proposition (USP) best suited to position the products to these segments, given what the research study revealed about the segment's attitudes, behaviors, motives, etc. Here again we see how understanding is translated into planning—in this case, the planning of a positioning strategy.

Positioning Analysis

Marketers may use several techniques for determining the appropriate positioning for a brand. Whether the brand is new or old, focus groups and in-depth interviews may be helpful in providing insights from consumers. In addition, survey and experimental research approaches may provide useful positioning data. Lifestyle information and a technique known as perceptual mapping can also be helpful in positioning decisions.

Lifestyle Positioning

Consumer AIOs (activities, interests, opinions) can be used in designing a marketing strategy. For example, the U.S. Army found dramatic differences between young people favoring and those not fa-

TABLE 6.4. Worthington Foods Positioning and Communication Strategies

	Vegetarians (CDs, AAs)	Meat restrictors (AFs, TSs)
Positioning	Morningstar Farms (MSF) provides vegetarians with the most convenient, healthy way to enjoy good-tasting vegetarian entrees.	For people trying to eat healthier by reducing their meat consumption, Morningstar Farms provides the taste appeal and satisfaction of meat in convenient, meatless foods.
Unique selling proposition	Only Morningstar Farms enriches your vegetarian diet by providing the best combination of taste and convenience in a wide variety of meatless entrees.	Only Morningstar Farms gives you the satisfaction of meat without the cholesterol or saturated fat because Morningstar Farms offers convenient, meatless foods with all the meat taste you crave.
Support	• MSF Garden Patties are made from the vegetables you love. • Other MSF foods are meat free and made with a tasty blend of grains and vegetable protein. • MSF foods have no cholesterol, are lower in fat, and contain no animal fat. • MSF has the most complete line of micowaveable foods. • They are conveniently available in supermarkets.	• MSF foods are meat free and made from a wholesome blend of grains and vegetables. • MSF goods are real meat substitutes—they look and taste like meat. • MSF foods have no cholesterol and are low in fat. • MSF has the most complete line of meat-free microwaveable foods.

AA = Alternative Advocates; CD = Convenience Driven; AF = Alternative Fans; TS = Time Savers

voring the army as a career. Data suggest that it may be a mistake to position the army as a continuous party in which discipline is relaxed and nobody is required to stand in line, clean rooms, follow orders, or shoot guns. Young men and women who agree that the army is a good career appear to be unusually patriotic and conservative and are willing to accept hard work, discipline, and direction. An ad copy for the U.S. Army ("Why should the Army be easy? Life isn't . . . Army.") illustrates the creative response to such findings.

Perceptual Mapping

The previous discussion suggests that consumers' perceptions of products are developed in a complex way and are not easily determined by the marketer. However, a technique known as perceptual mapping may be used in exploring consumers' product perceptions. Since products can be perceived on many dimensions (such as quality, price, and strength) the technique is multidimensional in nature. That is, it allows for the influence of more than one stimulus characteristic on product perceptions. Typically, consumers fill out measuring scales to indicate their perceptions of the many characteristics and similarities of competing brands. Computer programs analyze the resulting data to determine those product characteristics or combinations of characteristics that are most important to consumers in distinguishing between competing brands. Results of these analyses can be plotted in a perceptual "map" (see Figure 3.3 in Chapter 3), which displays how consumers perceive brands and their differences on a coordinate system.

SUMMARY

This chapter completes the two-chapter sequence begun in Chapter 5 on marketing planning. Chapter 6 has focused on the development of an annual operating marketing plan. The intent of the operating marketing plan is to identify the strategies and tactics at the product/market level that put the longer-range strategic plan into action. Four steps are involved in constructing the operating plan—conducting a situation analysis, setting objectives, defining a strategy, and identifying the means of monitoring and controlling the implementation of the plan.

One important part of any marketing plan is selecting a target market. A method of measuring the attractiveness of market segments to aid in selecting target markets was discussed, along with various targeting strategies. Also discussed was target marketing under different market conditions and positioning the product for the target market.

Chapter 7

Implementing Marketing Plans

In this chapter we move to a different stage of our effective marketing management model—implementation (see Figure 7.1).

Members of a target market do not see and react to a marketing strategy, they see and react to the *implementation* of that strategy. A brilliant strategy with disastrous implementation does not turn out well. On the other hand, brilliant implementation of a fair strategy will usually generate very good results. Good implementation of a good strategy may generate great results. In this chapter the major issues involved in the implementation of marketing strategies will be explored, including internal marketing, total quality management, and implementing the marketing mix.

Societal marketing orientation

↓

Understanding

↓

Planning

↓

Implementing
Implementation issues: Chapter 7

↓

Connecting with customers

FIGURE 7.1. The Effective Marketing Management Process

INTERNAL MARKETING IMPLEMENTATION ISSUES

Chronologically, strategy development precedes implementation. Conceptually, both should occur simultaneously. That is, strategy, when it is conceived should be thought through to the point of implementation. Otherwise, strategic plans and goals might be impractical or at least inefficient, requiring far more resources than might have been the case if some thought had been given to implementation issues when the strategy was devised.

One of the most important considerations when devising a marketing strategy is to foster *ownership* of the plan. Several means can be used by management to foster ownership of a marketing plan:[1]

1. *Detailed action plans*—One effective way of getting key people to own the strategy is to develop a detailed plan for implementing the strategy. Such a plan sets responsibilities for specific actions for individuals, and includes a measure and time frame of the action. For example, a strategy to add a direct sales program to a channel that previously used only retailers would specify a number of actions and responsibilities. One action might be for the company to secure a list of 6,000 current customers' names and addresses from the in-home database within the next three days. By specifying what actions specific individuals will be accountable for, management can ensure that plan ownership has been achieved. Those activities required for the plan's successful implementation will be assigned and will not go wanting because no one took responsibility for them.

2. *Champion and ownership team—Champions* are individuals who see their overall responsibility as the successful implementation of the marketing strategy and marketing plan. Better yet is a team of people with different expertise who can make sure the assigned responsibilities are fulfilled within their spheres.

3. *Compensation*—Another proven means of getting ownership of a plan is to tie people's compensation to the performance of those actions involved in the plan's implementation. These performance measures can be results oriented for both internal revenue/profit measures and external market numbers such as product trial rate, market share, brand awareness, percent of stores stocking the brand, low out-of-stock occasions, etc.

4. *Management involvement*—Top managers must sustain a commitment to the plan and review its implementation progress periodi-

cally. Other people involved in the plan's implementation will look to management for cues on the interest and importance placed in its implementation.

Obviously, marketing managers must do a good job of "internal marketing" if marketing plans are to be translated into successful implementation activities. Internal marketing refers to "the managerial actions necessary to make all members of the marketing organization understand and accept their respective roles in implementing marketing strategy."[2] "All members" means that everyone from the production line workers to the president must understand that what they do impacts the delivery of customer satisfaction via the implementation of the planned strategy. This requires everyone to understand and be committed to the underlying tenets of the marketing concept (see Chapter 1), which may mean that marketers devote time to training and sensitizing employees into a customer philosophy. Thus, internal marketing necessitates segmenting the groups of people within the organization; analyzing their needs, motives, objectives and level of understanding of marketing philosophy; devising specific training programs for each segment; and then carrying out the training and motivating and measuring the success of these programs.

IMPLEMENTATION SKILLS

To be successful, implementation skills must be developed within an organization. From an implementation perspective, an organization must translate strategy into a series of assigned activities in such a way that everyone can see their job as a set of value-added actions. These actions should be seen as contributive to the organization because they ultimately result in greater value being delivered to the customer. Bonoma suggests four types of skills to be utilized in implementation activities:[3]

Allocating skills are used to assign resources (e.g., money, effort, personnel) to the programs, functions, and policies needed to put the strategy into action. For example, allocating funds for special-event marketing programs or setting a policy of when to voluntarily recall a defective product are issues that require managers to exhibit allocating skills.

Monitoring skills are used to evaluate the results of marketing activities. Chapter 8 discusses how these skills can be used to determine the effectiveness of the marketing program.

Organizing skills are used to develop the structures and coordination mechanisms needed to put marketing plans to work. Understanding informal dynamics as well as formal organization structure is needed here.

Interacting skills are used to achieve goals by influencing the behavior of others. Motivation of people internal as well as external to the company—marketing research firms, advertising agencies, dealers, wholesalers, brokers, etc., is a necessary prerequisite to fulfilling marketing objectives.

Figure 7.2 shows how Eli Lilly might have used these four skills to implement the strategy and objectives formulated at the corporate, SBU, and product/market levels of planning. In this example there is a consistency between every level and every action taken with respect to the various manifestations of strategy and tactics. Contemporary marketing managers, perhaps unlike their predecessors, would find it important to tell the sales force and external agents why these assignments were being made and not just what and how much to do.

INTEGRATING A SOCIETAL MARKETING ORIENTATION THROUGHOUT THE ORGANIZATION

One of the key indicators of whether a true societal marketing orientation exists within a company is the degree to which its philosophical tenets are held by people outside the marketing function. It is critically important to inculcate everyone within the organization, as well as the external agencies with which the company works, into having customer orientation in the execution of their jobs. Often it is necessary to institute training sessions to explain why such an orientation is needed in the globally competitive markets in which the organization competes, as well as set forth the management expectations for achieving the goal of generating satisfied, loyal customers. Several books have been devoted to the subject of building a customer focus within an organization. Kotler illustrates the problems

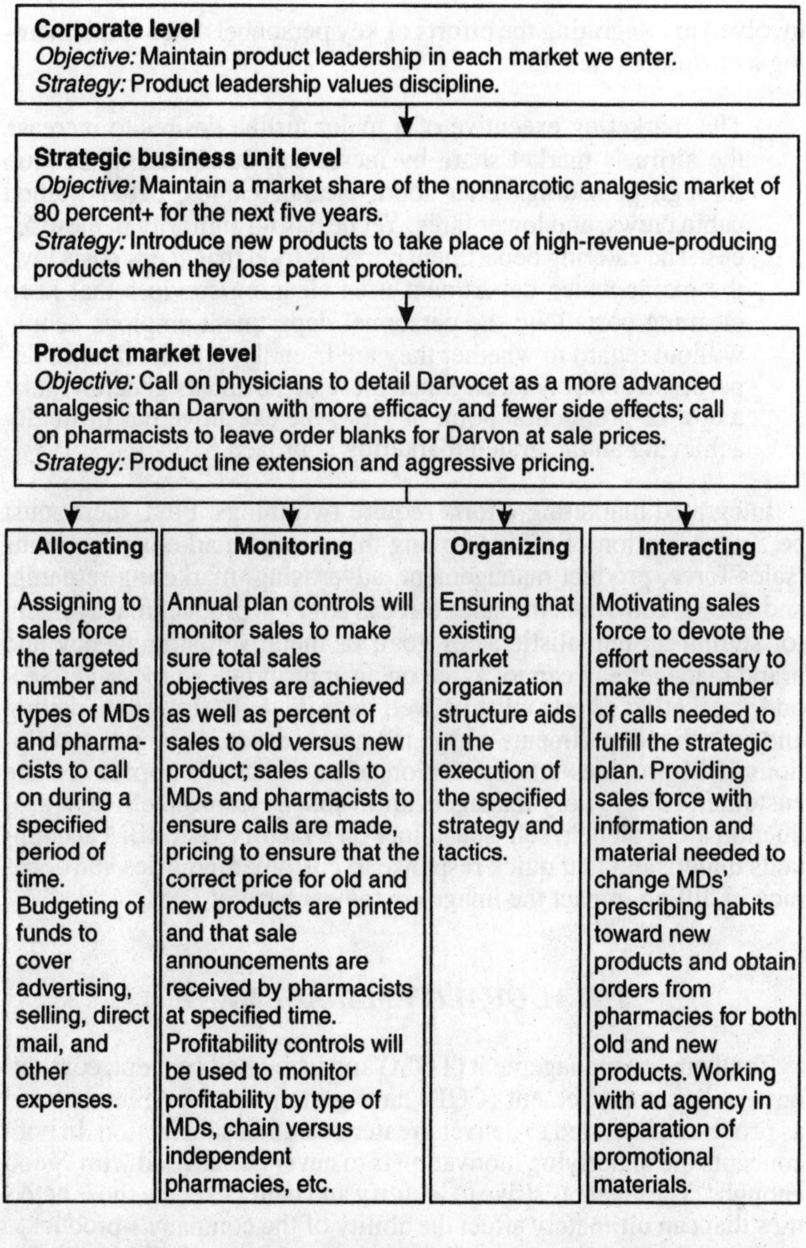

FIGURE 7.2. An Example of Objectives and Strategy Implementation at Eli Lilly

involved in integrating the efforts of key personnel when implementing a customer orientation.

> The marketing executive of a major airline desires to increase the airline's market share by increasing customer satisfaction through providing better food, cleaner cabins, better trained cabin crews, and lower fares. Yet he has no authority in these areas. The catering department chooses food that keeps costs low; the maintenance department uses cleaning services that keep cleaning costs low; the personnel department employs people without regard to whether they are friendly; and the finance department controls fares. Since these departments generally take a cost or production point of view, the executive has difficulty achieving an integrated marketing approach.[4]

Integrated marketing efforts require two things. First, there must be a coordination of efforts among the various marketing functions (sales force, product management, advertising, marketing research, and so on). Too often, the sales force is angry at product management for setting an unrealistic sales goal; or the advertising agency and brand management cannot agree on an appropriate ad message. Second, marketing efforts must be well coordinated between marketing and the other departments within the organization. In its job descriptions IBM provides an explanation of how that job impacts on the customer. IBM factory managers know that a clean and efficient production area can help sell a customer on a factory visit. IBM accountants understand that quick response to customer inquiries and accuracy in billing impact the image customers have of IBM.

TOTAL QUALITY MANAGEMENT

Total quality management (TQM) and its related concept, continuous quality improvement (CQI), have gotten considerable attention as processes intended to deliver greater customer satisfaction. In both concepts the underlying motivation is to never be satisfied with "good enough." These tenets strive to identify and better execute those activities that can ultimately affect the ability of the company's product to generate satisfied customers. To a marketer, the "quality" of a product or service is defined as its ability to address a customer's needs.

Therefore, TQM involves evaluating how everyone in the organization can integrate their activities to address customer needs, and CQI involves evaluating how each activity can be measured and improved as a means of delivering need satisfaction.

Japanese producers have demonstrated these concepts in their success at building market share in a variety of business and consumer markets. By applying CQI and TQM they have shown that defective goods are not inevitable, continuous improvement is a mandatory goal, benchmarking the top-performing product in each product category is the starting place for such improvements, and that high quality ultimately costs *less* because of retaining customers and avoiding the expenses of correcting problems. Increasing quality involves not just avoiding the production of defective parts, however, it means improving the product's design so that it is capable of delivering satisfaction of customer needs.

Attention to TQM means focusing on activity-delivery schedules, customer service, billing accuracy, clear advertising strategies, etc., which can impact customer satisfaction. Taking the customer's point of view (a basic principle of the marketing concept) provides a perspective on how a company can continuously improve those implementation activities. For example, an airline reservation system might benchmark all the actions involved in making a reservation (e.g., ease of recall of the "800" phone number, waiting time to talk with reservationist, message/music while waiting, knowledge/friendliness/helpfulness of reservationist, accuracy of taking reservation, etc.). The company can then set goals for how to continuously improve by always looking at the service *from the customer's perspective. Defects* are defective ways of addressing customer needs; *improvements* are better ways of satisfying customers. TQM goals will remain empty rhetoric, however, unless employees are empowered with the authority and responsibility to make customer-related decisions on the spot. Of course, those decisions must be consistent with the company's missions and customer service policies. Without such empowerment, customers may get frustrated with not having their needs immediately addressed.

Total quality management can benefit an organization in several ways. Financially, the company can expect lower operating costs, better returns on sales and investments, and a high-quality image which allows for premium pricing of goods and services. Other benefits include more rapid introduction of innovations, improved access to global markets, better retention of customers, better corporate image, and better employee morale.[5]

ORGANIZING FOR IMPLEMENTATION

In the past two decades, management theorists have increasingly turned their attention to the interactions of people, systems, corporate cultures, and organizational structures as the key to understanding successful implementation of marketing strategy.[6] Each of these components will be discussed as contributors to the successful implementation of marketing strategy.

People

Success within organizations does not come from everyone doing their best but rather from everyone doing their best at an assigned role to achieve an objective everyone understands and works to achieve. Managers need to gain the cooperation of involved parties to successfully achieve the implementation of marketing strategies. One study revealed that implementation was improved if the manager seeking change:

1. Is invested with the authority and seniority to oversee the process and evaluate performance.
2. Can demonstrate that changes are needed when performance falls below competitive benchmarks.
3. Can demonstrate the feasibility of altering practices to improve performance.
4. Establishes a task force to identify those implementation procedures that are inefficient or ineffective and suggests improvements.
5. Approves improved practices.
6. Monitors changes and demonstrates their value to the organization.[7]

This approach is more effective than implementation by edict, persuasion, or more democratic/participative approaches. By using this approach the manager unfreezes old beliefs, norms, attitudes, and behaviors and engages in supervision of the change process.

An experienced manager can identify subordinates with superior ability to accomplish assigned tasks. These people usually receive the assignments most demanding and critical to the implementation process. Taken to the extreme, however, this approach of "giving the busy person the job you need done well" may overburden even the most competent executive. Establishing systems that allow senior management to review assigned tasks and responsibilities for implementation of a program can ensure that bottlenecks are not created by making too many demands on talented executives.[8]

Systems

A number of systems are relevant to the implementation of marketing strategies. Among these are accounting and budgeting systems, information systems, and measurement and reward systems. The system most directly involved in the implementation of marketing plans is the project planning system, which involves the scheduling of specific tasks for carrying out a project. Some of the better-known planned project implementation tools are the program evaluation review technique (PERT) and the critical path method (CPM).

Using CPM in the implementation of a marketing strategy requires completion of the following steps:

1. Specific activities and sequences must be identified in the marketing strategy.
2. Specific dates for completion and review points for progress are identified.
3. Specific individuals are assigned responsibility for completion of each task.[9]

To achieve success with the use of CPM, marketing managers must foster ownership of the process by means previously outlined in this chapter (i.e., detailed action plans, champion and ownership teams, compensation, and management involvement).

Mapping out the activities, sequencing, and time required to execute the actions makes it possible to identify the "critical path"—the sequence that will take the longest time to complete. Although other paths will have some slack time and delays these will not add to the overall time of the project. Only increases in the time it takes to perform the activities in the critical path will add to the overall time for the project. This increase could result in missed deadlines such as key buying dates, shipment deadlines, trade show dates, etc. If everyone understands the critical nature of performing his or her task in the allotted time the process can become self-managing. Everyone is dependent on one another for performing their tasks in sequence in a timely fashion and "peer pressure" prevents procrastination.

A competitive advantage can be obtained in certain markets by reducing the time it takes to implement a marketing strategy. Firms such as Toyota, Hitachi, Honda, Sharp, Benetton, The Limited, FedEx, and Domino's Pizza have gained a competitive advantage in their markets by greatly decreasing the time it takes to perform key implementation activities.

Corporate Culture

Organizational or corporate culture is the pattern of role-related beliefs, values, and expectations that are shared by the members of an organization. It is a social control system with norms as behavioral guides.[10,11] Rules and norms for behavior within an organization are derived from these beliefs, values, and expectations. Norms of behavior can actually exert more control over employee behavior than a set of objectives or sanctions, which people can sometimes ignore, because norms are based on a commitment to shared values. For instance, if a Nordstrom employee goes to heroic lengths to satisfy a customer, such behavior is seen as laudable by management and peers because it is consistent with the shared values of the organization's employees. Norms can also work to discourage sloppy work which would violate a set of shared values of excellence held by employees. In their book, *Built to Last,* Collins and Porras describe "cult-like" cultures as one of the traits of visionary companies. By this they mean that visionary companies tend to be cultlike around core ideologies, and not around charismatic individuals. According to Collins and Porras, such companies translate their ideologies into *tangible* mechanisms aligned to send a consistent set of reinforcing signals by indoctrinating people, and imposing a tightness of fit to create a sense of belonging to something special. They suggest the following:[12]

Hiring

- Tight screening processes during hiring and for the first few years
- Rigorous up-through-the-ranks policies—hiring young, promoting from within, and shaping an employee's mind-set from a young age

Training

- Developing internal "universities" and training centers
- Training programs that convey not only practical content but also teach ideological values, norms, history, and tradition
- On-the-job socialization with peers and immediate supervisors
- Using unique language and terminology (such as Disney's "cast members," and Motorola's "Motorolans")
- Corporate songs, cheers, affirmations, or pledges that reinforce psychological commitment and a sense of belonging to a special, elite group

Reward

- Incentive and advancement criteria explicitly linked to corporate ideology "buy-in" mechanisms (financial, time investment)
- Celebrations that reinforce successes, belonging, and specialness
- Awards, contests, and public recognition that reward those who display great effort consistent with the ideology; severe tangible and visible penalties or termination for breaching the ideology

Operations

- Plant and office layout that reinforces norms and ideals

The successful nurturing of a corporate culture as embodied by such visionary companies results in a governance of behavior sometimes described as a "clan." A clan system, utilizing norms, exercises control over employees by socializing individuals into an informal social system that stresses teamwork rather than strict adherence to a set of bureaucratic rules and regulations. If a corporation's ideology, which has been indoctrinated into the employee (see previous list), stresses customer service as a shared value, then the clan system operates to reinforce that value. A clan culture can aid in improving the implementation of marketing strategies in several ways.[13]

1. Goals and beliefs of the organization are shared by employees resulting in less goal conflict.
2. Clan members believe that their self-interest is best served through team cooperation, so they support one another.
3. Costs associated with formalized control methods are reduced because of the increase in commitment and reduction of politics and conflict associated with implementation activities.

Structure

When preparing an organization for implementation of marketing strategies marketing managers must build an internal structure capable of carrying out the strategic plans. Changes in an organization's strategy initiate new administrative problems which, in turn, require changes in the new strategy if it is to be successfully implemented. Chandler's study of seventy large corporations revealed this pattern: new strategy creation, emergence of new administrative problems, a decline in profitability and performance, a shift to a more appropriate organizational structure, and then recovery to more profitable levels and improved strategy execution.[14]

The axiom that structure follows strategy is well ingrained as a corporate heuristic. However, if an organization's current structure is so out of line with a particular strategy that it would be thrown into total turmoil to implement the strategy, then the strategy is not practical and is not realistic for that firm. Therefore, structure does to some degree influence the choice of strategy. However, structure should generally be of service to strategy, acting as a means of aiding people to pull together in carrying out their tasks toward implementation.

Organizational structure can actually refer to either the formal or informal structure. The formal structure can be seen with the organization chart. The informal organizational structure refers to the social relations among the organizational members. Wise marketing managers take both the formal and informal structures into account when planning strategy implementation. Three reasons have been offered to explain why this is so.[15] The first issue concerns whether the existing organizational structure is likely to facilitate or impede the successful implementation of the strategy. A strategy that requires the ability to make fast reactions to a changing market might be inhibited by a structure with multiple layers of management requiring approval before changes can be made. For example, General Electric found that it needed to eliminate several echelons of management and reorganize fifteen businesses into three areas in order to make fast responses to environmental change.

Second, decisions must be made regarding which management levels and specific personnel will be responsible for carrying out the various tasks involved in the implementation of strategy. Sometimes top management will need to be involved. Other times it is just a middle management issue. Finally, informal organizational structure can be used to facilitate the implementation tasks. For example, in one firm, several regional managers confer regularly on implementation issues. This type of informal network can be helpful in encouraging the adoption of changes in implementation tasks.

Type of Organizational Structures

Five strategy-related approaches can be used to structure organizations for implementation purposes: functional, geographic, divisional, SBUs, and matrix.

Functional. Organizational growth usually includes the development of several products and markets, resulting in structural change reflecting greater specialization in functional business areas. These structures tend to be effective when key tasks revolve around well-defined skills and areas of specialization. Performance of such functional area activities can enhance operational efficiency and build distinctive competence. Companies that are a single-business dominant-product type of enterprise or vertically integrated, usually adopt this type of structural design. In different types of organizations such functional structures might appear as: business firms: R&D, production, marketing, finance, personnel; municipal governments: fire, public safety, health, water and sewer, parks and recreation, education; universities: academic affairs, student services, alumni relations, athletics, buildings and grounds, and so on (see Figure 7.3).

Whatever the configuration, the disadvantages of this structural form center around obtaining good strategic coordination across the functional units. Thinking like a marketer, accountant, or engineer may in many ways be a good thing since an organization might need high levels of expertise in such fields. However, such tunnel vision can penalize a general manager seeking to resolve cross-functional differences, joint cooperation, and open communication lines between functional areas. In addition, functional structures are not usually conducive to entrepreneurial creativity, rapid adjustments to market or technology change, and radical departures from conventional business boundaries.

Geographic. Organizations who need to tailor strategies for the particular needs of different geographical areas might adopt this structural form. Some of its advantages include delegation of profit/loss responsibility to the lowest strategic level, improvement of functional coordination within the target geographic market, and opportunity to take advantage of the economics of local operations. Disadvantages include increased difficulty in maintaining consistency of practices within the company, necessity of maintaining large management staff, duplication of staff service, and problems with control of local operations from corporate headquarters (see Figure 7.4).

Divisional. Firms that develop or acquire new products in different industries and markets may evolve a divisional structural form. Divisional lines might be made on the basis of product lines (automotive, aircraft) markets (industrial, consumer), or channel of distribution (retail, catalog). Divisional mangers are given authority to formulate and implement strategy for their divisions but it may be difficult to coordinate strategies and turf battles may erupt (see Figure 7.5).

Strategic business units. CEOs with too many divisions to manage effectively may use a structure organized around strategic business

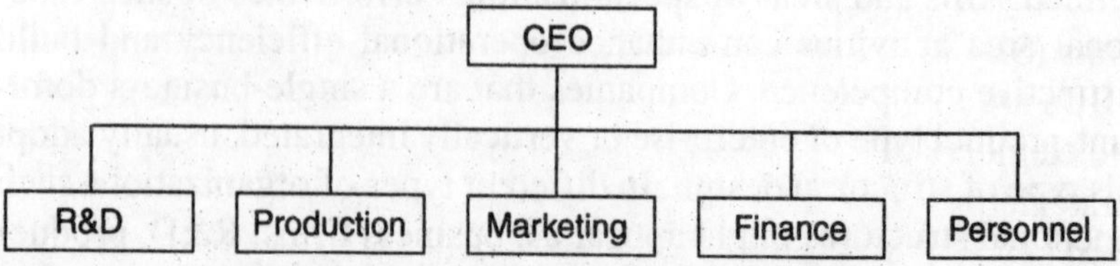

FIGURE 7.3. Functional Organization Structure

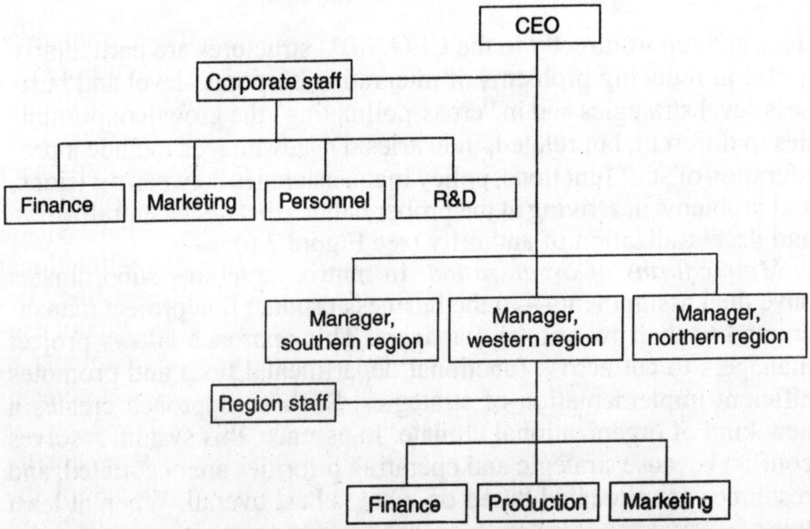

FIGURE 7.4. Geographic Organization Structure

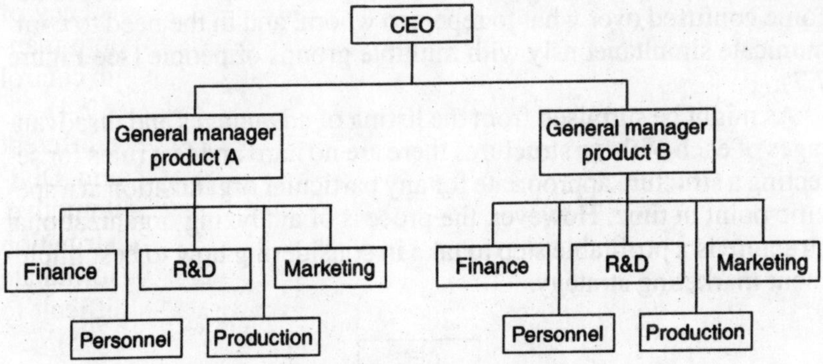

FIGURE 7.5. Divisional Organization Structure

units (SBUs). These forms are popular in large conglomerate firms. SBUs are divisions grouped together based on such common strategic elements as: an overlapping set of competitors, a closely related strategic mission, a common need to compete internationally, common key success factors, or technologically related growth opportunities. Vice presidents might be appointed to oversee the grouped divisions and report directly to the CEO. SBU structures are particularly useful in reducing problems of integrating corporate-level and business-level strategies and in "cross-pollinating" the growth opportunities in different, but related, industries. Disadvantages include a proliferation of staff functions, policy inconsistencies between divisions, and problems in arriving at the proper balance between centralization and decentralization of authority (see Figure 7.6).

Matrix forms of organization. In matrix structures subordinates have dual assignments—to the business/product line/project managers and to their functional managers. This approach allows project managers to cut across functional departmental lines and promotes efficient implementation of strategies. Such an approach creates a new kind of organizational climate. In essence, this system resolves conflict because strategic and operating priorities are negotiated, and resources are allocated based on what is best overall. When at least two of several possible variables (products, customer types, technologies) have approximately the same strategic priorities, then a matrix organization can be an effective choice for organizational structure. The primary disadvantage of this form is its complexity. People become confused over what to report to whom, and in the need to communicate simultaneously with multiple groups of people (see Figure 7.7).

As might be surmised from the listing of advantages and disadvantages of each of these structures there are no hard and fast rules for selecting a structure appropriate for any particular organization at a specific point in time. However, the process of analyzing organizational structure is a profitable step to take in considering how to best implement marketing strategy.

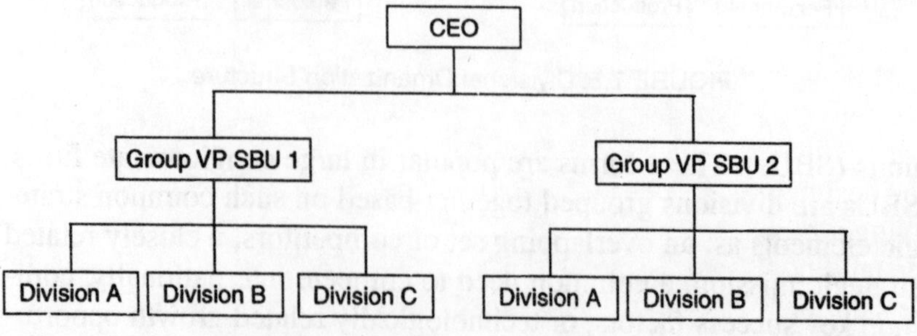

FIGURE 7.6. SBU Organizational Structure

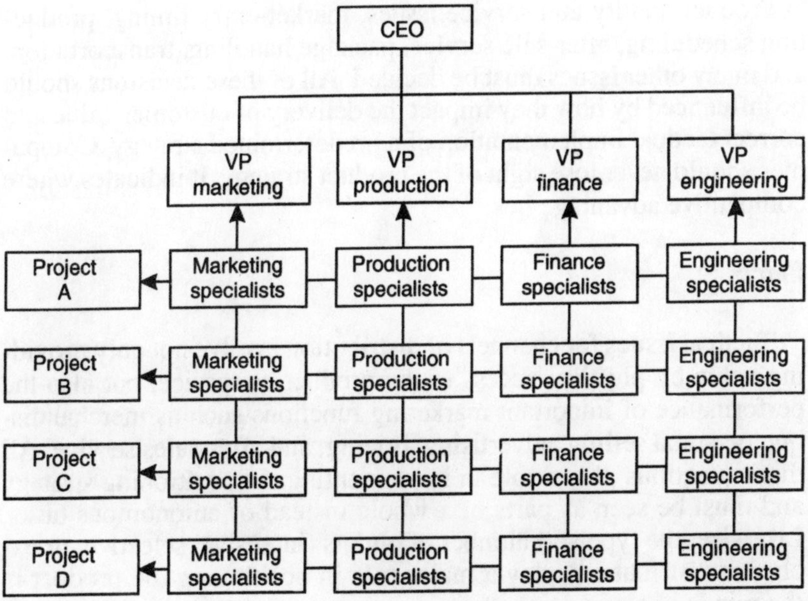

FIGURE 7.7. Matrix Organization Structure

TRANSITION FROM STRATEGY TO TACTICS

Implementation of a marketing plan includes turning the strategic elements of the marketing mix into tactics. Each of these elements is discussed next.

Product

Moving from a product positioning statement to a tangible product that delivers customer satisfaction in accordance with the positioning strategy and at a profit to the company is not easily accomplished. The design team must not lose sight of the product strategy while applying a high degree of creative and technical skills. They must understand not only the strategic needs in the product's design before the sale, but also the entire product use/consumption experience to make the product as "user-friendly" as possible. They must also consider the after-consumption disposal of the product and its packaging.

Product quality and service issues, market-entry timing, production scheduling, after-sale service, package handling, transportation, and many other issues must be decided. All of these decisions should be influenced by how they impact the delivery of customer value and correct tactical implementation of a predetermined strategy. Companies should never lose sight of the product strategy. It indicates where competitive advantage lies.

Place

Tactical issues for channels of distribution involve not only providing value by physical access to the product or service, but also the performance of important marketing functions such as merchandising, personal selling, advertising, pricing, and after-sales service. All these functions play a role in implementing the positioning strategy and must be seen as parts of a whole instead of autonomous tasks. Likewise, the type and number of outlets (intensive, selective, or exclusive distribution) play a major role in positioning the product in the minds of target-market consumers.

Promotion

Many models exist for selecting promotional media to maximize reach and frequency objectives for a given audience at a given budget. However, models are never a perfect substitute for managerial judgment in this area. Promotional tactics involve the actual presentation of messages to target audience members. These messages must be formulated to be the most effective means possible of presenting the essence of the positioning strategy to potential customers. Too many companies with sound positioning strategies have self-destructed at the implementation stage by choosing an advertising approach totally unsuited to conveying the image they wished to project for their company or product. Sales promotions, special-event marketing, trade show displays, collateral material, and all other forms of promotion should be carefully formulated to be the appropriate tactical implementation of the positioning strategy. Possible competitive reactions to promotional efforts should also be factored into tactical actions. Coherence with marketing strategy is as important with sales force tactics as it is with the other promotional elements. Sales training, sales support materials, and reward systems must be considered with overall strategy.

Price

Policies established in the pricing component of the marketing mix are essentially the implementation of a pricing plan which acknowledges that adjustments to price must be made to fit market conditions. Other price implementation issues include initiating price increases and responding to changes in competitors' prices.

As costs rise and productivity rises near the point of diminishing returns, companies feel the pressure to initiate price increases. The following types of price adjustments are commonly used:[16]

- *Adoption of delayed quotation pricing*—a price for a product is not set until the product is produced or delivered. In this way any price adjustment needed to maintain margins can be made once all costs have been determined.
- *Use of escalator clauses*—customers pay a price at time of order, plus any inflation increase that occurs before delivery is made. An escalator cause may be tied to a specific price index such as the cost-of-living index.
- *Unbundling of goods and services*—the product's price is maintained, but previously included services are now priced separately such as delivery or installation.
- *Reduction of discounts*—policy changes might be initiated that prevent the sales force from offering normal discounts.

Another pricing implementation issue is reaction to a change in competitors' prices. Market leaders, in particular, must determine how they will react to a drop in price by major competitors. Several options are available:[17]

- *Maintain price*—The market leader may decide to maintain its price without losing customers. This strategy can be risky in some circumstances but avoids both giving the attacker confidence and demoralizing the sales force.
- *Raise perceived quality*—Another option is to maintain price but improve the perception of value by strengthening products, services, or communications.

- *Reduce price*—The leader might decide to drop its price in response to a competitor. This is commonly motivated by a belief that buyers primarily make decisions on the basis of price, and that a failure to lower price will result in an unacceptable decline in market share. Quality should be maintained even if price is dropped, however.
- *Increase price and improve quality*—This approach is based on the belief that by establishing an elite image as the "best" on the market, a company can better capture the share of the market comprised of customers motivated by that status. Some firms pursuing this strategy simultaneously launch a less expensive "fighting brand," which is intended to compete against the lower-cost competitor.

Price implementation actions should be governed by the objectives a company sets for its price decisions.

SUMMARY

No marketing manager's job is complete without determining the implementation activities necessary to put a strategy into action. Internal marketing, or ownership of a strategy by those involved in the plan's implementation is an important first step. Likewise, a successful implementation program will include the development of skills such as allocating, monitoring, organizing, and interacting. If the organization is committed to total quality management and a societal marketing orientation, infusing these philosophies throughout the company is the job of marketing management. Appropriate organizational structure is key to successfully implementing marketing strategy. Several structures were discussed. The transition from strategy to tactics includes performing numerous activities for each element of the marketing mix.

Chapter 8

Evaluation and Control of Marketing Activities

In Chapter 8 we come to the final stage of the effective management process model: connecting with customers (see Figure 8.1).

As the previous seven chapters have demonstrated, connecting with customers does not happen by chance or just because the marketer wants it to. Connecting is the final result of a series of demanding steps, carefully and expertly executed. It begins with a firm commitment on the part of all employees that their jobs are not well done unless they contribute to this connection. When a firm achieves excellence in making this connection, it results in the kind of mutually beneficial exchange relationships that customers find so satisfying; competition is irrelevant. That is, customer loyalty is so firmly entrenched

Societal marketing orientation

↓

Understanding

↓

Planning

↓

Implementing

↓

Connecting with customers

Evaluation and control issues: Chapter 8

FIGURE 8.1. The Effective Marketing Management Process

that they do not evaluate competitors' products when making purchase decisions. When they decide to make a purchase—you are it. This is a rare kind of connection. Yet as difficult as it is to achieve, it is a worthy goal for marketers and can be the ultimate result of following the effective marketing management process. Evidence has shown the power of such connections, but also the difficulty in achieving them. Research results indicate that if customer satisfaction is measured on a 1-to-5 scale, with 5 representing "completely satisfied," those customers who are at a 5 are *six times* less likely to defect to competitors (i.e., are six times more brand loyal) than customers who are at a 4 on the scale.[1]

Achieving such a level of satisfying performance is obviously rewarding for both customers and companies. Organizations who are not satisfied with lesser performance devote considerable attention to the subject of this chapter. Establishing evaluation and control procedures keeps marketing managers informed of how well an organization has achieved connections with customers and where corrective action is needed.

INTEGRATION OF PLANNING AND CONTROL

Planning and control should be integrated processes. In fact, planning is defined as a process that includes establishing a system for feedback of results. This feedback reflects a company's performance in reaching its objectives through implementation of the strategic marketing plan. The relationship between planning and control is depicted in Figure 8.2.

The planning process results in a specific plan being developed for a product or service. This plan is then implemented (marketing activities are performed in the manner described in the plan) and results are produced. These results are sales revenues, costs, profits, and accompanying consumer attitudes, preferences, and behaviors. Information on these results is given to managers who compare them with objectives to evaluate performance. This performance evaluation identifies the areas where decisions must be made. The actual decision making controls the plan by altering it to accomplish stated objectives, and a new cycle begins. The information flows are the key to a good control system. Deciding what information is provided to which managers in what time periods is the essence of a control system.

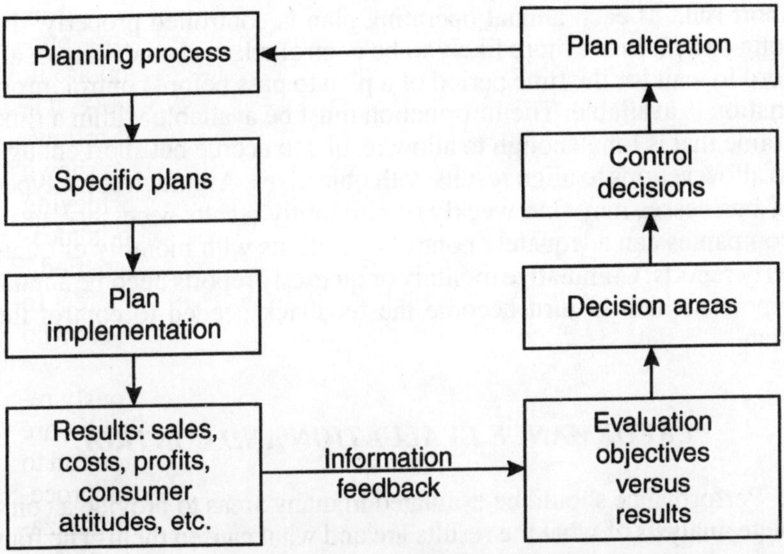

FIGURE 8.2. Planning and Control Model

The need for better control systems was clearly pointed out in a study of seventy-five companies of various sizes in several industries. The findings were as follows:

> Smaller companies had poorer control procedures than larger ones.
> Fewer than one-half of the companies knew the profitability of individual products, and, one-third had no system set up to spot weak products.
> Almost half failed to analyze costs, evaluate advertising or sales force call reports, or compare their process to competitors.
> Many managers reported long delays in getting control reports, and many of their reports were inaccurate.[2]

TIMING OF INFORMATION FLOWS

A strategic plan is comprised of many annual operating plans. An economist once noted that "we plan in the long run but live in the short run." If each annual operating plan is controlled properly, the long-run plans are more likely to be controlled. A planner cannot afford to wait for the time period of a plan to pass before control information is available. The information must be available within a time frame that is long enough to allow results to accrue but short enough to allow actions to align results with objectives. Although some types of businesses may find weekly or bimonthly results necessary, most companies can adequately control operations with monthly or quarterly reports. Cumulative monthly or quarterly reports become annual reports, which in turn become the feedback needed to control the plan.

PERFORMANCE EVALUATION AND CONTROL

Performance should be evaluated in many areas to provide a complete analysis of what the results are and what caused them. The four key control areas are sales, profits, consumers, and costs. Objectives have been established in three of these areas for the operating and strategic plans. The fourth area, costs, is a measure of marketing effort and is directly tied to profitability analysis.

Sales Control

Sales control data are provided from an analysis of sales by individual segments (products; territories, etc.), market share data, and data on sales inputs (sales force, advertising, and sales promotion).

Sales by Segment

Sales performance can be evaluated per segment by developing a sales performance report as shown in Table 8.1. Using this format, the

TABLE 8.1. Sales Performance by Product—Quarter 1

Product	$ Objective	$ Actual sales	$ Variation	% Variation	Sales index
A	100,000	90,000	–10,000	–10.0	.90
B	95,000	102,000	+7,000	+7.4	1.07
C	120,000	92,000	–28,000	–23.0	.77
D	200,000	203,000	+3,000	+1.5	1.02

sales objectives stated in the annual operating plan are broken down on a quarterly basis and become the standard against which actual sales results are compared. Dollar and percentage variations are calculated because in some instances a small percentage can result in a large dollar variation.

A performance index can be calculated by dividing actual sales by the sales objective. Index numbers of about 1.00 indicate that expected and actual performance are about equal. Numbers larger than 1.00 indicate above-expected performance, and numbers below 1.00 reveal below-expected performance. Index numbers are especially useful when a large number of products is involved because they enable managers to identify those products that need immediate attention.

Analysis of net sales can provide some insight into a firm's sales pattern and historical market share, but more specific information is needed. This information can be obtained through analyses of sales by segments—products, product groups, customers, divisions, geographical areas, and so on. An example of this type of analysis is shown in Table 8.2 for a manufacturer of industrial parts. In this table, a two-way classification of sales is presented: by product and by region. This analysis provides data of three different types. First, it shows the contribution of each product to total sales volume; second, it shows the contribution of each region's sales to total sales; and finally, it shows the contribution of each product in each region.

This type of analysis is most revealing when it is first completed because it shows the composition of the total sales volume. This detailed information is needed because decisions are made on the basis of individual products, territories, customers, etc., and not on the basis of totals. In fact, the good performance of one product may offset

TABLE 8.2. Sales Analysis by Product and Region for Industrial Parts

		$ Sales by region			
Product	**Total sales**	**Southwest**	**Southeast**	**Northwest**	**Northeast**
Grinders	127,806	34,606	27,901	48,600	16,699
Drills	238,700	58,731	62,800	54,601	62,568
Drill bits	158,208	39,653	47,288	34,046	37,221
Buffers	252,900	63,985	65,126	54,631	69,158
Sanders	328,500	75,858	84,720	85,952	81,970
Total sales	1,106,114	272,833	287,835	277,830	267,616

the bad performance of another product, which could be unnoticed if only total net sales were examined. This has been called the "iceberg principle" in that total sales (the top of the iceberg), can cover up the sales by segments (the hidden part of the iceberg). Usually, the submerged part of the iceberg causes the problems.

Another basic finding in this type of analysis has been referred to as the 80/20 principle or rule. This generalization states that 80 percent of the business is accounted for by 20 percent of the products, customers, or territories. The percentages, of course, will vary, but the point is that there will be an uneven proportionate contribution to total sales by certain segments. In Table 8.1, for example, two products, buffers and sanders, account for 52 percent of sales, and for grinders, three regions account for 87 percent of sales. If a manager is aware of these types of situations, attention and marketing effort can be allocated appropriately. However, unless this type of analysis is made, a misallocation of effort can occur. This means more effort is directed at a part or a segment—a specific region, for example—than its potential contribution would warrant. If, in the example, 25 percent of the marketing budget and effort for grinders were directed at the Northeast region, too much effort would probably have been exerted in that region. Its contribution to sales is only 13 percent.

This type of analysis begins to provide a clear picture of "where we are" for specific products and services and for any other segments that are analyzed. It offers a much more solid basis for planning than merely a general analysis of sales volume. Since these data are not part of a regular accounting system, they must be requested and sometimes generated by the marketing planner. Computer manipulation would facilitate detailed analysis of sales volume.

The same procedures can be followed to analyze sales performance by customers or territories. They could also be combined to check performance of products in various territories or sales to various customer types.

Market Share Data

Other important types of sales control data are provided through a market share analysis. A firm's performance should be compared to competitors'. A common method is to calculate a firm's share of a market. External forces do not affect all firms in the same way, and their impact can be analyzed through market share analyses. To calculate market share, the relevant market must be identified. Market share can be analyzed on at least two bases.

1. *Share of total market:* This is the firm's sales divided by the total sales in the markets in which the firm is exerting marketing effort.
2. *Relative market share:* This is one firm's share of the market held by the top two, three, or four firms. It reflects the firm's share of the market captured by the major competitors.

Unless some effort is made to understand why a firm's market share has changed or failed to change, this analysis is more of a scorekeeping task. If the components of market share are analyzed—such as the number of customers reached, product loyalty, repeat purchases—meaningful control decisions can be made.

Sales Input Data

A great deal of analyses of performance can be done on sales inputs. For the sales force these inputs can be divided into qualitative and quantitative inputs.

Qualitative inputs:

1. Time management
2. Planning effort
3. Quality of sales presentation
4. Product knowledge
5. Personal appearance and health
6. Personality and attitudes

Quantitative inputs:

1. Days worked
2. Calls per day
3. Proportion of time spent selling
4. Selling expenses
5. Nonselling activities
    a. Calls to prospects
    b. Display setups
    c. Service calls
6. Miles traveled per call

Analysis of these factors will help a sales manager evaluate the efficiency of the sales effort. For many of these factors, a sales force average can be computed to serve as a standard for analyzing individual salespersons. For example, if the number of sales calls per day for one salesperson is three and the company average is six, this case warrants attention. The low calls per day could be caused by a large, sparsely populated territory or it could be that the salesperson is spending too much time with each customer. Whatever the problem, management must be alerted to its existence.

Advertising inputs are difficult to evaluate but must be dealt with nonetheless. Several factors can be evaluated to help determine the efficiency of advertising:

1. Competitive level of advertising
2. Readership statistics
3. Cost per thousand
4. Number of sales inquiries stimulated by an ad
5. Number of conversions of inquiries to sales
6. Changes in store traffic generated by an ad campaign

Tracking these data over several years can help identify successful appeals, ads, or media.

Many promotional sales tools can be directly evaluated if objectives are set before their use. For example, if a firm is going to enclose a cents-off coupon in a packaged product, the number of coupons redeemed is one measure of the results. The number of people who visit a trade show, the number of customers who try a product through in-store demonstrations, etc., are all examples of how data can be used.

The key to evaluating sales input performance is the setting of objectives, which become the standards by which actual performance can be evaluated.

Cost Control

Several methods are available for establishing cost control procedures. These include budgets, expense ratios, and segment and functional costs analysis. Budgets are a common tool used by most organizations for anticipating expense levels on a yearly basis. The budget is often established by using historical percentages of various expenses as a percent of sales. Thus, once the sales forecast is established, expense items can be budgeted as a percent of total sales. If zero-based budgeting is used, the objectives to be accomplished must be specified and the expenditures necessary to accomplish these objectives estimated. The estimates are the budgeted expenses for the time period.

Once the budget is established, an expense variance analysis by line item or expenditure category is used to control costs. Although it is not possible to establish standard costs for marketing expenditures, the budget amounts are the standards used to perform the variance analysis. A typical procedure is to prepare monthly or quarterly budget reports showing the amount budgeted for the time period and the dollar and percentage variation from the budgeted amount, if any exists. Expenditure patterns that vary from the budgeted amounts are then analyzed to determine why the variations occurred.

Expense ratio analysis is another tool used to control costs. An important goal of every plan is to maintain the desired relationship between expenditures and revenues. Calculations of expense ratios provide information on what this relationship is at any time. Monthly, quarterly, and yearly ratio calculations should satisfy most managers' needs for these data.

Common expense ratios are as follows:

1. Profit margins
2. Selling expense ratio
3. Cost per sales call
4. Advertising expense ratio

Many other financial ratios, such as asset turnover, inventory turnover, and accounts receivable turnover, also provide measures that can be used to reduce or maintain cost levels.

Sales analysis, even by segments, is only a part of the information needed to understand the nature of a firm's current marketing operations. Sales analysis, when considered alone, can even be misleading: a product low in sales volume may not be low in its profit contribution. Sales and profitability can be determined only through sales and cost analysis.

There are three basic types of cost analysis: (1) analysis of ledger accounts, (2) functional or activity cost analysis, and (3) segment cost analysis. These analyses are not part of the accounting system, and a manager must request this information and in most cases work with the information supplier in coordinating the analysis.

The simplest type of cost analysis involves examining costs, over a period of time, as they appear in the accounting system. The interest is in the absolute size and growth of an account, such as the change in sales salaries over time. One tool frequently used in this analysis is the common-size income statement shown in Figure 8.3. This statement shows each item as a percentage of sales. When several years are compared, the actual percentage growth and relative value of a given expense can be evaluated. A manager can then begin to question why a given expense has grown or why it represents such a large

Net sales		100.0%
Cost of sales		–72.0%
Gross profit		28.0%
Selling expenses:		
Sales salaries	5.5%	
Travel and entertainment	.9%	
Sales supplies used	.5%	
Advertising	5.6%	
Other selling expenses	.5%	
Total selling expenses	13.0%	
Administrative expenses:		
Office salaries	4.9%	
Office supplies used	.8%	
Office rent	.8%	
Taxes and insurance	.6%	
Depreciation of equipment	.3%	
Other administrative expenses	.1%	
Total administrative expenses	7.5%	
Total operating expenses		20.5%
Net operating income		7.5%
Less income expense		.5%
Net income		7.0%

FIGURE 8.3. Common-Size Income Statement, 20__

part of total expenses. These analyses help explain why an expenditure pattern exists and enable planners to understand expenditure patterns.

Functional Cost Analysis

Functional or activity cost analysis involves allocating costs from the natural accounts to accounts set up for each marketing function or activity. This analysis serves two purposes. First, it provides information on the total costs of performing the various marketing activities, and, second, it is an intermediate step to segment cost analysis. Knowing the total cost of performing a function or activity is useful in major strategic decisions such as altering the physical distribution system. This type of analysis is illustrated in Table 8.3. When costs are allocated to a category, such as a product, questions about the costs for a specific product can be answered.

Functional costs allocated to a specific category are determined by the nature of the function. For example, storage costs would usually be allocated to products on the basis of the number of square feet of warehouse space used to store each product. If storage costs were allocated to geographical areas, sales volumes in each area would usually be used as the basis for allocation unless there were storage facilities in each area.

Segment Cost Analysis

Segment cost analysis is illustrated in Tables 8.4 and 8.5. The objective in segment cost analysis is to determine the contribution of a segment—products, customers, territories— in relation to total profitability. Two alternate approaches can be used in allocating costs. These approaches are the full cost approach and the contribution margin approach. In the full cost approach, illustrated in Table 8.4, all costs—direct and indirect—are allocated to a specific category, such as a product. This determines the net profit contribution of each product to total profit.

However, this approach poses a problem. It forces allocation of indirect costs to individual products. Indirect costs are those costs that are not eliminated even if a given product is dropped. For example, the sales manager's salary is an indirect cost of a particular product. If you eliminate that product you would not eliminate the manager's

TABLE 8.3. Activity Cost Analysis

	Ledger total	Activity cost groups						
		Direct selling	Advertising and promotion	Transportation and shipping	Storage	Credits and collections	Financial and clerical	Marketing administration expenses
Sales force commissions	$312,000	$312,000						
Sales force salaries	120,000	120,000						
Office supplies	13,320	2,400	2,040	1,560	1,200	1,200	4,200	720
Media space and time	120,000		120,000					
Advertising salaries	30,000		30,000					
Administrative salaries	108,000	19,200		8,400	8,400	7,200	16,800	48,000
Rent	16,920		1,800	3,840	4,200	2,304	2,256	2,520
Taxes and insurance	13,500	2,040	960	2,760	3,000	1,260	1,260	2,220
Heat and light	7,020		960	1,620	1,620	1,020	1,020	780
Depreciation	9,240	960	600	2,040	2,640	480	1,920	600
Miscellaneous	4,560	420	960	600	780	960	660	180
Totals	$754,560	$457,020	$157,320	$20,820	$21,840	$14,424	$28,116	$55,020

TABLE 8.4. Income Statement by Product: Full Cost Approach

	Total	Drills	Drill bits	Grinders
Net sales	$3,600,000	$1,200,000	$600,000	$1,800,000
Less cost of goods sold	2,520,000	880,000	440,000	1,200,000
Gross margin	$1,080,000	$320,000	$160,000	$600,000
Less operating expenses				
Direct selling	$457,020	$132,536	$82,264	$242,220
Advertising and sales promotion	157,320	56,635	23,598	77,087
Transportation and shipping	20,820	7,912	5,205	7,703
Storage	21,840	8,955	5,678	7,207
Credits and collections	14,424	4,472	2,596	7,356
Financial and clerical	28,116	8,997	7,873	11,246
Marketing administrative	55,020	18,707	8,803	27,510
Total operating expenses	$754,560	$238,214	$136,017	$380,329
Net profit before income taxes	$325,440	$81,786	$23,983	$219,671

salary. To allocate indirect costs, a basis of allocation must be selected. Three commonly used allocation methods are (1) allocating equally to each part of a segment; (2) allocating in direct proportion to sales of each part of a segment; or (3) allocating in direct proportion to the direct cost of each part of a segment. If you choose to allocate the sales manager's salary equally to each product and the salary was $30,000, then each product would be assigned $10,000 as its share of that indirect cost. Although all indirect costs must be allocated to arrive at a net profit figure by product, this process can be misleading. For example, a product that is not showing a profit should be eliminated, thereby increasing total profitability. However, if a product is eliminated only direct costs are eliminated, and the indirect costs have to be reallocated to remaining products.

To overcome this problem, the contribution margin approach is commonly used. With this approach only direct costs are allocated to each part of a segment (see Table 8.5). The contribution margin is the amount each product contributes to cover indirect costs and earn a profit after all its direct costs are subtracted. As long as a product's contribution is positive, the firm is better off keeping it—i.e., its sales cover all of its costs and make a contribution to indirect costs and

TABLE 8.5. Income Statement by Product: Contribution Margin Approach

	Total	Drills	Drill bits	Grinders
Net sales	$3,600,000	$1,200,000	$600,000	$1,800,000
Less cost of goods sold				
Labor and materials only	2,520,000	880,000	440,000	1,200,000
Gross margin	$1,080,000	$320,000	$160,000	$600,000
Less direct operating expenses				
Direct selling	$370,186	$107,354	$66,634	$196,198
Advertising and sales promotion	99,112	33,698	13,876	51,538
Transportation and shipping	8,328	2,748	2,082	3,498
Storage	7,862	2,359	1,965	3,538
Credits and collections	7,645	2,828	994	3,823
Financial and clerical	10,122	3,037	1,822	5,263
Total direct expenses	$503,255	$152,024	$87,373	$263,858
Contribution margin	$576,745	$167,976	$72,627	$336,142
Less indirect operating expenses				
Direct selling	$86,834			
Advertising and sales promotion	55,208			
Transportation and shipping	15,492			
Storage	13,978			
Credits and collections	6,779			
Financial and clerical	17,994			
Marketing administrative	55,020			
Total indirect expenses	$251,305			
Net profit before income taxes	$325,440			

profit. This type of analysis does not reveal why costs or contributions are the way they are. It simply analyzes what is happening in specific areas of the firm's business.

The analytical methods discussed in this chapter can provide specific detailed data about markets and products. The analyses are not done in many companies because marketing planners may not understand the procedures. Another factor that may limit their use is that the planner must submit a detailed request in order to secure the information that is so vital to effective planning. Since the analyses are not part of a typical accounting system, additional expenditures are necessary to complete the analyses and make them available for use in planning. This investment in information should produce a very high and quick payback in the form of better marketing plans.

Profit Control

Profit control begins with profitability analysis by products, territories, and customers. This involves a breakdown of sales and costs by various market segments to determine either a profit contribution or a contribution to cover indirect costs and earn a profit. Profitability analysis is the only way to identify the strong and weak products, territories, or customers. Until specific products can be identified as unsuccessful no action can be taken to correct the situation. Managers need specific information about a product or customer on both sales revenues generated and the costs associated with a given level of revenue.

Once specific information on profitability analysis is available action can be taken to achieve profit control. Table 8.6 shows data on order size for a grocery wholesaler. In this example, many of the customers were placing small orders, which actually resulted in losses. When the cost of goods sold and other direct expenses such as sales commission, order picking, and delivery were calculated, there was a negative contribution margin for orders under $200. Sales revenues did not cover direct expenses. A naive decision would be simply to stop selling to these customers. This would reduce sales revenue, but the decrease in direct expenses would more than offset the decrease in revenues.

TABLE 8.6. Number of Customers by Order Size

Number of customers	Order size
31	Over $1,000
50	$800-$999
80	$600-$799
90	$400-$599
75	$200-$399
65	Less than $200

A more analytic approach would determine why the orders were small and what could be done to increase their size. Possibly, these are all small retailers, and little can be done to increase order size; or these retailers may be splitting orders with several wholesalers. Following are some corrective actions.

1. Get several small retailers to pool their orders.
2. Have the salespeople call on them less frequently, thus increasing the size of individual orders.
3. Start a cash-and-carry operation to deal with these retailers.
4. Have these retailers order by phone or via Internet product listings.
5. Encourage them to concentrate their purchases with one source of supply.

Several possible corrective actions could improve order size and permit the wholesaler to continue to deal with these retailers. If none of the corrective actions evaluated is feasible, a minimum-size order could be established. This decision could eliminate some customers, but it cannot be avoided if profitability is to be improved.

Customer Feedback

Performance evaluation on customers involves analysis of customer awareness, knowledge, attitudes, and behaviors. Communication efforts should be goal oriented. The goals are to have consumers become aware of products, services, or stores; possess certain knowledge; and exhibit certain attitudes and behaviors. These should be specified in the operating and strategic objective statements and then become the standards to which current consumer data are compared.

Data on consumers must be collected either by the company or a research firm. Many research firms specialize in providing commercial data to companies, either as a one-time research project or on a regular basis. Store audits, awareness studies, and attitudinal surveys are available by subscription for most consumer goods. Several research firms specialize in industrial markets and provide appropriate data on these customers.

Consumer data are especially valuable if collected over a long period of time. Information such as awareness levels, attitudes, and purchase behavior can be analyzed to reveal trends and areas for further investigation. Also, changes in consumers' attributes can be related to marketing activities, such as coupons or the introduction of a new advertising theme.

Consumer feedback can also be obtained by customer-attitude tracking. Following are the main customer-attitude tracking systems:

1. *Complaint and suggestion systems.* In this system, companies record, analyze, and respond to written and oral complaints from customers. Management should attempt to correct whatever is causing the most frequent types of complaints. Many organizations provide suggestion cards to encourage customer feedback.

2. *Customer panels.* Some companies use panels of customers who agree to periodically communicate their attitudes through phone or mail surveys. These panels provide a broader range of customer attitudes than customer complaint and suggestion systems.

3. *Customer surveys.* Periodic questionnaires directed to a random sample of customers can be used to evaluate the friendliness of the staff, the quality of the product or service, and so on. Customers can respond to questions on a scale ranging from, e.g., very dissatisfied, to dissatisfied, neutral, satisfied, and very satisfied. The responses are summarized and provided to local managers and to higher-management levels. Results show how the various components were rated in the current period compared to the last period, to the average of all the local units, and to the standard.

4. *Mystery shoppers.* In this system, people are recruited to pose as potential customers and report on their experiences shopping and buying the product or service.

Ratio Analysis

Another useful type of analysis is called ratio analysis. In ratio analysis one financial value is shown in relation to another value. The resulting ratio can show the absolute standing of the company in a given area but is best used in comparison with previous time periods or industry averages. Some of the most commonly used ratios are discussed as follows.

Profitability Ratios

Gross profit margin. This is an indication of the total margin available to cover operating expenses and yield a profit. It is calculated as shown in the following equation.

$$\text{Gross profit margin} = \frac{(\text{Sales} - \text{Cost of goods sold})}{\text{Sales}} \tag{8.1}$$

Net profit margin or net return. This shows aftertax profits per dollar of sales. Subpar profit margins indicate that a firm's sales prices are relatively low, its costs are relatively high, or both.

$$\text{Net return} = \frac{\text{Profit after taxes}}{\text{Sales}} \tag{8.2}$$

Return on total assets. This is a measure of the return on total investment in the enterprise. Sometimes it is adjusted by adding interest to aftertax profits to form the numerator of the ratio since total assets are financed by creditors as well as by stockholders; hence, it is accurate to measure the productivity of assets by the returns provided to both classes of investors.

$$\text{Return on total assets} = \frac{\text{Profit after taxes}}{\text{Total assets}} \tag{8.3}$$

or

$$\frac{(\text{Profit after taxes} + \text{interest})}{\text{Total assets}}$$

Liquidity Ratios

Current ratio. This ratio indicates the extent to which the claims of short-term creditors are covered by assets that are expected to be converted to cash in a period roughly corresponding to the maturity of the liabilities.

$$\text{Current ratio} = \frac{\text{Current assets}}{\text{Current liabilities}} \qquad (8.4)$$

Quick ratio (or acid-test ratio). This ratio measures a firm's ability to pay off short-term obligations without relying on the sale of its inventory.

$$\text{Quick ratio} = \frac{\text{Current assets} - \text{inventory}}{\text{Current liability}} \qquad (8.5)$$

Leverage Ratios

Debt-to-assets ratio. This measures the extent to which borrowed funds have been used to finance a firm's operations. It provides another measure of the funds provided by creditors versus the funds provided by owners. It is also widely used to measure the balance between debt and equity in a firm's long-term capital structure. This ratio also measures the extent to which earnings can decline without a company becoming unable to meet its annual interest costs and is a more inclusive indication of a firm's ability to meet all of its fixed-charge obligations.

$$\text{Debt-to-assets ratio} = \frac{\text{Total debt}}{\text{Total assets}} \qquad (8.6)$$

Debt-to-equity ratio. This provides another measure of the funds provided by creditors versus the funds provided by owners.

$$\text{Debit-to-equity ratio} = \frac{\text{Total debt}}{\text{Total stockholder's equity}} \qquad (8.7)$$

Times-interest-earned ratio. Measures the extent to which earnings coverage can decline without the firm becoming unable to meet its annual interest costs.

$$\text{Times-interest-earned ratio} = \frac{\text{Profit before taxes}}{\text{Total interest charges}} \qquad (8.8)$$

Activity Ratios

Inventory turnover. When compared to industry averages, this ratio provides an indication of whether a company has excessive or perhaps inadequate inventory.

$$\text{Inventory turnover} = \frac{\text{Sales}}{\text{Average inventory}} \tag{8.9}$$

Asset turnover. This is a measure of the turnover and utilization of all of a firm's assets; a ratio below the industry average indicates that a company is not generating a sufficient volume of business, given the investment of its assets.

$$\text{Asset turnover} = \frac{\text{Sales}}{\text{Total assets}} \tag{8.10}$$

Accounts receivable turnover. This ratio measures the time it takes the firm to collect credit sales.

$$\text{Accounts receivable turnover} = \frac{\text{Annual credit sales}}{\text{Average length of turnover}} \tag{8.11}$$

None of the performance evaluation data described are going to be available unless they are requested and funds are made available to finance analyses. Thus data-collecting and reporting procedures must be set up by the marketer in consultation with managers who are going to use the control data in decision making.

The procedures will usually change over time as some types of analyses or reporting times are found to be better than others. The most important requirement is that the data meet the needs of managers in taking corrective actions to control marketing activities.

THE MARKETING AUDIT

In some situations an organization may want to extend the evaluation process to include the entire marketing process. This is referred to as a marketing audit. The concept of a marketing audit was derived from the accounting field in which audits have traditionally been used as a procedure for internal financial control. A marketing audit is "a *comprehensive, systematic, independent,* and *periodic* examination of a company's—or business unit's—marketing environment, objectives, strategies, and activities with a view to determining problem areas and opportunities and recommending a plan of action to improve the company's marketing performance."[3] A *marketing audit* is a critical, unbiased review of the philosophies, personnel, organization, purpose, objectives, procedures, and results associated with some activity. It is a review of everything associated with the marketing process within a company.

Audits are appropriate for virtually any type of organization—new to old, small to large, healthy or ailing—engaged in providing services or physical products. The need for a marketing audit may stem from changes in: target markets, competitors, internal capabilities, the economic environment, etc. Consequently, an audit may have many purposes:[4]

- Appraisal of the total marketing operation
- Evaluation of policies and objectives and their underlying assumptions
- Diagnosis and prognosis of the marketing program
- Searches for market opportunities and how to capitalize on them
- Searches for weaknesses and ways to eliminate them
- Identification of preventive as well as palliative marketing practices

The marketing audit process can be lengthy and complex. A great deal of prior planning and preparation is necessary. Ultimately, it involves (1) deciding who will do the audit; (2) agreeing on its objectives, scope, and breadth; (3) identifying sources of data; and (4) deciding on the format used to present its results.

Audit Personnel

Kotler has offered six ways in which a marketing audit may be conducted: (1) self-audit, (2) audit from across, (3) audit from above, (4) company auditing officer, (5) company task-force audit, and (6) outsider audit. Generally speaking, the best audits are likely to come from experienced outside consultants who have the necessary objectivity and independence, broad experience in a number of industries, some familiarity with this industry, and the undivided time and attention to give to the audit.[5]

Basically, the choice is between internal and external auditors. Internal auditors have the advantage of working relationships and familiarity with a company's operating environment. An audit performed by higher level executives or an auditing staff can be less time-consuming and perhaps less costly. However, internal auditors cannot be myopic in their knowledge of planning procedures. That is, they must have a good understanding of how planning should take place in any organization and not just in their particular company. Analysts must possess the depth and breadth of knowledge needed in marketing to make effective judgments.

If their experience is broad-based, external auditors can provide some of the breadth of knowledge needed. Consulting firms specializing in marketing may bring a perspective to a firm's planning process that could not otherwise be obtained, especially for firms with inbred executives. The major disadvantage of using external auditors is the time needed for them to gain an understanding of the company's approach to planning and the qualifications and training of the people involved in the planning process. A long-term relationship with the same consulting group would help alleviate this shortcoming.

Objectives, Scope, and Breadth of Audit

A meeting between the company officer(s) and the marketing auditor(s) should result in an agreement on the objectives, coverage, depth, data sources, report format, and the time period for the audit. Auditing time and cost can be kept to a minimum by carefully preparing a detailed plan for who is to be interviewed, the questions to be asked, the time and place of contact, and so on. The marketing audit should include data and opinions from not only company executives but also customers, dealers, and other outside groups to better understand how they see the company.[6]

The audit is most effective when its philosophy is built on three attributes: comprehensive, systematic, and periodic. An audit should not be considered comprehensive unless all aspects of planning are analyzed. A sales force audit or promotional audit by itself provides depth but is not comprehensive enough to evaluate relationships among personnel, organizations, and procedures. The audit should contain an examination of six major components of the company's marketing situation:[7]

Marketing environment: Analyze the major macroenvironmental forces and trends that are key components of the company's environment such as: markets, customers, competition, distributors, suppliers, and facilitators.

Marketing strategy: Appraise how well the company's marketing objectives and strategy are adapted to the current and forecasted marketing environment.

Marketing organization: Evaluate the capability of the marketing organization to implement the necessary strategy for the forecasted environment.

Marketing system: Examine the quality of the company's system for analysis, planning, and control.

Marketing productivity: Examine the profitability of different marketing entities and the cost effectiveness of different marketing expenditures.

Marketing function: Conduct in-depth evaluations of the major marketing-mix components.

A systematic audit follows logical, predetermined steps. The areas covered (based upon the major components of the marketing situation) and the types of questions asked provide the basis for analyzing a company's procedures. Figure 8.4 provides one such approach to conducting an audit.

This systematic approach should uncover a great deal of data about the planning process within a company. The continual questioning of why? about procedures, decisions, and controls is the key to uncovering who did what with what efficiency and provides input for answering, Are we doing the right things?

The audit should be undertaken with sufficient periodicity to avoid crisis circumstances. Many firms do not audit their managerial activities until a crisis occurs, but in many cases a crisis can be avoided by an audit. Few marketing planning processes are so successful that yearly or second- or third-year audits should not be used.

Part I: The Company Marketing Environment

A. Purpose
   1. Has a meaningful statement of company purpose been developed?
   2. Has it been effectively communicated to all marketing personnel?

B. Organization
   1. Has the responsibility for developing the marketing plan been assigned within the organization?
   2. Are the right people involved in preparation, review, and approval of completed planning documents?

C. Market analysis
   1. Has a general environmental analysis been completed that identifies salient factors in the company's operating environment?
   2. Has an environment analysis been completed to identify the product/market's boundaries (i.e., set of customer needs for particular customer segments served by alternative technologies)?
   3. Have the movements along these product/market dimensions been tracked over time to identify evolving trends?
   4. Have the major market factors been identified and their relation to revenue studied?
   5. Have these market growth factors been properly forecasted for planning periods?
   6. Have the key success factors for the product/market been identified?
   7. Has an analysis of sales and cost been conducted by market segment served?

D. Customer analysis
   1. Have customers' needs been carefully studied by market segments?
   2. Are sufficient data on customers available for planning? What is the nature and time period covered by these data?
   3. Have customers' motivations been analyzed? What approaches were used to accomplish this?
   4. Has purchase behavior been studied in detail over time? What patterns were identified?
   5. What conclusions were reached about customers' needs, motivations, and behavior?
   6. Have the product/markets been segmented? Have the segment profiles been determined? Have segments been targeted?

E. Competitive analysis
   1. Has the nature of competition in the market been analyzed? Defined?
   2. Have competitive activities been systematically evaluated?
   3. What competitive advantages were uncovered?

F. Opportunity analysis
   1. Were the opportunities identified and described in detail?
   2. Were sufficient data used to evaluate these opportunities?
   3. Was the compatibility of these opportunities studied in relation to the resources of the firm?
   4. Were economic, legal, technological, and cultural factors analyzed for each opportunity? What decisions were made?

FIGURE 8.4. The Marketing Audit Format

Part II: Objectives

A. Nature of objectives
   1. Were specific objectives developed?
   2. Did these objectives meet the requirements of good objectives? How was this tested?

B. Types of objectives
   1. What types of objectives were established?
   2. Was a sufficient database used to establish realistic objectives?

Part III: Strategy

A. What basic strategy was used? Was it appropriate?
B. Were alternative strategies evaluated? How?
C. What approach was used in establishing prices? Products offered? Place? Promotional mixes?
D. Were sufficient resources available to implement the strategy?
E. Was the financial impact of the strategy evaluated? How did this influence strategy decisions?

Part IV: Monitoring and Control Feedback

A. Was a control system established in the planning process?
B. What types of data were collected with what periodicity?
C. Were these data and time periods appropriate?
D. What results were achieved? Were these compared to objectives?
E. Was performance evaluation completed on all products by market segment? What types of performance were evaluated?
F. Was corrective action taken as a result of this feedback? What specific actions were taken?

FIGURE 8.4 *(continued)*

Audit Data and Reporting Format

The data for the audit must be provided through source documents (sales reports, sales training procedures, advertising budgets, media schedules, etc.) and interviews with personnel involved in marketing planning. Top management must ensure that auditors have complete cooperation from these personnel and access to any needed information, especially when external auditors are used. Failure to provide access to the same data available to the planners is sure to lead to a superficial audit and can result in an incomplete and misleading audit report.

Most companies assign one high-level executive to work with the auditor. Information requests routed through that executive carry authority by "virtue of office."

A variety of reporting formats is possible but one of the most appropriate is a written report of findings and recommendations. In such a report, the auditors' findings are written out for each area of study and a specific recommendation for improvement is stated for each finding. Thus the reporting format is action oriented, and specific actions can be evaluated for improving the planning process.

SUMMARY

The final step in the effective marketing management process is connecting with customers—establishing long-term, mutually satisfying relationships. Optimal performance in an organization depends upon having controls in place to identify where efforts need to be targeted to improve marketing activities directed at making such connections. This chapter reviewed the need for control, described what is to be controlled, and discussed control procedures. Sales control, cost control, and profitability control methods were discussed, along with consumer feedback mechanisms, ratio analyses, and the rationale and content of a marketing audit.

Cases

Case 1

Watercrest Park

Robert E. Stevens
David L. Loudon
Bruce E. Winston

Jim Owens was under considerable strain as he worked on a marketing plan for his new employer, Watercrest, Inc. He completed a consumer survey and a rough draft of the plan but was still unsure of the details of the rest of the document. Time was a factor in his concern since the deadline was one week away.

The designers of Watercrest originally envisioned the park as an outdoor water-related recreational facility. It was to include a wave pool, water slides, swimming pools, jogging trails, and several water rides. In addition, the plan included dressing rooms, a snack bar, a souvenir shop, a large space for sunbathing, and space for special events such as outdoor concerts. The idea seemed sound after a consulting group conducted a feasibility study that confirmed the original ideas on the need and potential profitability of the concept. The next step was to create enough interest in potential investors to raise the $4 million needed to launch the project.

However, Sid James, originator of the Watercrest project, wanted to supply potential investors with a copy of the feasibility study as well as a complete marketing plan to help convince them of the project's viability. Mr. James hired Jim Owens, a recent marketing graduate, to prepare the plan and help manage the facility when it opened.

Jim's early work was relatively easy because the consulting team collected much of the environmental and competitive data for the feasibility study. The parts of the plan Jim completed are shown in the following analysis, including a summary of the study revealing consumers' reactions to the proposed project.

Situation Analysis

Environmental Trends

Although the Watercrest concept is new and therefore does not have a history, recreation in general and water-related recreation specifically, has a long and interesting history. The following trends and forecasts for recreation were taken from recent industry literature:

- Americans have a growing preoccupation with outdoor recreation.
- Based on past trends, a doubling of recreational expenditures can be expected in the next eight to ten years.
- Expenditures for leisure activities are increasing faster than consumer spending as a whole.
- More and more people are moving to the Sun Belt; the South and Southwest are expected to be major growth areas, and people tend to be more recreationally active there.
- Leisure spending does not appear to be as heavily influenced by adverse economic conditions as other expenditures.
- Total leisure spending is expected to reach \$250 billion by next year and \$350 billion in five years.
- Admissions revenues for sporting events grew from \$3.6 billion to \$15 billion over the past five years.
- The most popular sport in the United States is swimming—some 103 million people regularly swim.
- Water-related activities account for five of the top twenty-five outdoor recreational activities.
- Experts say that participation in summer outdoor recreational activities is four times greater than forty years ago.
- Many theme parks are currently in trouble financially because of saturation, competition, and inflation.
- Experienced theme park operators have learned how to keep guests for several hours and offer many alternative ways to spend money.
- A major cost problem for theme parks is the attempt to add a newer, more thrilling ride every two years—at continuing inflated costs.
- Big Surf outdoor water recreation project is successful. It appeals mainly to youths, ages eight to twenty-three; very few families participate.

Although large theme parks have recently had financial trouble, there is an overall favorable climate for outdoor recreation ventures, and water-related activities in the Sun Belt historically have enjoyed a high probability of success.

Consumer Analysis

Table C1.1 lists potential market segments for Watercrest. Two major characteristics of the market segments influenced planned marketing activities. One was the size of the parties involved. Research from this project confirms that the primary markets for this project are youths and single adults. Also, many consumers indicate they would probably go with a group to this type of attraction. Although the plan will not ignore families, the size of the family segment, compared to the other two, warrants less marketing effort.

Another market-segment variable that the plan must consider is "resident versus tourist." Again, the plan will not ignore the tourist segment but primary emphasis will focus on the resident segment because of the size and accessibility of this group. Research reveals that the major motives for going to this type of park are:

1. *Fun:* a key word used by many consumers.
2. *Peers:* people like to be with others of their own age.
3. *Physical attraction of combination of sun and water:* people like to be near water in hot weather.
4. *Boredom:* people want other activities than staying home, watching television, and so on.

Consumers appear willing to spend five to eight dollars per person for this type of activity, and most youths report spending fifteen to twenty dollars a month on outdoor recreational activities during the summer.

There also appears to be a high degree of consumer acceptance of water-related activities such as water slides. Most youths have been to a water

TABLE C1.1. Market Segments

	Size of party		
Type of party	**Individuals/couples**	**Families**	**Groups**
Area residents	Youths ages 8-18, single adults ages 19 and over, young couples	Young/no children, older/young children, older/older children	Church, college groups
Tourists	Single adults, young couples	Young/no children, older/young children, older/older children	Church, school groups

slide and most adults with children are aware and approve of water slides. This translates to a favorable consumer mind-set for Watercrest.

The demographics of the market are favorable in terms of the major segments of Watercrest customers. Table C1.2 shows the size of the market by age. Population projections show a near doubling of the area population in the next twenty years.

Income statistics for the proposed location also reveal a very strong market. Table C1.3 shows a recent estimate of household buying income and the comparative local-state-nation percentage. Income in the area is not much different from the state. Overall, the area provides a stable economic base with future population growth and income levels that support additional recreational facilities.

Competitive Analysis

Although there are many competing recreational activities in the area, none offers a facility comparable to Watercrest. In fact, at current prices for water slides in the area, Watercrest should draw most consumers because of the cumulative attraction of other Watercrest activities and the positive Watercrest value. Each alternate recreational facility is a competitor for Watercrest; but given the nature of the project, there is no major daytime or nighttime competitor to Watercrest. Competitive data are shown in Tables C1.4 and C1.5.

TABLE C1.2. Population Distribution by Age Groups

Age group	Total number
6-17	70,758
18-34	150,134
35-64	92,700

TABLE C1.3. Household Income (Last Census)

Income ($)	Proposed location (%)	State (%)	United States (%)
Up to 15,000	26.4	27.3	25.4
15,001-25,000	7.3	6.9	6.6
25,001-35,000	17.5	17.6	18.0
35,001-45,000	26.9	28.7	30.8
45,001 and over	21.9	19.5	19.2

TABLE C1.4. Indoor Recreational Daytime Competitors

Types	Number	Average price
Theaters	23	$4.50/12 years and over
Skating rinks	4	$1.50/person
Bowling alleys	5	$1.70/person
Racquetball courts (public)	2	$5.50/person
Arcades	10	$0.25/game
Pistol ranges	3	$2.00/person

TABLE C1.5. Outdoor Recreational Daytime Competitors

Types	Number	Average price
Water slides	2	$2.00/1/2 hour
		$3.50/1 hour
		$6.00/all day
Race cars	1	$1.25/lap
		Usually $10/person
Skateboard parks	1	$2.50/3 hours
Swimming pools (public)	6	$1.60/person
Miniature golf	3	$2.00/person
Tennis courts (public)	6	$2.00/person
Amusement parks	2	3-4 tickets per ride ($1.00)

Although Jim had laid the groundwork for the rest of the marketing plan, he was still unsure about which overall positioning strategy to use and how to effectively promote the park to generate enough sales to make the venture profitable. If the profitability of this venture followed other theme parks, high volumes of sales could be expected during the first two to three years. This would be followed by declines as competition increased and the novelty of the park made it less attractive to customers. His attendance projections are shown in Table C1.6.

TABLE C1.6. Attendance Projections

	Attendance		
	Alternative first-year forecasts		
Facts/assumptions	**Low**	**Most likely**	**High**
Attendance/penetration			
Local market—target population			
Target market (ages 10-25)	112,000	112,000	112,000
Penetration	.65	.70	.85
Attendance	72,800	78,400	95,200
Local market—general population			
Population	103,087	103,087	103,087
Penetration	.03	.05	.07
Attendance	3,100	5,100	7,200
Regional market			
Population	90,000	90,000	90,000
Penetration	.10	.15	.20
Attendance	9,000	13,500	18,000
Tourist market			
Population	225,000	225,000	225,000
Penetration	.03	.05	.07
Attendance	6,750	11,250	15,750
Group sales market			
Attendance	18,275	20,350	25,700
Repeat business attendance	72,800	78,400	95,200
Total attendance (sum of above)	182,725	207,000	257,050

Low forecast: $1,827,250 (182,725 × $10); most likely: $2,070,000 (207,000 × $10); high forecast: $2,570,500 (257,050 × $10).

Sid James had indicated that the investors would be expecting at least a 15 percent return on investment for the $2 million dollar costs associated with fixed and operating capital needed for the park. Since there would be high fixed costs, the key to profitability was generating a high level of sales for the park.

CASE APPENDIX

The Consumer Study

This section of the report discusses the methods for collecting consumer information and presents the results of the consumer study. Assessment of consumer attitudes on this new concept began with a series of focus-group interviews. Each focus group included twelve teenagers between the ages of twelve and eighteen. There was an even mix of males and females, and most of the participants would be considered opinion leaders to some extent.

The interviews proceeded from a general discussion of recreation to outdoor activities to water-related activities. The moderator asked participants to comment on the Watercrest concept as well as many questions about participation, price, repeat trips, and so on. The consumer survey confirmed the findings of the focus group interviews and revealed a consistent pattern of responses from both data collection techniques. The method and findings of the consumer survey follow.

Introduction

Purpose. The purpose of this study was to provide data for market analysis and planning for the Watercrest project. The study provided data and a wide range of topics related to outdoor recreational activities and market participation.

Research objectives. This study sought to accomplish several research objectives:

- Identify the type of recreational activities residents participate in and the extent of participation by family unit.
- Determine the price levels anticipated by consumers for an outdoor recreational activity such as Watercrest.
- Determine exactly which consumer segment was most likely to be attracted to the project.
- Identify reasons for anticipated participation or lack of participation in the proposed project.
- Identify socioeconomic characteristics of the anticipated target markets.

Methodology

Sampling. Researchers selected respondents for this study through a cluster-sampling procedure of area residents listed in the current telephone book. The original clusters consisted of 1,500 residential listings. This rather large number was necessary to produce a sample of 300 respondents—225 adults and 75 young people. The researchers anticipated problems such as (1) disconnected numbers, (2) respondents who would not cooperate, and (3) potential respondents who could not be reached. Therefore the sample needed to begin with a large number of residents to ensure the desired sample size.

Survey Instrument and Data Collection

The researchers developed a telephone questionnaire and pretested it for validity. The following topics were covered in the survey:

- Participation in outdoor recreational activities
- Types of outdoor activities participated in
- Vacationing recreational activities
- Total family expenditures anticipated for an outdoor activity
- Familiarity with and reaction to water slides
- Motivation for participation in water-related recreational activities

Socioeconomic Classification Data

The study used a separate questionnaire for young people to ensure collection of data from consumers most likely to use a recreational facility such as Watercrest. Researchers collected data during the second week of February using interviewers selected and trained by the consultants. Although the interviewers encountered little difficulty in obtaining cooperation or administering the questionnaires, many interviews were aborted completely because respondents were not participants in outdoor activities or were unfamiliar with water-related activities. The average adult interview took ten minutes for completion while the youths' interviews took approximately five minutes.

Data Tabulation and Analysis

The data were tabulated by computer and organized by topical area. The researchers calculated descriptive statistics to represent the basic response modes of consumers and permit further analysis of the data.

Findings

Outdoor recreational participation. Most of the respondents interviewed in the study (71 percent) participated in outdoor recreational activities with the most popular activities being swimming, jogging, and tennis. These data are consistent with earlier findings from the focus group interviews. Outdoor activity was clearly seen as an activity for youths by both adults and young people interviewed.

The majority of adults with children indicated a preference for staying and watching their children participate in an activity if the facility offered a comfortable place. Adults also seemed extremely concerned with safety for their children in this type of activity. Eighty-five percent of the respondents identified safety as their major concern.

Expenditure Data

Respondents were asked how much they would spend per person to participate in an outdoor recreational activity if they could stay for eight to ten hours as a family. The median response was $8.00 per person. When asked how much they would be willing to spend for one of their children to participate, the average response was $10.50. Youths' average response was $10.00 when asked the same question.

The current price for an all-day pass at a water slide in the area is $6.00. Youths reported spending an average of $26.00 per month for recreational activities during the summer.

Socioeconomic Characteristics of Respondents

A typical adult respondent in this study can be profiled as follows:

1. Median income of a little over $25,000
2. About thirty years old

3. Male
4. Caucasian
5. Works in a professional or technical occupation
6. Median level of education was some college work completed

The majority of youths interviewed were between the ages of twelve and seventeen.

Summary and Conclusions

Based on the findings outlined in this study, the following conclusions and summary statements emerged:

- The majority of adults and youths view water-related activities such as a water slide as being for young people—not for families or older adults.
- A price of ten to twelve dollars or more for the Watercrest complex is entirely in line with what adults and youths would expect to pay.
- The major reason for participation in water activity is summed up in one word—fun. Also, hot weather and water activities appear to be part of the consumer mind-set.
- The major concern of adults for this type of activity is safety in use.
- Most youths appear to be interested in participating in this type of activity with a group of friends.

Findings of this study parallel the earlier focus group interviews—a consistent pattern of responses in viewing outdoor recreational activities.

Many families are involved in outdoor recreational activities when at home and while on vacation. However, the variety of activities is much more limited when on vacation.

Case 2

Superior Electrical Contractors: Residential Services Division

Robert E. Stevens
David L. Loudon
Bruce E. Winston

As Jim Bell, owner of Superior Electrical Contractors, studied monthly sales figures for the last three months, what he feared he would see became clear. Last year, sales declined 37 percent and the year before those sales declined 20 percent. In light of this trend, Jim questioned the survival of his firm. He believed that the firm could survive if the newly created Residential Services Division could bring in the sales lost in the commercial market.

Background

Jim Bell began Superior Electrical Contractors eleven years ago in a medium-sized city in the South. The company's primary service was electrical wiring of commercial buildings. As a secondary line, the firm also sold and serviced residential and commercial heating and air-conditioning units. Since the company's inception, electrical contracting services had accounted for 70 percent of sales with the remaining 30 percent coming from the sales and service of heating and air-conditioning units. Routine maintenance services in the secondary line included Freon checks, filter replacements, and system repairs.

Most commercial electrical contracting work is given to the firm with the lowest bid on the project. Superior Electrical prepared each bid from electrical specifications furnished by the general contractor, or in a few cases, the client/company itself. If Superior submitted the winning bid, it would receive the contract and had to complete all work within the specified time at the bid price. Jim developed his own computer applications to assist in preparing cost estimates that helped him achieve a 98 percent average accuracy on job cost estimates.

Sales History

Superior Electrical Contractors grew from a sales volume of less than $100,000 in the first year to over $900,000 within a period of four years. Years six through nine showed sales figures holding consistent at around $1 million; however, as the state's economy faltered, sales volume declined. Figure C2.1 shows sales figures for the company. Although Superior's market share remained the same, there simply were not enough new jobs to bid. Tables C2.1 and C2.2 show the company's income statements for the past two years and the current balance statement.

Jim realized that he had to do something to reverse the trend in sales volume. The company began this fiscal year with the lowest level of contract work since the firm's first year of operation. He was convinced that the firm had to either expand the geographic area that the company operated in to find additional commercial work or find new sources of revenue in the current geographic area.

The Residential Services Division

Although the company generated some revenue each year from sales and services performed for residential customers, this business

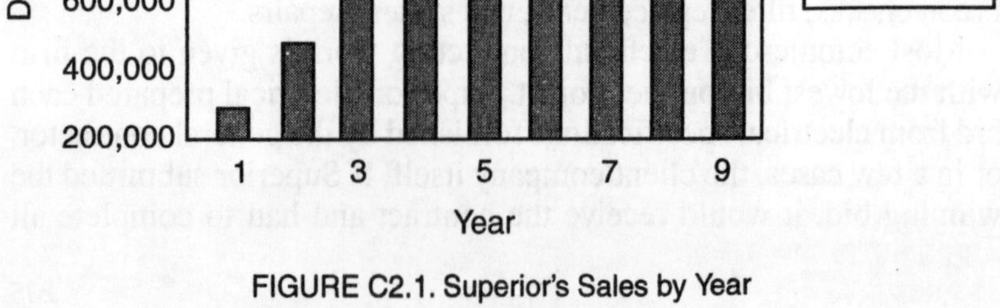

FIGURE C2.1. Superior's Sales by Year

TABLE C2.1. Comparative Statements of Income and Expenses for the Most Recent Years Ended June 30

	Two years ago		Last year	
	Percentage	**Dollars**	**Percentage**	**Dollars**
Income				
Contract income	100.00	937,317	100.00	594,624
Direct job costs				
Materials	41.15	385,716	39.42	234,417
Labor	23.24	217,870	25.13	149,404
Payroll taxes	2.64	24,739	2.66	15,795
Truck and travel	2.04	19,117	2.32	13,772
Subcontract	.42	3,950	1.64	9,744
Equipment rental	2.26	21,141	2.06	12,259
Miscellaneous	1.23	11,487	.08	556
Total direct job costs	72.98	684,020	73.31	435,947
Gross profit	27.02	253,297	26.69	158,677
Operating expense	26.88	251,958	37.94	225,591
Income (loss) from operations	.14	1,339	(11.25)	(66,914)
Other income				
Interest income	.18	1,700	.03	168
Gain on sale of fixed assets	.21	1,930	.00	–
Total other income	.39	3,630	.03	168
Income (loss) before taxes	.53	4,969	(11.22)	(66,746)
Federal and state income taxes	.00	0	.00	0
Net income (loss)	.53	4,969	(11.22)	(66,746)

was never aggressively developed or promoted. The firm always viewed this work as a way to keep crews busy between contracted jobs. Many competitors in this market perform a variety of electrical services for home owners, such as (1) light/fan fixture installations, (2) repair/replacement of electrical switches and breakers, as well as (3) sales and service of heating and air-conditioning units.

TABLE C2.2. Balance Sheet, June 30, Last Year

	Value	Totals
Current assets		
Cash in bank	$10,030	
Accounts receivable—employees	216	
Accounts receivable—trade	54,571	
Materials inventory	54,667	
Costs and estimated earnings in excess of billings	14,575	
Prepaid expenses	8,890	
Total current assets		$142,949
Fixed assets, at cost		
Machinery and equipment	63,083	
Accumulated depreciation	(55,936)	
Net fixed assets		7,147
Other assets		
Note receivable—officer	11,072	
Stock, at cost	500	
Refundable deposits	300	
Total other assets		11,872
Total assets		161,968
Current liabilities		
Accounts payable	$23,942	
Payroll taxes payable	3,068	
Accrued interest	2,459	
Accrued insurance	5,517	
Notes payable—bank	103,160	
Billings in excess of cost and estimated earnings	79	
Total current liabilities		$138,225
Long-term liabilities		
Notes payable—bank		82,393
Total liabilities		220,618

	Value	Totals
Stockholders' equity		
Common stock	33,520	
Treasury stock	(3,380)	
Retained earnings	(88,790)	
Total stockholders' equity		(58,650)
Total liabilities and stockholders' equity		161,968
Balance at beginning of year—July 1, two years ago		(22,044)
Add: Net income (loss)		(66,746)
Balance at end of year—June 30, last year		(88,790)

A customer experiencing an electrical problem would usually use the yellow pages to locate an electrical sales/service firm or rely on word-of-mouth recommendations from friends and neighbors. If customers were satisfied with the electrical sales/service firm, they would continue to call the same firm as other needs arose.

The idea for increasing the emphasis on the residential market came about by necessity but also through a conversation with another contractor at a national convention. This contractor explained to Jim that his firm had doubled its sales volume within two years by offering a maintenance contract to home owners. The maintenance contract provided (1) two maintenance calls on each home to check out the central heating and air-conditioning system; (2) add refrigerant, if needed; (3) oil motors; (4) clean or replace filters; and (5) check for leaks and potential problems. The contract specified one filter and two pounds of refrigerant free per year. Customers paid for any additional supplies or parts required to repair a unit, separately upon approval to perform the work. The contractor said that he sold the maintenance contract for $99, which covered the cost of providing the service. However, additional services identified through the maintenance service, in addition to repeat business on other requested electrical services and word-of-mouth advertising, doubled his sales volume. The contractor told Jim that each maintenance contract generated an additional $300 in business and $150 in profits.

Jim asked a team of marketing students at the local university to conduct a survey to determine consumer interest in the idea of a maintenance contract. The results were very encouraging.

Market Survey Results

The survey of 100 area residents screened out non–home owners and home owners with homes valued at less than $75,000 to make sure the information represented higher-income consumers. Jim felt that the higher-income segment was most likely to respond favorably to such an offer. Those respondents who were extremely interested or somewhat interested were higher-income males with at least a college education (see Table C2.3).

Market Area Data

The market area served by Superior Electrical Contractors includes a population of 500,000 people and approximately 112,428 homes. Information from the tax assessor's office on the value of homes is shown in Table C2.4. Jim estimated that twenty percent of these homes were rental properties; however, he was certain that the rental homes were valued under $75,000. Jim believed that this left a large market potential for the maintenance agreement even with the under-$75,000 homes factored out.

Pricing Strategy Options

Jim believed that two alternative pricing strategies were available (see Table C2.5 for consumer price expectations). The first was a low price of under $100. This low price, though, would generate very little, if any, contribution to profit. However, a higher penetration of

TABLE C2.3. Level of Consumer Interest in Maintenance Agreement

Response	Percentage
Extremely interested	11.1
Somewhat interested	50.0
Not at all interested	26.4
Don't know/not sure	12.5

TABLE C2.4. Tax Assessment of Home Values (Current Year)

Home value	Number	Percent
Less than $25,000	3,375	3
$25,000 to $50,000	13,491	12
$50,001 to $75,000	25,857	23
$75,001 to $100,000	30,356	27
$100,001 to $125,000	20,236	18
$125,001 to $150,000	11,243	10
$150,001 to $175,000	4,497	4
$175,001 to $200,000	2,249	2
Over $200,000	1,124	1
	112,428	100

TABLE C2.5. Expected Price for a Maintenance Agreement

Expected annual price	Percentage
$50 or less	21.5
$51 to $75	26.9
$76 to $100	29.3
$101 to $125	16.2
$126 to $150	4.6
over $150	1.5

homes would achieve greater exposure for Superior that might lead to additional revenue from other services.

The other strategy would price the agreement between $120 and $125 per customer generating between $20 and $25 contribution/margin per customer. The trade-off would be lower market penetration and less opportunity to generate additional revenues from maintenance agreement customers.

Time was running out on choosing the right strategy. Jim had to call the printer so the price could be included in the brochure that was to be mailed to past customers. Jim was undecided on how best to promote the service to other home owners. The brochure cost $1,500 for 1,000 copies and represented one-tenth of his advertising budget. In addition to selecting the media and the message, Jim also had to decide on how long to run the promotional campaign.

Case 3

Gateway Medical Waste Transport of Colorado

Robert E. Stevens
David L. Loudon
Bruce E. Winston

Kathy West, vice president of marketing at Gateway Medical Waste Transport of Colorado, sat at her desk reading the home office's request for a strategic marketing plan for the next three years including pro forma income statements. She had thought about this project off and on for the past couple of months and now faced the daunting task of actually creating the overall strategy and the mix of personal selling and advertising. The home office expected substantial growth from the Colorado operation and Ms. West searched for growth options to meet the desired sales/profit levels.

Background

Medical waste first came to the attention of the general public in the 1980s when it washed up on New Jersey beaches. Because of the media exposure of this event and others pertaining to undesirable disposal practices as well as fear of AIDS, public hysteria resulted and pressure was put upon regulatory officials to develop comprehensive regulations to prohibit such occurrences. The Medical Waste Tracking Act (MWTA) of 1988 was passed requiring the federal Environmental Protection Agency (EPA) to begin an investigation to determine whether federal legislation was necessary. The EPA provided their findings in 1991 which led to federal regulations on medical waste disposal.

Also, the Occupational Safety and Health Administration (OSHA) has begun to fine waste generators for improper disposal practices within their facilities and most states have adopted some type of regulation pertaining to infectious waste disposal requirements. The concern was not just for human medical waste but also animal medical waste since farmers and ranchers inoculate animals including beef, pork, and poultry.

The MWTA initially applied to facilities in Connecticut, New Jersey, and New York. Illinois, Indiana, Michigan, Minnesota, Ohio, Pennsylvania, and Wisconsin also were included within the original scope of the MWTA but were permitted to, and each elected to, opt out of coverage. The federal government permitted other states to opt into coverage under the MWTA, but only Rhode Island and Puerto Rico elected to be included. The MWTA only covered medical waste generated in any of the covered states. Conversely, the MWTA did not cover medical waste transported from a noncovered state to a covered state for treatment and/or disposal.

The EPA issued regulations (MWTA regulations) listing applicable generators, identifying the wastes that had to be tracked, and outlining standards for separating, packaging, and labeling medical waste. Facilities producing less than fifty pounds of waste per month are exempt from the tracking requirements. The MWTA regulations impose record-keeping requirements on all generators, transporters, and destination facilities and each facility must maintain all tracking records for three years. The program requires the use of a specified uniform tracking form. Additional requirements and operating procedures are applicable to transporters, and treatment, storage and disposal facilities. Generators exporting medical waste to a foreign country for treatment, destruction, or disposal must receive written confirmation of receipt within forty-five days; otherwise, an exception report must be filed by the forty-sixth day.

Company History

Gateway Medical Waste Transport, Inc. (GMWT) emerged in late 1988 in response to concerns expressed by federal, state, and local regulators regarding biomedical waste disposal practices and their impact upon human health and the environment. At that time, in most market areas, only BFI Medical Waste Systems and/or Waste Management, Inc. offered biomedical waste management services; and, as a result, those companies enjoyed a near monopoly in the marketplace, which reflected itself in the prices charged by those companies.

Since signing its very first account in March 1989, GMWT has grown to be the largest provider of biomedical waste management services in the state of Oklahoma where it currently manages 450,000 pounds of biomedical waste per month.

GMWT opened a subsidiary office in Denton, Texas, in early 1990 and enjoyed significant success throughout the Dallas-Fort Worth market area. This branch presently contracts with 23 hospitals that generate a total of 150,000 pounds of biomedical waste each month. The Dallas-Fort Worth Hospital Council recently endorsed GMWT as the preferred provider of biomedical waste management services to its member hospitals. This endorsement should lead to greater presence in the market.

In addition to serving Oklahoma and Northern Texas, GMWT also presently services numerous medical facilities in Kansas, Missouri, Arkansas, Colorado, and Wyoming. GMWT received endorsement from Voluntary Hospitals of America (VHA) for its biomedical waste disposal service to VHA member facilities.

A major factor in the success of GMWT, in addition to its quality of service and competitive pricing, is the exclusive use of a newly constructed, fully permitted incinerator with a capacity of 100 tons per day. This incinerator was designed specifically for biomedical waste (including antineoplastic/chemotherapy wastes) and is located in Oklahoma. GMWT routinely arranges for potential clients to tour this impressive facility which instills confidence regarding the disposition of biomedical wastes.

The Colorado Department of Health recognized GMWT's stature as a major provider of biomedical waste management services when a Denver biomedical waste management company requested GMWT to assist in the immediate removal and incineration of nearly one million pounds of biomedical waste that the company had stored in trailers in the Denver area. GMWT successfully completed this project within the twenty-one-day compliance time frame imposed by Colorado authorities.

All GMWT employees directly involved in the hands-on management of biomedical wastes receive training in the proper use of personal protective equipment and appropriate corrective actions relating to spills, including decontamination techniques and procedures. All GMWT employees, including drivers, submit to GMWT's proactive substance abuse program, which includes drug testing upon employment and random testing thereafter. All GMWT drivers must also meet U. S. Department of Transportation driver qualification standards, including physical exams and an annual review of their driving records. In addition, GMWT employs a team of emergency responders who must complete a forty-hour emergency response course conducted by Oklahoma State University.

GMWT's corporate management includes an environmental attorney licensed by the state of California whose other credentials include a master's-level certification in hazardous materials management from the Institute of Hazardous Materials Management. He also serves as an adjunct extension program faculty member in environmental management at Oklahoma State University.

GMWT is permitted to manage biomedical materials including infectious wastes (wastes capable of producing an infectious disease), chemical wastes (such as pharmaceutical wastes), laboratory wastes, antineoplastic drugs, other chemicals, and those items that are not regulated as hazardous wastes. The infectious wastes that GMWT manages include the following:

1. Cultures and stocks of infectious agents and associated biologicals
2. Human blood and blood products
3. Pathological wastes
4. Contaminated sharps
5. Contaminated animal carcasses, body parts, and bedding
6. Wastes from surgery, autopsies, and other medical procedures
7. Laboratory wastes
8. Dialysis unit wastes
9. Isolation wastes unless determined to be noninfectious by the infection control committee at the health care facility
10. Any other material and contaminated equipment that, in the determination of the facility's infection control staff, presents a significant danger of infection because it is contaminated with, or may reasonably be expected to be contaminated with, etiologic agents. An *etiologic agent* is a type of microorganism, helminth, or virus that causes, or significantly contributes to the cause of, increased morbidity or mortality of humans.

The chemical wastes handled by GMWT include the following:

1. Pharmaceutical wastes
2. Laboratory reagents contaminated with infectious body fluids
3. All the disposable materials in contact with cytotoxic/antineoplastic agents during the preparation, handling, and administration of such agents. (Such waste includes, but is not limited to, masks, gloves, gowns, empty IV tubing bags and vials, and other contaminated materials.)
4. Other chemicals that may be contaminated by infectious agents as designated by experts at the point of generation of the waste

The Colorado Operation

GMWT opened a subsidiary office in Denver to provide quality, competitively priced biomedical waste management services to the medical community in Colorado. Mr. Rick Stewart and Ms. Kathy West manage this office. Ms. West was formerly employed by BFI in Oklahoma, where she helped set up its medical waste program and ranked first in sales and service throughout that company in its biomedical waste operations. Her background and training enabled her to assist medical facilities in their efforts to properly manage biomedical wastes in a safe and economical manner consistent with all regulations and joint commission guidelines. This office, in one three-month period, signed obligations generating enough revenue to cover 60 percent of the subsidiary's operating costs.

GMWT currently serves thirty-five clients in the eastern part of the state and will soon provide service to all of Colorado. The GMWT office located in Denver, Colorado, currently has a staff of four with vast experience in the areas of medical waste and transportation. GMWT of Colorado offers its clients a comprehensive medical waste management program and assists them in a consultative role. This includes assessment of their current system and recommendations for improvement. If a program does not exist, GMWT helps to develop one. This process can take several days for a large hospital or a few minutes for a small office. Once service begins, GMWT adds the clients onto a pick-up route that allows GMWT to conform to a schedule and gives the client assurance of timely service. GMWT provides all clients with containers for waste disposal and also documentation confirming receipt of waste and an actual date of incineration. GMWT currently uses a twenty-foot bobtruck, which collects the waste at the generator's site. At the end of a route, a trained technician transports the waste to GMWT's transfer facility and off-loads it into a fifty-three-foot trailer. When full, GMWT transports the trailer to the incinerator in Oklahoma. No operational incinerator currently exists in Colorado. Incineration is the only method of disposal that GMWT of Colorado uses.

For GMWT to be competitive, long-haul-transportation costs must stay at a minimum. GMWT currently uses Ranger Transportation, Inc., a nationwide transportation company that provides all trailers and transport to Stroud, Oklahoma, within a forty-eight-hour period from pickup. Ranger's drivers must complete a special spill-response training course.

Colorado presently requires generators to have a comprehensive infectious waste management plan in place, documentation of proper disposal, written standard operating procedures, and regular monitoring of the disposal practice. Noncompliance with these requirements subjects the generator to civil penalties.

Currently, ninety-one hospitals in Colorado generate a total of approximately 35,146 pounds of infectious waste per day. In addition, there are also several thousand physicians and dentists as well as hundreds of clinics, laboratories, and other infectious waste generators. About 73 percent of hospitals and 20 percent of clinics and others use commercial disposal companies (the clinics and others are just now beginning to use this type of service). This yields an average annual revenue potential of about $500,000.

Competition in the marketplace favors GMWT because of its strength in disposal capacity and capabilities, technology, service, track record, as well as expertise. BFI Medical Waste Systems (BFI), Waste Management, Inc. (WMI), and others operating in the area all acknowledge major weaknesses. BFI had been a tough competitor until recently when it made the decision to autoclave waste for Colorado rather than incinerate. *Autoclaving* involves steam sterilization of waste and disposal in a landfill. WMI also autoclaves as do the other competitors. GMWT, on the other hand, uses state-of-the-art incineration in Oklahoma and has a staff of specialized industry experts.

Marketing Activities

Marketing activities in Colorado have mirrored the activities used in other locations. GMWT has focused on personal selling since an on-site inspection of a generator's facility is required to determine whether it meets current codes for handling waste and the volume of waste on a monthly basis.

Colorado's sales force consists of three people who received specialized training in medical waste disposal issues. The salespeople provide comprehensive waste stream assessments, comparative cost analyses, intensive staff training in servicing, as well as ongoing consultation in regulatory compliance issues. GMWT had not yet contacted all the hospitals statewide. Ms. West thought that cold calling, as well as telemarketing support and a mail-out campaign might be the best way to reach the potential customers.

Financial Performance

GMWT of Colorado, Inc. is beginning to become more financially independent. Current accounts are generating enough revenues to cover approximately 60 percent of operating costs. With the addition of new accounts weekly, it projects a break-even point to occur within a six-month period based on calculations comprised of income statements and budget projections. Due to the nature of the business and the size of the market, GMWT of Colorado had forecasted a profit after the first year of business. Kathy West also feels that a 25 percent growth over the next three years is a very realistic projection for the company (see Table C3.1).

After the initial three years of growth, West expects increased competition and slower growth. She is concerned about the company's ability to continue this growth pattern and wonders how this might affect GMWT's ability to attract additional investors to support expansion. She also wonders about ensuring other strategic options that might be available rather than expanding the business to other geographical areas.

TABLE C3.1. Gateway Medical Waste Transport of Colorado, Inc.

Financial projections	Year 1	Year 2	Year 3
Estimated sales revenue	$511,000.00	$880,000.00	$1,303,500.00
Estimated costs of goods sold	204,000.00	348,000.00	515,000.00
Estimated gross margin	307,000.00	532,000.00	788,500.00
Variable expenses	13,200.00	13,200.00	14,000.00
Utilities/communications	3,600.00	4,000.00	5,000.00
Office expense	2,500.00	3,000.00	4,000.00
Auto expense	1,200.00	1,500.00	2,000.00
Fuel	8,700.00	10,000.00	15,000.00
Repairs and maintenance	2,000.00	2,000.00	5,000.00
Marketing/advertising	6,000.00	6,000.00	6,000.00
Accounting/legal	1,200.00	1,500.00	1,500.00
Miscellaneous	1,200.00	1,500.00	2,000.00
Total variable expenses	39,600.00	42,700.00	54,500.00
Margin for fixed expenses and net income	267,400.00	489,300.00	734,000.00
Fixed expenses			
Salaries	130,000.00	150,000.00	200,000.00
Rent	14,700.00	14,700.00	20,000.00
Taxes	12,200.00	13,000.00	15,000.00
Loan payments	20,400.00	22,000.00	30,000.00
General liability insurance	11,616.00	13,000.00	20,000.00
Worker's compensation	10,800.00	12,000.00	20,000.00
Medical/life insurance	4,800.00	6,000.00	10,000.00
Unemployment, federal/state	3,000.00	4,000.00	10,000.00
Total fixed expenses	207,516.00	234,700.00	325,000.00
Estimated net income before taxes	59,884.00	254,600.00	409,000.00
Estimated income taxes	11,977.00	76,380.00	159,510.00
Estimated net income after taxes	47,907.00	178,220.00	249,490.00
Estimated income earnings per share (100,000 shares)	0.48	1.78	2.50

Case 4

National Foundations, Inc.

Robert E. Stevens
David L. Loudon
Bruce E. Winston

Kent Smith sits at his desk reviewing his notes on a new product that his company is considering adding. The product, a foundation stabilizing system, could dramatically change the company's product line and growth potential.

Bill and Kent Smith established National Foundations, Inc., in 1978 as a residential foundation repair company. Both brothers worked in another foundation repair company before starting their own business. National Foundations specializes in repair of residential foundations and does no commercial jobs. The need for foundation repair arises when a foundation—usually a concrete slab—settles due to shifting soils, expansion or contraction of soils, or inadequate construction of the original foundation. Repairs normally consist of digging under the existing foundation, jacking the foundation back into position with hydraulic jacks and then pouring new concrete under the foundation. Cosmetic repair of bricks, shrubs, and grass may also be needed to restore the home to an acceptable condition after repair.

The new product under consideration involves the use of a "seep hose" which can be tied to a home's water system to maintain the moisture content of the soil under a foundation. When the moisture content of the soil decreases, the seep hose would replace the moisture to maintain a constant level. The constant moisture content of the soil would conceivably prevent the soil from expanding or contracting when long dry spells or extremely wet spells occurred, thus, preventing foundation problems. However, the founder and patent holder, Dr. Harold Jenkins, had not completed any field-testing of the product.

Consumer Analysis

Smith realized that the need for residential foundation repairs and/or preventive systems is based on two factors: (1) the number of structures existing at a given point in time, and (2) the proportion of these structures experiencing foundation failures of sufficient magnitude to warrant repair. He also knew that the number of existing structures is influenced by population, family formations, income levels, and interest rates; while the proportion of structures needing repairs or preventive systems is determined by bearing soil and climatic conditions and/or inadequate foundation construction. Kent understood that he needed to check each of these factors for reliability before he could estimate the sales volume of the new product.

Residential Housing in the United States

Using the U. S. Census housing data, Smith found that the number of existing residential houses in the United States was 109,800,000 units. Growth in housing units, as measured by new housing starts, has followed the pattern shown in Tables C4.1 and C4.2.

TABLE C4.1. Percent of Homes by Year Built

Year range	Percent of homes built
1990-1994	6
1985-1989	8
1980-1984	8
1975-1979	11
1970-1974	11
1960-1969	15
1950-1959	13
1940-1949	8
1930-1939	6
1920-1929	5
1919-earlier	9
Total	100

TABLE C4.2. New Housing Starts by Year (in Thousands)

Year	Number
1992	1,200
1993	1,228
1994	1,457
1995	1,354
1996	1,477
1997	1,476

Source: National Association of Home Builders (NAHB) housing starts, available online at <http://www.nahb.com/starts.html>.

More relevant to National's planning was the number of homes in the areas most likely to experience the soil and climatic conditions that cause foundation failures. In the continental United States seventeen states have been labeled "problem states" as far as foundation failures are concerned. These states are listed in Table C4.3 along with the number of existing houses in 1999.

Smith planned to use these data to calculate market potential for the sales of the foundation stabilization system in the seventeen problem states. He learned that an estimated 60 percent of all houses built on expansive soils will experience foundation problems of some type. Ten percent of these are estimated to experience problems significant enough to warrant repair. Smith thought that, perhaps, 70 percent of the houses in the seventeen problem states were built on expansive soils.

Market Potential

Table C4.3 shows the total number of houses in each of the seventeen problem states. These data would serve as a basis for estimating total market potential in these states. Table C4.4, in turn, shows the total number of houses for the four cities in which National would initially do business.

TABLE C4.3. Housing in the Seventeen Problem States, 1999

State	Number of houses (in thousands)
Alabama	1,834
California	11,599
Colorado	1,493
Florida	5,474
Kansas	1,194
Mississippi	1,140
Montana	410
Nebraska	781
New Mexico	635
North Dakota	324
Oklahoma	1,546
Oregon	1,354
South Dakota	346
Texas	6,936
Utah	613
Washington	2,111
Wyoming	235
Total	38,025

Source: Robert Wade Brown, *Residential Foundations: Design, Behavior, and Repair,* Second Edition (New York: VanNostrand Reinhold, 1984), p. 18.

TABLE C4.4. Housing in Four Selected Cities

City	Number of houses (in thousands)
Tulsa	195
Oklahoma City	221
Dallas	488
Fort Worth	195
Total	1,099

Consumer and Builder Input

The Smith brothers realized that before they could make a decision on their new venture, they needed to know what home owners and builders thought about foundation problems and repairs. Consequently, they spent many hours interviewing respondents from both groups.

The consumer interviews involved a random sample of home owners in the Tulsa area. The Smiths talked with fifty respondents from a group of home owners who had experienced foundation problems and repairs. This information was used to more precisely estimate repair costs, market share, and interest in the foundation stabilizing system under consideration.

Kent Smith summarized the findings from the home owner survey as follows: of the fifty respondents, frame (wood) (32.3 percent), all brick (31.3 percent), and brick and frame (23.2 percent) were the most popular types of homes. Of the ten respondents who were extremely interested in the system, half (five) had all-brick homes with only one individual with a wood frame home. Brick homes that show exterior cracks are the prime target for such a system.

- Although the homes with crawl spaces (53.7 percent) outnumbered the homes with slabs (43.2 percent), twice as many individuals who were extremely interested in the system had slab foundations.
- The majority of the homes in the survey were 2,000 square feet or less. None of the respondents with 3,000 square feet or more were interested in the system. This is not to say that those individuals with large homes are not interested in such a system. Larger homes may be perceived as better constructed and thus not in need of the system. Interest in the stabilizing system did increase if respondents were aware of problems in their neighborhood. Of those aware of the problems, 44.4 percent said they were extremely interested in the system. This compares with only 6.6 percent who were not aware of problems.
- Those who experienced foundation problems were not more interested in the system than those who had not. The stabilization system may be viewed as either preventing foundation problems

for those who have not had problems or as a stabilization system for those who have experienced problems.

- Of the respondents who experienced foundation problems, 77.8 percent listed foundation settling as the primary type of problem. Exterior cracks were the usual indication of problems. Only 55.6 percent of the respondents had repaired their foundation. The average cost was less than $2,500. Most individuals making repairs spend only a minimal amount while a few must make major costly repairs. Thus, the average cost of repairs is expected to be much greater than just $2,500.
- Of those who were extremely interested in the system and responded to the question on what they expect to pay for the system, more than half responded with greater than $5,000. Thus, for those extremely interested, the present cost of $4,000 does not seem unreasonable.
- When asked if they were still interested if the system costs $4,000, 60 percent responded that they were still extremely interested.
- Of those extremely interested in the system, 50 percent said that they wouid prefer to pay over time; 71.4 percent of those that were only somewhat interested in the system were interested in paying over time. The availability of credit appeared to be important in marketing the system.
- Of those extremely interested in the system, all were married, and of those 90 percent had children at home. No singles or marrieds without children were extremely interested in the system.
- The primary age category extremely interested in the system was thirty-five to forty-four years old. Of the individuals in this age category, 20.83 percent said they were extremely interested in this system. The next interested age categories were the twenty-five to thirty-four and fifty-five to sixty-four age categories with a combined 15.4 percent.
- Educational levels did not differentiate interest in the system. Those with higher levels of education were slightly less likely to be interested.
- Of those who said that they had experienced foundation problems, 55.6 percent had all-brick homes. Again, these respondents were likely to have noticed exterior cracks. Respondents

with other types of homes may have experienced foundation problems but were unaware of them.

- Most of the homes with foundation problems (88.9 percent) had a market value of less than $85,000. More expensive homes may be constructed in such a way as to minimize foundation problems.
- Those likely to purchase the system usually made more purchases than planned compared to those not likely to purchase the system. Thus, the ten individuals who said they were extremely interested in the system may be acting on impulse and may not purchase the system when offered.

Interviews with ten home builders from the area provided insight into their interest in the system. Table C4.5 summarizes the results.

Financial Considerations

The stabilization system is estimated to cost an average of $3,650 per installation. A cost breakdown is shown in Table C4.6.

An engineering report, provided by a civil engineering firm on a fee-for-service basis, along with soil samples, determine the depth at which to install the system for maximum foundation stabilization. The average price per installation is expected to be about $4,500 yielding a 19 percent markup or a contribution-per-installation of $850. Since many consumers were expected to want to finance the system over at least five years, a local bank agreed to finance creditworthy home owners.

Although the addition of the stabilization system was seen as a complementary product to the repair business, Smith anticipated a substantial investment in materials, crew training, and equipment. In addition, the firm would need to locate additional capital as new areas were developed. Estimates of the initial investment needed for each market area are $150,000. This includes all the expenses of opening a new branch office; leasing office and storage space; hiring a general manager, sales staff, secretary, and work crews; equipment rentals; purchase of tools; and working capital of $25,000 per branch.

Since the firm was already in business in the Tulsa market, the initial investment was expected to be only about $50,000 for that market. However, since the concept of a stabilization system was new,

TABLE C4.5. Home Builders' Survey

Name	Home value	Comments
Mike Freeze Mike Freeze, Inc.	$65,000 to $85,000	Uses home owner's warranty (HOW) and does not see benefit of foundation stabilization system.
Larry Ogden Ogden Properties	$90,000 to $250,000	System is a good idea and he is interested in concept.
Dave Millsap Dave Millsap, Inc.	$150,000 to $400,000	Had a bad experience with the system on five different occasions. He indicates that system does not work and that it cannot be properly maintained.
Bill Hood Timberwood Custom Homes	$160,000 to $400,000	He is not interested in the system. He indicated that if foundation were put in properly you would not have problems. Get a soil test before building to determine soil type. He does not believe system works on some soils that do not need moisture.
William Howard Timbercrest	$55,000 to $90,000	He feels the same as previous respondent.
Perry Cox, President Cox Properties	$50,000 to $90,000	He feels the same as previous respondent.
Boyd Preston Prestige Homes	Over $120,000	He may be interested for higher priced homes of $250,000 or more.
Leonard Frye Frye Homes	Over $200,000	He may be interested if building in an area with unstable soil.
Jim Glenn Glenn Homes	$150,000 to $400,000	He thinks the system is a good idea and that this type of system is needed. He uses french drains on most homes.
Gary Smith Smith Homes, Inc.	$70,000 to $150,000	Every home is piered, which he believes will solve the problem.

TABLE C4.6. Cost per Installation

Item	Cost
Material	$1,800
Labor	$1,200
Engineering report	$200
Sales commissions	$450
Total cost	$3,650

promotion expenses were expected to run about $50,000 a year for the first three years of operation and at least $25,000 to $30,000 a year thereafter for all locations.

Additional crews could be added and equipment rented within a short period of time to allow for wide variations in demand for the system. In the Tulsa market, a 2 to 5 percent penetration would yield a substantial base from which to expand into other areas of the country.

The Smiths needed to calculate the expected returns they would make from an investment in the foundation system. In a proposed venture, the net inflows of cash expected from a project should be equal to or greater than the net profit after taxes plus depreciation. The analysis should terminate after ten years with zero salvage at that time, which would force the new company to stand alone with only the near-term cash flows determining operational feasibility. The company wanted the new venture to generate an internal rate of return of at least 15 percent if it were to be launched.

Case 5

Mildred's Caddy

Robert E. Stevens
David L. Loudon
Bruce E. Winston

Mildred Sanders was trying to decide what she should do about her latest invention—an ironing board caddy. Mildred is an entrepreneur at heart, although she spends most of her work time in a real estate firm in Jackson, Mississippi, in which she is a partner. Mildred's creative energies, though, always seemed to focus on new products. She already received a patent on a previous invention as well as the new Ironing Board Caddy (see Figures C5.1 and C5.2).

The Ironing Board Caddy is a clip-on attachment that holds a bottle of spray starch or sizing, scissors, safety pins, and needles and thread. This device prevents items from falling off the ironing board, and if needed, permits the user to repair a garment while ironing.

Mildred asked a friend who did marketing research to help her design a questionnaire to collect data from consumers to estimate acceptance of the product idea. Mildred's friend hired two people to conduct 100 telephone interviews in Jackson using a random sample of potential consumers. In addition, Mildred's friend collected secondary data on households in several southern states. Mildred felt the results of the consumer survey were favorable and that the prospect for sales at very low levels of penetration could produce a substantial profit potential.

This case was prepared by Robert E. Stevens, PhD, Professor of Marketing; David L. Loudon, PhD, Professor of Marketing and Head, Department of Management and Marketing, University of Louisiana at Monroe; and Bruce E. Winston, PhD, School of Business, Regent University. Names, selected data, and corporate identities have been disguised.

FIGURE C5.1. Mildred's Ironing Board Caddy

Mildred obtained production estimates from three possible manufacturers. These cost estimates ranged from $2.35 to $2.45 per unit in lots of 5,000 or more. Packaging costs were expected to be about .40 per unit. The manufacturer selected would require an injection mold for the product that would cost $26,500. Mildred located a reputable package design firm and secured an estimate of $3,500 for a final design. Each of the three manufacturers agreed to store and ship the units in cases of 24 at an additional cost of .10 per unit or $2.40 per case.

At a wholesale price of $6.50, a retailer could sell the product for $12.95 and make a profit of about 50 percent. This markup would make the product fairly attractive if a large volume was sold. To obtain retail distribution, Mildred could use manufacturers' reps. Reps require a 15 percent commission on new products. These reps could also reach fabric/sewing outlets—a key channel in Mildred's thinking.

A regional promotional campaign to launch the product was expected to cost between $75,000 and $100,000 if newspaper inserts and direct mail promotion were used. Mildred was not sure how she could reach potential users more directly.

As a first step in assessing market potential for the southeastern United States, Mildred's marketing research friend gathered data on the number of households in twelve southeastern states. This information is shown in Table C5.1.

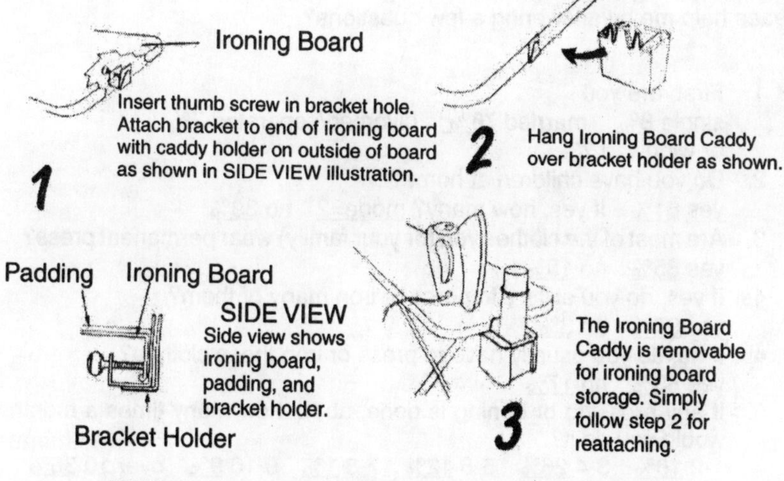

FIGURE C5.2. Ironing Board Caddy Instructions for Use

TABLE C5.1. Number of Households in the Southeastern United States

State	Number (in thousands)	State	Number (in thousands)
Alabama	1,342	Arkansas	816
Florida	3,744	Georgia	1,872
Kentucky	1,263	Louisiana	1,412
Mississippi	827	N. Carolina	2,043
S. Carolina	1,030	Tennessee	1,619
Virginia	4,452	W. Virginia	1,705

Source: U.S. Bureau of the Census

Mildred then sought to identify characteristics of potential consumers through the questionnaire shown in Figure C5.3. This questionnaire produced data on (1) marital status, (2) family composition, (3) incidence of ironing, (4) spray starch/sizing usage, (5) problems related to functions performed on the ironing board, and (6) reactions to features/price of the proposed new product.

Hello, my name is _________________, and I am doing a survey for Marketing Research Associates in Jackson, Mississippi, on the care of clothing. I am not selling anything, and nothing will be mailed to you. Would you please help me by answering a few questions?

1. First, are you
   single 8% married 78% divorced/separated 7%
   or widowed 7%
2. Do you have children at home?
   yes 61% If yes, how many? mode=2 no 39%
3. Are most of the clothes you (or your family) wear permanent press?
   yes 85% no 15%

4a. If yes, do you still try to press or iron many of them?
   yes 97% no 3%

4b. If no, do you usually have to press or iron these clothes?
   yes 83% no 17%

5. If any pressing or ironing is done, about how many times a month would you do it?
   1-2 16% 3-4 26% 5-6 12% 7-8 1% 9-10 9% over 10 36%
6. Do you use an ironing board?
   yes 98% no 2%
7. Do you use spray starch or sizing?
   yes 70% no 30%
8. If yes, about how many cans of starch/sizing would you use in a year?
   1-3 40% 4-6 22% 7-9 3% 10-12 10% 13-15 3% 16-18 3%
   19 or more 19%
9. Do you ever do mending, sewing, or altering on the ironing board?
   yes 64% no 36%
10. If yes, do you ever experience problems of:
    a. starch/sizing can falls off the ironing board? 77% yes
    b. no convenient place to keep pins, scissors, etc., close to your ironing board? 72% yes

FIGURE C5.3. Market Potential Survey for Ironing Board Caddy

11. If an inexpensive product were on the market that held your spray starch, scissors, pins, etc., and would attach to your ironing board, would you buy it?
    yes 56% no 21% maybe 19% don't know 4%
12. How much would you expect to pay for such a product?
    $8.00 or less 0% $10.01 to 11.00 1%
    $8.01 to 9.00 16% $11.01 to 12.00 2%
    $9.01 to 10.00 45% over $12.00 36%

Thank you very much for your help.

FIGURE C5.3 *(continued)*

TABLE C5.2. Profile of Potential Buyers Based on Jackson Market Study

Characteristic profile*	Answers
Marital status	78% married
Children at home	71% children at home
Type of clothing	82% most are permanent press
Pressing of clothes	100% press clothes
Frequency of pressing	6-7 times per month
Use of ironing board	100% use ironing board
Use of spray starch/sizing	100% use spray starch/sizing
Problems—can falling off	95% experienced this problem
Problems—no place for pins, etc.	89% experienced this problem
Expected price	$9.75 median price expected

*The values shown are for those respondents who said they would purchase the product if available.

By cross tabulating the responses to the questions, it was possible to develop a profile of the potential purchasers of the caddy. Table C5.2 shows the profile derived from the respondents who said yes to the question about buying the product. Mildred thought these characteristics pointed to clearly identifiable market segments interested in this product.

Mildred estimated that she would need a minimum capital investment of about $132,200 to launch the product if she decided to market the product herself. This included $75,000 for a regional promotional campaign, $12,200 for production of the first 5,000 units, $26,500 for the injection mold, $3,500 for package design, and another $15,000 to cover packaging and administrative costs. She knew she had access to that amount because of her real estate holdings but wondered if she should risk it in the venture or simply try to license another company to manufacture and market the product.

Mildred knew she would only get about 10 percent per unit under a licensing arrangement but that the manufacturer would assume the risk of the venture. She also wondered what would be involved in a thorough and complete marketing strategy for the ironing board caddy if she were to implement it herself and not license the product. Production and marketing of a previous product idea had produced disappointing results. She also knew she needed to decide soon before someone else came up with a similar idea and she also wanted to get back the $9,500 she had already spent in getting the product patented.

Case 6

Jay's Travel Trailer Park

Robert E. Stevens
David L. Loudon
Bruce E. Winston

Jay Fenton had just completed his first year in the travel trailer park business. The purchase of the park a year earlier was Jay's "retirement" investment. The $300,000 purchase price seemed to be a way to invest some of his retirement funds in an area close to relatives but still provide an attractive annual income.

The thirty-nine-unit park was located off a main highway leading to a lake in one of the state's most beautiful and biggest resort areas. The park contained an office, swimming pool, laundry room, rest rooms, sanitary dump, and picnic areas. In addition, the park had the potential to add more trailer sites with water and electrical hookups. The park was located on the corner of a forty-acre plot, leaving plenty of room for expansion. Although there was no current access to a creek that bordered the property, there was potential for developing beach and boat access to the creek as well as other attractions.

The lackluster performance of the park caused Jay to consider other options. One possibility was to invest more money in park development and promotion to create a "destination park" rather than the current "pass-through" park orientation. Destination parks were developed with more amenities and guests averaged longer stays, while pass-through parks offered minimum amenities and were designed for guests en route to another destination. In searching for some answers, Jay obtained data on parks and camping from the state's tourism department.

Tourism and Recreation

The state has developed and supported a great deal of tourist and recreationally oriented attractions during the past decade. The development of a lake and dam gave impetus to more rapid development of this area.

The northwest area is the second-ranked area in the state for overnight visitors. Of the total 24,107,500 overnight visitors to the state last year, about 22 percent were in the northwest area (see Table C6.1).

Smith County attracts the greatest number of overnight visitors. Although Washington County is far behind as a destination, it leads the entire region as the economic and population center. As such, Washington County could be a source of weekend business during the slow seasons.

Overnight Campers

Overnight campers represent a specific segment of the tourism market. They accounted for about 7.2 percent of the state's overnight visitors last year (see Table C6.2).

More pertinent to this overnight segment is the number of group nights (shown in Table C6.3), which is the total number of parties (three to four people) times the number of nights' stay in a particular area. Table C6.3 shows the actual nights in total for the state and then estimated nights for the northwest area.

These two tables together show that last year, for example, 97,904 camping parties came to the area, stayed an average of 7.6 days, and

TABLE C6.1. Overnight Visitors in the Northwest Area

County	Visitors	State share (in percent)
Smith	2,543,340	10.55
Rankin	2,143,155	8.89
Simpson	26,515	0.11
Washington	605,100	2.51
Totals	5,318,110	22.06

TABLE C6.2. Camping Activity for the Past Three Years

	Two years ago	One year ago	Last year
Overnight campers	1,788,700	1,885,470	1,730,900
Parties	506,030	496,175	443,810
Average stay (nights)	7.4	6.8	7.6
Persons per party	3.6	3.8	3.9
Person-night	13,236,380	12,821,196	13,154,840
Spent per party-night	$31.45	$33.87	$35.97
Annual economic impact	$117,768,360	$114,277,040	$121,325,220
Percent by category			
Truck-camp	33.5%	32.0%	32.5%
RV-camp	49.6%	50.0%	49.0%
Tent-camp	16.9%	18.0%	18.5%
Total	100.0%	100.0%	100.0%
Trip nights	3,744,622	3,373,990	3,372,956

TABLE C6.3. Camper Party Nights: State and Northwest Region

	State			Northwest Region		
	Two years ago	One year ago	Last year	Two years ago	One year ago	Last year
Parties	506,030	496,175	443,810	103,129	109,010	97,904
Avg. stay	7.4	6.8	7.6	7.4	6.8	7.6
Group nights	3,744,622	3,373,990	3,372,956	763,155	741,268	744,070

used 3,641,594 RV campsites and 137,653 tent campsites. The area's share of campers is 63 percent of all overnight visitors, and that the percentage of campers by type is basically the same in the northwest area as for the state as a whole.

Competitive Analysis

Jay found that three basic marketing strategies are used by private trailer park facilities. One strategy is aimed at the overnight or pass-through market. These parks are designed to appeal to travelers en route to some predetermined destination or those who are in a location for a short (one- to three-day) period. These parks are usually close to major highways and offer few amenities to guests.

A second strategy is aimed at those travelers who are planning an extended stay (four to seven days) in a particular area—usually a resort or other major tourist attraction. Although these trailer parks do not contain many amenities, they are located very close to if not adjacent to the attraction.

A third strategy is geared toward the extended traveler, and includes all, or most, of the amenities in the park itself. Thus the park becomes the attraction and offers facilities and services geared to guests who will remain in the area for a few days.

Jay's research of competitors revealed that all three strategies existed in the northwest area of the state. The major competitors in the Washington-Smith County area are shown in Table C6.4. This table clearly demonstrates the differences in services offered in this area. Yogi Bear's Jellystone Park is by far the most complete—using the concept of a self-contained resort; it offers the full range of services. KOA and Safari basically use the same strategy but with fewer amenities. KOA's location on a major state highway also appeals to overnighters. Safari is being expanded at the present time to offer more sites and amenities.

Jay's Travel Trailer Park uses the strategy of not providing amenities but locating close to them. It is within a mile of the Corps of Engineers Recreational Area. The park offers nothing more than a place to park a trailer; however, a grocery store, boats, bait, picnic tables, and other amenities are all close to the park. A couple of mobile home parks in the area offer overnight hookups but cater strictly to overnighters and probably the overflow of other RV parks.

A new proposed park located only 100 yards off a major highway is planned and is awaiting a zoning decision. Judging from the location and amount of land used in development, it would appear to be aimed at the pass-through or short-stay market.

TABLE C6.4. RV Trailer Parks by Type of Amenities

RV trailer park	Coffee snack bar	Group shelter	Rest rooms	Laundry room	Swimming pool	Sanitary dump	Showers	Picnic tables	Rec room	Boats	Teen hut	Planned activities	All hookups	Tennis courts	Barbecue grill	Tent area	Playground	Number of units
KOA	X		X	X	X	X	X	X	X				X			X	X	60
Yogi Bear's Jellystone Park	X	X	X	X	X	X	X	X	X	X	X	X	X	X	X	X		60
Safari	X		X	X	X	X	X		X					X	X			24
Jay's Travel Trailer Park			X	X	X	X		X					X					39
Karl's Mobile Home Park					X			X										10

The real opportunities in the RV park business appear to be destination parks. These parks are close to major population centers (up to four hours driving time) and offer urban RV owners a chance for fun on weekends and vacations.

Destination parks require a major financial commitment because they offer many activities to keep guests busy. A typical list of activities and related facilities includes: swimming, fishing, and boating; golf (including miniature golf); children's playgrounds; horses; jet skis; waterskiing; separate recreational buildings for adults and youths; tennis; hayrides; picnic areas; Ping-Pong; shuffleboard; horseshoes; archery; hiking and bicycle trails; restaurants/bars; general store; laundries; movies; etc. Most important is a planned recreation program for children, teenagers, and adults. Such parks earn about half of their revenue from fees other than for space. The goal is fun, fun, fun for everybody, so that visitors stay longer and return frequently.

A second category of destination parks requires less investment in facilities but usually much higher costs for land. Located near a major attraction, such as Disney World, visitors to such parks are attracted by fun and sightseeing activities in the surrounding area.

RV park rates are rising rapidly, however, this has not affected RV travel; it is still more economical than other modes of travel.

Although the rate of return for a successful RV park investment is higher than for a mobile home park, the risk is much greater. Feasibility studies for RV parks are more subject to error; in contrast, such studies for mobile home parks are almost foolproof. One problem with RV park investments is that mortgage money is more difficult to obtain. The financial community is aware of the successful record for mobile home parks. RV parks are much newer and have no well-established financial record.

As Jay considered his options, he also reflected on the need for an effective marketing strategy. One consistent observation he made of private, nonfranchised trailer parks is that they lacked an effective marketing program. Thus, he realized that the marketing activities would be part of the overall effective management of the park.

Target Market

Although Jay carefully identified several potential market segments, he was not sure which of these he should target. The segments included the following:

1. *Cross-country travelers* en route to a predetermined destination looking strictly for overnight hookups.
2. *Cross-country travelers* en route to a specific area of the country but with no definite destination in mind—looking for some overnight and some short-stay (two to four days) accommodations.
3. *Local area residents,* usually weekenders, on short trips with a predetermined destination—tourist attractions, horse shows, lake recreation area, etc. They mostly want overnight hookups but also need some short-stay accommodations.
4. *RV clubs, large multiunit family groups, sport spectators* may be local area residents and/or nonlocal residents, depending on the nature of the group involved. They may want only overnight accommodations for a short stay.

Jay knew that the marketing mix (consisting of location, amenities, price, and promotion) should be put together with a specific group in mind. For example, a strictly overnight park would be located close to a major highway, offer few amenities, and not require a park theme. Figure C6.1 shows some of the possible positions available for a new or redesigned park attempting to "fit in" with existing offerings.

The current trend in travel trailer parks is in the direction of the high amenity concept such as Yogi Bear's Jellystone Park. These parks appeal to the extended-stay market (five to seven days) with a complete array of amenities from laundry rooms to planned activities for children. At the other end of the scale are mobile home parks, which have a few sites for travel trailers and offer no specific amenities.

Low Amenities				**High Amenities**
Karl's Mobile Home Park	Jay's Travel Trailer Park	KOA	Safari	Yogi Bear's Jellystone Park

FIGURE C6.1. Positioning a Trailer Park

Price

The prices charged by different trailer parks reflect three things: (1) competition, (2) amenities offered, and (3) usage or costs associated with serving guests. More amenities mean a higher price. Typical prices for RV parks reflect these factors and are shown in Table C6.5.

This price structure reflects current competitive prices for a park with several amenities. Jay's Travel Trailer Park currently offers few amenities and charges a flat rate of $10.50 per night.

Using current revenue and expense data, Jay knew he could estimate revenue and expenses for expansion to a 100-site destination-type park for average occupancy levels. The park had a 45 percent occupancy rate last year, and Jay felt that repositioning the park as a 100-site destination park would increase occupancy rates to at least 65 percent. If expansion was feasible, Jay knew he would still need an effective marketing plan to increase occupancy.

Jay estimated that an additional $1,110,000 would be needed for expansion of the park and to reposition it close to the Yogi Bear's Jellystone Park. This included sixty-one more sites, additional pools, a water slide, access to the river, a canoe rental shop, a riding stable, driving range, and other amenities needed to reposition the park as a destination park. (See Table C6.6 for income statement information.)

A less aggressive strategy would be to add some amenities and position the park close to the KOA-Safari position. Jay felt that this would result in a 55 percent occupancy rate and would require an investment of $500,000. Table C6.7 offers a breakdown of the cost estimates for adding additional amenities.

Jay was still undecided about what he should do next. He knew he could not continue the current losses but wondered if a more effective promotional campaign might increase occupancy without any additional capital investment.

TABLE C6.5. Typical RV Park's Services and Rates

Amenities	Price per night
All hookups (two people)	$19.95
Water or electricity only	$15.50
No hookups	$10.50
Charge for each additional person	$1.00
Air conditioner or heater surcharge	$5.00

Table C6.6. Last Year's Income Statement

Income and expenses	Income
Occupancy, based on seven-month season (210 days)	45%
No. of spaces rented	3,686
Gross income	$38,703
Extra occupancy	2,126
Vending machines, laundry	2,835
Store sales	28,350
Total Income	$72,014
Less cost of goods sold	27,010
Gross profit	$45,004
Less expenses	
Salaries	$10,500
Payroll taxes	1,994
Property taxes	2,723
Insurance	2,160
Advertising and signs	3,000
Office expense and supplies	300
Telephone	600
Electricity	3,835
Water	1,834
Maintenance—bldg and ground, trash	200
Maintenance—pool	1,000
Maintenance—roads	300
Depreciation	9,226
All other expenses	2,500
Total expenses	$40,172
Income before debt service and taxes	$4,832
Interest expense	12,000
Taxes	0
Profit	($7,168)

TABLE C6.7. Amenity Cost Estimates

Amenity	Cost
Land preparation/landscaping	$180,000
Site preparation (61)	61,000
Paving roads	250,000
Drainage/sewage	75,000
Large pool (40' x 80')	38,000
Small pool (25' x 60')	33,000
Recreation building (adult)	125,000
Recreation building (youth)	112,000
Water slide	30,000
River access	25,000
Canoes/rental building	15,000
Concession stands (2)	6,000
Stable and horses	15,000
Driving range	25,000
Miniature golf range	25,000
Equipment	30,000
Miscellaneous supplies	15,000
Additional working capital	50,000
Total additional capital	$1,110,000

Case 7

The Box Factory, Inc.

Robert E. Stevens
David L. Loudon

Charles Smith was wondering what his next move should be in developing the market for his die-cast toy car display case. He knew he had to use a cost-effective marketing strategy based on his limited financial resources. He did not feel he had developed his ideas well enough to secure a bank loan or to interest potential investors, but he knew he had a product with good potential sales if he could just get it launched. He was even more encouraged when a friend showed him all the Web sites related to collecting die-cast toy cars and trucks and the widespread interest in these collectibles.

Background

Charles and Cindy Smith incorporated Box Factory, Inc., in 1994 for the purpose of making and selling woodwork crafts. The Box Factory developed a product for the storage and display of die-cast toy cars. The basic design of this product is a wooden shadow box in the form of an eighteen-wheeler truck (see Photo C7.1). Encouraged by friends and relatives, the Smiths set up a mail-order system for consumers to purchase the product. The Box Factory advertised the display case in *Country Sampler* magazine in April 1994. Response to the advertisement was overwhelming, so the Smiths decided to keep concentrating on mail-order sales. The success of the wooden product prompted the Box Factory to research producing the truck in plastic and distributing it through retail outlets. A patent was obtained for the plastic display case.

To act as an agent for the production and sale of the plastic product, the Box Factory entered into an agreement with a design company. A

PHOTO C7.1. The Wooden Display Unit

prototype of a plastic, injection-molded truck was developed and displayed at a convention in 1995. At this time, a major toy manufacturer requested a proposal on licensing the product from the design company. The design company responded to the Box Factory with a new agent agreement that drastically increased the design company's commissions. The Smiths refused to sign the new agreement and all communication with the design company ceased. Since that time, no further attempts to commercialize the product have taken place.

The contract established with the design company expired in August 1997, thus releasing the Box Factory from any obligations. This created the opportunity for the Box Factory to enter the market with the plastic, injection-molded, wall-mounted display case for die-cast toy cars. Die-cast toy cars considered to be collectibles ranged in price from .99 to $99.00.

Market Analysis

Collecting stamps, baseball cards, or bottle caps has always been a favorite pastime; this does not differ in the case of die-cast toy cars. Many people collect Hot Wheels and Matchbox brand cars; like most collectors, these individuals want to showcase their collections.

Customers of Box Factory, Inc., are mainly adults. Men mostly collect Hot Wheels and Matchbox cars, while women tend to buy them as gifts for collectors or for their children. The Internet contains numerous Web sites devoted to the collection of Hot Wheels and Matchbox toy cars. These data reinforce the belief that a market for the Box Factory's product exists.

Parents will buy the product to fulfill two purposes: first, to provide a place for their children to store the cars when they are not playing with them, and, second, as a way to decorate their children's rooms. Collectors need a place to store their cars, showcase their prized collectibles, and organize their collections.

Since the majority of the purchases are gifts, sales for the wooden display case typically increase during the months between October and January (due in large part to Christmas). Women make the majority of the purchases of the display cases, and men make most of the individual toy car purchases.

Product Analysis

A wooden version of the mounted display case enjoyed a great deal of sales success in the years leading up to this point. Advertising in only one hobby magazine produced sales of over $50,000 in the first year. These magazine ads generated sales for five years, with a number of sales occurring after the ads were cut at the beginning of 1996. The sales of the wooden display case provided evidence that a market for this type of product existed. Table C7.1 shows the sales of the wooden display case; however, promotions for this product were cut in 1996.

The new product would be an injection-molded, wall-mounted display case designed to house twenty die-cast cars (Hot Wheels and Matchbox cars). The case is fashioned in the design of an eighteen-wheeler truck; it is 28 inches long, 8 1/2 inches high, and 3/4 inches deep. The estimated production cost per unit is $3.50.

The product would be shipped in a protective cardboard box, the same type of package used by the Box Factory to send the wooden display cases to its customers. This package costs approximately $.40 per unit.

TABLE C7.1. Sales by Year

Year	Sales (in dollars)
April 1991 to December 1993	200,000
January 1994 to December 1994	60,000
January 1995 to June 1995	20,000
July 1995 to December 1996	20,000

The two target markets identified by the Smiths (collectors and children) complicate the product decision. In order for the same product design to relate to different market segments with such vast distinctions, the product must differ in some way. One inexpensive means of changing the product might be accomplished by varying the color. For the product to appeal to the collectors' market segment, a wood finish appearance could be used. The children's segment could implement a more "playful" image with red, blue, and yellow to better relate to this target market.

Competitive Analysis

Presently, there was no direct competition for the Box Factory's mounted display case. However, a few similar products could pose a threat. A handful of companies produce plastic display cases designed and marketed to display much larger cars. These cases could be used to showcase seven to ten die-cast cars; however, they do not have any eye-catching features. They are made up of plastic bases and clear plastic detachable domelike boxes. Some companies also produce these cases to mount on a wall. Another possible more direct competitive threat is carrying cases for small die-cast cars. Numerous types of cases are designed to house many die-cast cars yet they are not fashioned to be fixed display cases. Rather, they are designed to transport or store the toy cars. Table C7.2 shows current competitive cases available and their prices.

TABLE C7.2. Carrying Cases and Prices

Product	Price
Hot Wheels Sto & Go (drag race case and playset)	$12.99
Hot Wheels City Playset	6.99
Hot Wheels Sto & Go (parking and service)	14.99
Hot Wheels Sto & Go (super city playset)	14.99
Hot Wheels Cargo Plane	14.99
Hot Wheels Super Rally Case	9.99
Tara Toy 48 Car Case	6.99
Fast Lane (Toy Car Briefcase)	9.99
Garage (Toy Car Storage Case)	5.96

Financial Analysis

The Smiths need to develop an analysis of their breakeven point for the plastic display case based on sales of the product directly to consumers as well as through retailers. If the product is sold to retailers, the price would have to provide an adequate markup. Table C7.3 presents the expected cost structure for the Box Factory display case.

The production cost of $3.50 was based on a production run of 5,000 units in one color. At 10,000 units production cost would drop to $2.75 per unit. The company that would produce the plastic unit had a production capacity of 25,000 units a year. The injection model itself would have to be designed and manufactured by a design company. The cost of the mold was estimated to be about $7,500.

The Smiths need to estimate how much additional investment is needed to launch the new product (including the injection mold, purchase of an inventory of shipping boxes, and an investment in inventory of 5,000 display cases) and how much operating capital is needed to cover expenses until the sales volume is high enough to cover operating expenses.

TABLE C7.3. Display Case Cost Structure

Costs	Per item
Variable costs	
Production	$3.50
Packaging	$0.40
Shipping (from factory)	$0.50
Comment card and postage	$0.45
Total variable costs	$4.85
Fixed costs	
Storage	$500.00
Salaries	$25,000.00
Advertising	$600.00
Insurance	$250.00
Total fixed costs	$26,350.00

Marketing the New Display Case

The financials for the product indicated that even at sales of 5,000 to 10,000 units, the product could be very profitable. The Smiths' previous marketing approach had been fairly successful for the wooden display case, although they felt they were in the dark about what past customers thought. The Smiths wondered how, in the future, they could obtain feedback from purchasers and exactly what information should be sought to be managerially useful.

The ads they had run produced sales for several years. However, they were not sure about how to reach the children's market or how to get their product into retail stores. The Smiths wondered if there might be a number of children's magazines in which to promote the product or if there were some good specialty magazines carrying unique products that could generate mail orders. They had also thought about approaching one of the toy car manufacturers and trying to negotiate a license agreement to manufacture and distribute the display case but were not sure about the implications of such a move.

Their accountant had also suggested contacting one or more major retail chains as possible distributors. The volume that could be generated by any one of these large retailers would probably be enough to handle their current production capacity, especially if they were producing three different colors of the case.

All of these options were evaluated before a decision was made about proceeding with trying to raise the money to launch the new product.

Case 8

Central Bank: Automatic Teller Machines

Robert E. Stevens
David L. Loudon
Bruce E. Winston

As Mark Chappell, vice president and manager of the Automatic Banking Services department at Central Bank, reviewed the latest month's ATM transaction data and the consumer survey on ATM usage, he wondered about what pricing strategy to recommend to the executive committee. Should he recommend an annual fee for all cardholders, continuation of the current \$.50 fee transaction, or a raise in the current fee to \$1.00 per transaction? The impact of this decision could dramatically affect the bank's earnings and ATM usage.

Background

Automatic teller machines (ATMs) emerged in the early 1970s and have experienced relatively widespread acceptance by both the industry and its customers with many financial institutions aggressively promoting the use of ATMs to their customers. Increasing the base of ATM users can contribute to an institution's profitability in a number of ways. Such transactions can help the institution to (1) stabilize or reduce staff, (2) cut paper processing costs, (3) generate fee income, (4) generate investment funds from high average balance accounts, and (5) reduce labor hours or avoid extending hours. The key to obtaining these benefits is to direct market to those consumers who are most likely to obtain and use an ATM card on a regular basis.

ATMs are extremely important to Central Bank's overall strategy for two reasons: (1) the bank is domiciled in one of the last states to eliminate antibranch banking laws which prohibit a bank from building branches, and (2) studies had shown that the bank's cost per transaction for an ATM was only about $.50, compared to $1.00 per transaction with a "live" teller. Since an earlier test case declared that ATMs did not constitute a branch, their proliferation gives banks the opportunity to expand geographically to reach new markets. Central Bank currently has fifteen ATMs in various locations throughout the city with a monthly average of 5,576 transactions per ATM (see Table C8.1). The services offered at each ATM are (1) cash withdrawals, (2) balance inquiries, (3) account transfers, and (4) deposits. The cash withdrawals may be from a checking account, savings account, or credit card. All of the bank's ATMs (except for the one in the bank's main lobby) are "stand alones," meaning not inside a store but in their own constructed facility. All the ATMs can be accessed twenty-four hours a day, seven days a week. Each ATM is also equipped with a phone for recorded messages on how to use the ATM or what to do if a problem occurs.

TABLE C8.1. Average Transactions per Machine

Machine number	Average monthly transactions
1	3,894
2	7,227
3	6,423
4	8,270
5	3,721
6	2,112
7	6,340
8	7,432
9	4,565
10	5,541
11	5,212
12	4,613
13	4,825
14	6,130
15	7,328
Total	83,633

The average use per machine of 5,576 per month was higher than the national average of 4,310. Chappell attributed this to the state antibranch banking laws that prohibited branches prior to 1985. Consumers became more dependent on ATMs to conduct banking transactions and carried on these behavior patterns even after branches were permitted.

The Consumer Study

The bank hired a marketing research firm to study ATM usage in the area to determine reasons for ATM use, services used most, average usage, problems encountered in use, and questions about ATM fees. During a six-week period, the marketing research firm conducted a telephone survey of a random sample of 500 area residents who used the services of a financial institution. The sample is believed to be representative of Central Bank's 10,500 noncommercial clients.

ATM Usage

Tables C8.2 and C8.3 show ATM usage patterns among respondents. Table C8.2 shows that withdrawals and deposits were the two most frequently used functions among study respondents. These figures correspond to national percentages on usage characteristics.

Table C8.3 shows frequency of use among respondents. The first two categories of users were called *active users* based on their frequent use of ATMs. These consumers have altered their banking patterns to include frequent use of ATMs.

TABLE C8.2. Function Performed by ATM Users

Function	Percentage*
Deposits	35.6
Withdrawals	77.6
Transfers	3.80
Balance inquiry	3.80
Bill payment	1.00

*Percentages add to more than 100 percent due to respondents giving more than one answer.

TABLE C8.3. Usage Frequency

Frequency of ATM use	Percentage*
Three or more times per week	26.4
One or two times per week	35.2
Once every two weeks	9.90
Once every three weeks	12.1
Less than once a month	8.80
Don't use anymore	7.70

*Does not add to 100 percent due to rounding

Price Sensitivity Among Cardholders

Price sensitivity was measured by asking respondents about (1) current card charges, if any, (2) desired transaction charge alternatives—annual fee versus transaction fee, and (3) maximum charge under their choice of fee payment before they would stop using their card. This permitted establishing a method of payment and a level of payment for card usage.

Seventy percent of the respondents reported that they were not currently paying a fee for ATM use. About 17 percent said they were paying a fee and about 13 percent did not know whether they were paying a fee at the current time.

When respondents were asked their preference for an annual fee or a fee per transaction, 46.3 percent preferred an annual fee, 29.1 percent preferred a fee per transaction, 20.1 percent said they would not use their card if a fee were charged, and 4.5 percent were undecided. Active cardholders showed a stronger preference for an annual fee than inactive cardholders. Only 23.8 percent of the inactive cardholders reported that they would not use their card if the bank charged a fee.

The fee schedules for both the annual fees and the fees per transaction were presented as alternatives by asking if the respondents would be willing to pay a given amount. These results are shown in Tables C8.4 and C8.5. The percentages shown in each column represent the proportion of respondents who were willing to pay a maximum given fee before they would stop using their card.

TABLE C8.4. Alternative Fee Levels for an Annual Fee by Card Ownership

Maximum annual fee	Central Bank %	Non–Central Bank %	Both combined %	All cardholders %
Less than $5 a year	4.7	6.1	0.0	5.5
Pay $5 a year	32.6	24.2	9.10	25.3
Pay $10 a year	30.2	33.3	9.10	29.7
Pay $15 a year	9.30	27.3	54.6	20.9
Pay $20 a year	11.6	0.00	18.2	7.70
Pay $30 a year	9.30	0.00	0.00	5.50
Over $30 a year	2.30	9.10	9.10	5.50

TABLE C8. 5. Alternative Fee Levels for a Fee per Transaction by Card Ownership

Transaction fee	Central Bank %	Non–Central Bank %	Both combined %	All cardholders %
Less than $.25 per transaction	9.1	18.0	0.0	12.5
Pay $.25 per transaction	27.3	33.3	66.7	34.7
Pay $.50 per transaction	45.5	28.2	33.3	31.9
Pay $.75 per transaction	13.6	7.70	0.00	11.1
Pay $1.00 per transaction	4.60	10.3	0.00	8.30
Over $1.00 per transaction	0.00	2.60	0.00	1.40

For those who preferred an annual fee (46.3 percent), almost all (95.4 percent) would be willing to pay $5 a year for the use of their card. For those who preferred a fee per transaction (29.1 percent), at least 90 percent were willing to pay at least $.10 per transaction to use their card. There were no significant differences between active versus inactive cardholders and all cardholders combined on fee preferences and fee levels.

Awareness of ATMs in the study area was very high overall (94.3 percent), but awareness of specific transactions was concentrated on cash withdrawals and deposits. About 64 percent of the adult population reported owning a card that could be used in an ATM.

Among cardholders, 64.5 percent were classified as active, i.e., they used their card at least once every two weeks. Of the active cardholders, 36.4 percent used their card three times a week and 51.2 percent used their card one to two times a week. The majority of cardholders (68.1 percent) used their cards close to home, on Friday, Saturday, and Sunday, and between 3 p.m. and 10 p.m., which corresponds with the hours banking facilities are traditionally closed.

The overriding motivation for ATM usage was "convenience." Cardholders ranked "overall convenience" more frequently (51.9 percent) than any other reason for getting an ATM card. The second-highest ranking reason was "open twenty-four hours a day" (17.3 percent) which implies convenience and availability.

The Pricing Dilemma

Chappell's review of banking literature revealed three schools of thought about pricing ATM services. The first was not to charge customers at all for ATM use. This was based on the cost savings associated with ATM use compared to "live" tellers. Since financial institutions actually cut costs through ATMs, not charging a service fee should encourage their use.

The second approach was to charge customers for the use of ATM services either with an annual fee (fifteen to twenty dollars per year) or a fee for each transaction ($.50 to $1.00 per transaction at Central Bank's ATMs). This would create an additional source of revenue for the institution and help recover the cost of ATM installations. (ATM installations ranged from $35,000 for an in-store location to $100,000 plus for a "stand-alone" location.)

A third school of thought, which was gaining popularity among banks, was to provide some free transactions, say three to four per quarter, and then charge for additional transactions on a quarter-by-quarter basis.

Chappell was convinced that the bank should continue to charge for ATM services but wondered if the annual fee might cause nonusers of ATMs to complain or even switch to a competing financial institution.

Case 9

Cell Tech

Janet Bear Wolverton
Philip C. Fisher

In 1995, the Oregon Department of Agriculture listed algae harvested from Upper Klamath Lake and associated waterways as the state's seventh largest agricultural dollar crop with estimated overall annual sales between $140 and $150 million. Products made from algae were sold as nutritional dietary supplements. Although there were at least nine firms actively harvesting, processing, and marketing algae from Upper Klamath Lake, the largest of these by far was Cell Tech.

Cell Tech marketed its products through over 350,000 distributors with the trademark Super Blue Green Algae (SBGA). These products included tablets, concentrates, beverage mixes, capsules, wafers, and pet foods.[1] The fervor and enthusiasm of the distributors and users of the Cell Tech products were readily apparent from their many Web site acclamations. This enthusiasm was demonstrated in the following statement:

> Anyone who eats SBGA can tell almost immediately why it is called the super food. It contains virtually all the vitamins and minerals the body requires. . . . SBGA is virtually the only plant on earth that contains all the essential amino acids. These are present in the exact proportions for optimal metabolism. . . . SBGA also contains many pigments known for their ability to boost the body's immune system. . . . Cell Tech was established for the sole purpose of harvesting, processing and marketing this valuable natural resource.[2]

The company's excitement and belief in the products was evident—algae were referred to as "nature's perfect food." Algae were believed to cure many medical problems ranging from depression to allergies and arthritis. In addition, algae's proponents listed many benefits including feelings of increased energy, vitality and stamina; reduction and alleviation of stress, anxiety, and depression; relief from the discomforting symptoms of fatigue, hypoglycemia, poor digestion, and sluggishness; improved memory and mental clarity; and a wonderful feeling of well-being and stronger sense of self-direction.[3]

Cell Tech company publications emphasized the nutritional and health benefits of its products. Distributors were encouraged to use the products to enjoy better health, think more clearly, and have more energy.[4] Cell Tech literature repeatedly stressed the safety and quality of its products; however, outside the Cell Tech community the detractors expressed their concerns for false claims and public safety. Eating algae was a topic that produced strong feelings and opinions in both believers and nonbelievers.

Cell Tech

Daryl Kollman was the headmaster of a Montessori school in South Carolina when he became interested in research on algae as a possible nutritional supplement. His experiences as a teacher had led him to speculate that poor nutrition was responsible for the lack of energy and the short attention span he observed in schoolchildren. He quit his job and tried for seven years to cultivate, grow, and market algae as a dietary supplement. He was not successful until someone familiar with his work sent him a sample of blue-green algae from Upper Klamath Lake. Blue-green algae flourished naturally in Upper Klamath Lake without cultivation.[5]

In 1982 Daryl and his wife Marta formed Cell Tech. The business needed capital, however, and two venture capitalists from Nevada provided the initial financing and took 100 percent ownership of the company. Daryl was hired to operate the company with an opportunity to buy it back with its profits. The Kollmans worked for several years doing the hands-on work of harvesting and processing the algae.[6]

Initial sales were disappointing, and in the spring of 1983, the investors threatened to pull out. Daryl persuaded them to let him try network marketing. They agreed, provided he took a 50 percent pay cut.[7] In network marketing products are available only through distributors and cannot be purchased in retail stores. To become a distributor one must be sponsored by another distributor. For Cell Tech, new distributors could start with an order for as little as forty dollars plus shipping and handling charges and were paid commissions once their sales reached an annual level of $250.[8] Once a new distributor had been registered, he or she could order products directly from the company, which then shipped directly to the new distributor. Network marketing succeeded for Cell Tech. By the fall of 1983, Cell Tech had 26,000 distributors who were generating $1.6 million in monthly sales.[9]

Sales continued to increase and in 1990, the Kollmans bought out the investors.[10] By 1995, according to Marta Kollman, Cell Tech was processing 100,000 pounds of algae daily,[11] and its portion of the algae market in 1995 was reported to be $133,600,000. In 1996 Mrs. Kollman stated, "This year, we're processing 800,000 pounds a day."[12]

In an article in *Success* magazine, the Kollmans outlined their "four principles of precision networking": (1) build an information base, (2) build a buyer network, (3) build intimate communication with distributors, and (4) make haste slowly.[13]

To build their information base, the Kollmans amassed a wealth of information about the nutritional benefits of algae. Cell Tech published a journal, *New Leaf,* a monthly newsletter, *Letter from Daryl,* and periodic catalogs. These publications were replete with information about nutritional research and the claimed benefits of eating blue-green algae. The buyer network was built through distributors for whom nutrition was an important consideration. The *Success* magazine article quoted Marta Kollman as saying, "Many of our distributors are the sort of people who belong to Greenpeace and Save the Whales, wear Birkenstock sandals and eat granola."[14] Commission levels were based on cumulative sales so the financial incentives to sell the products increased as time passed. This led long-time distributors to remain interested in selling the company's products.

Cell Tech's intimate communications were achieved through the *New Leaf* magazine, the newsletter, and company teleconferences.

Computer support was available that provided distributors with up-to-date copies of their distribution networks and earnings reports on demand. (Since distributors signed up other distributors, who then signed up others, it was difficult for the initial distributors to know just who was in their downlines or "genealogies.") Although the rapid growth of Cell Tech seemed to belie the philosophy of "make haste slowly," the Kollmans believed that all 280 million people in the United States needed their algae.[15]

In their articles and newsletters, the Kollmans emphasized the physical, spiritual, and mental benefits of their products as a means for self-actualization. For example, the December 1996 *Letter from Daryl* included the following:

> **IT WORKS!** Eating Super Blue Green Algae makes me feel different physically, mentally, and spiritually. **I love this Algae!** I've never found anything I could eat that made such a huge difference in my life. I had an instant and very dramatic change in my physiology.[16]

Cell Tech's harvesting facilities are located a few miles south of Upper Klamath Lake along the "A" canal whose waters came from the lake.[17] The company extracts 1 gram of algae from 50 gallons of water and uses a vacuum drum to squeeze out the excess water. Cell Tech's product reaches the freezer within five minutes of being extracted from the Klamath Falls canal according to Kollman.[18]

By late 1996, it was estimated that distributors were selling $18 million worth of SBGA per month to an estimated 1 million users of the product in Canada and the United States.[19] The distributors did all the selling and advertised the product directly to customers by talking about their personal experiences. In an article on blue-green algae, Judith Mandelbaum-Schmid pointed out that algae eating has gone from relative obscurity into a national craze in just the past few years.[20]

Cell Tech has worked hard to promote its image as a visionary organization whose mission is to improve nutrition throughout the world. The Kollmans also remain interested in children's nutrition. Cell Tech had a program called "The 10 percent Solution" in which it claimed to provide 10 percent of the algae harvests to "people who have the greatest need and the fewest resources."[21] The result of this program was the distribution of algae products to children in Nicaragua, Cambodia, Dominican Republic, Guatemala, as well as in the United States. Cell Tech worked with an organization called Hope L.A. Horticulture Corps. When asked if the kids really ate SBGA, the program director of Hope L.A., George Singleton, replied, "It's like a sacrament to them."[22]

Klamath Lake's blue-green algae products supplied by Cell Tech were used in studies in Nicaragua where many important vitamins and minerals have been lacking in children's diets. A 1995 study distributed by Cell Tech indicated that the addition of algae to the diets of the children resulted in increased learning abilities and improved physical condition of those children taking them on a regular basis.[23] Claims were made of the Nicaraguan children's schoolwork showing great improvement. "Average test scores skyrocketed from 64 percent to 85 percent," according to Cell Tech.[24] But critics pointed out that any source of nutrition provided to children who are malnourished could show similar results.

Products

In 1997 Cell Tech's product line included nutritional supplements, probiotics, enzymes, animal food, and skin and hair care products. The nutritional products were sold in capsules, tablets, liquid, wafers, and powders which could be mixed with water or used as ingredients in baking or cooking other foods. These products were advertised as providing vitamins, trace minerals, chlorophyll, protein, amino acids, and beta carotene.[25]

Probiotics contain "friendly bacteria" designed to improve the functions of the digestive system. Enzymes improve the efficiency of digestion by helping in the breakdown of the natural nutrients in food so that they can be used by the body.[26]

Users of Cell Tech products are encouraged to begin with a six-week regimen that eventually includes all three types of products: supplements, probiotics, and enzymes. The daily cost of using Cell Tech products ranges from $1.25 for the nutritional supplements to $2.50 for a regimen including all three types of nutritional products.[27]

Cell Tech offers a line of five skin care products including cleansers, creams, and moisturizers. Hair care products include shampoo, a hair conditioner, and a scalp cleanser. Company advertising emphasizes that the products are natural and enriched with Super Blue-Green Algae.

The animal food product is a blend of algae products that are advertised as rich in vitamins, minerals, enzymes, and amino acids. Claims stated that the product provided "building blocks for strengthening your animal's immune system."[28]

Cell Tech products are part of a rapidly growing dietary supplement industry that includes vitamins, herbal products, mineral supplements, ginseng, garlic products, and algae. Annual sales of dietary supplements were estimated at $4 billion in 1995.[29] Although sales of vitamins were estimated to be growing at 6 percent annually, sales of other dietary supplements were growing at 35 percent annually.[30]

Distribution

Cell Tech's products are sold through a system called network or multilevel marketing. In this form of marketing, products are sold only by individuals who are enlisted by other distributors. Each enlisted seller has the right to buy from the company and resell to consumers. Each seller can also become a distributor by enlisting others to sell the products. Distributors get a commission both on the sales they make to consumers and the products sold to the sellers they have enlisted. If their sellers become distributors and enlist others, the original distributor receives a commission on their sales as well. In this way, some distributors may have literally thousands of distributors and sellers in their networks and receive commissions on all their sales. Critics call this type of marketing a pyramid scheme.

Network marketing is fairly prevalent in the nutritional supplement industry. Herbalife is another company selling dietary supplements and using network marketing. The system is used in other fields. Mary Kay and Amway are well-known companies that use some variety of this method of selling.

Cell Tech distributors promote the company's products using company brochures and video and audiotapes. Some distributors produce their own video and audiotapes. Cell Tech distributors also make extensive use of the Internet. It was estimated that in June 1997 there were approximately 4,000 distributor Web sites. Some but not all of these sites display a Cell Tech approval number.

Cell Tech distributors have praised network marketing as a fun way to make money through sharing a good product with friends, relatives, and acquaintances. They point out that traditional distribution methods also contain multiple levels, and that retail prices are often more than double manufacturing costs. Network marketing is said to be particularly effective when the product being sold requires consumers to have a lot of information before they purchase it.[31]

Cell Tech distributors receive commission checks from Cell Tech on all their sales. Cell Tech also sends commission checks to the sponsor for all products ordered by distributors they sponsored. All distributors are encouraged to sponsor other distributors so that they earn commissions on the products they sell to consumers but also on products sold to the sponsored distributors.[32]

Information provided by Cell Tech distributors was that approximately 55 percent of the retail price of Cell Tech products was returned to the distributor, the distributor's sponsor, the sponsor's sponsor, etc. Price lists published by the distributor showed that Cell Tech distributors received a 25 to 30 percent margin on the products they retailed.[33]

Ethical and Legal Problems with Network Marketing

Critics of network or multilevel marketing argue that it is inherently flawed. The most fundamental flaw is that the demand for any product is finite. Since network marketing distributors are always encouraged to sign up more distributors, the distribution network tends to grow exponentially. Eventually, market saturation occurs and results in distributors having products for which there are no customers. Other objections are that the network marketing companies make blatant appeals to materialism and greed, that the claims for products being sold are often unsubstantiated, and that distributors are encouraged to use their relationships with family members and friends to sign them on as distributors. The eventual collapse of the multilevel organization then brings disillusionment and alienation.[34]

Some companies using multilevel marketing have been found to be in violation of federal law. A publication of the United States Postal Inspection Service[35] listed three elements which would make a multilevel marketing program illegal: (1) expectation of a monetary or other gain from participation, (2) the monetary gain being dependent on the efforts of others in levels below you, and (3) a fee to participate.[35]

Blue-Green Algae

Blue-green algae are a group of microorganisms known scientifically as cyanobacteria. Although early scientists thought the cyanobacteria were true algae, research resulted in their classification as a major group of bacteria in 1971. The popular name *blue-green algae* is derived from the coloring of their blooms, and the fact that both these bacteria and true algae carry out photosynthesis.[36]

Blue-green algae are aquatic organisms that grow rapidly when several conditions occur simultaneously: a quiet or mild wind, and water having a balmy temperature that is neutral to alkaline with an abundance of nitrogen and phosphorus nutrients.[37] In late summer, under these ideal conditions, the blue-green algae come together to form water blossoms as they float to the surface to obtain light for photosynthesis.

One of the world's prime growing sites for blue-green algae is Upper Klamath Lake in Oregon. An estimated 100,000 tons of algae develop in this 125-square-mile shallow lake each year.[38] "In August and September layer upon layer of the living organisms make wide areas of Oregon's largest recreational body of water impossible to see into."[39] During this time, while the blooms are on the surface, the blue-green algae are harvested for human consumption. Since the 1990s a growing number of companies have harvested the algae from the lake as well as from canals south of the lake.

Federal Regulation

Under the 1958 Food Additives Amendments to the Federal Food, Drug, and Cosmetic Act, the Food and Drug Administration (FDA) regulated dietary supplements to ensure that they were safe and that their labeling was truthful. However, federal regulation of dietary supplements was severely curtailed with the passage of the Dietary Supplement Health and Education Act of 1994 (DSHEA). With this act Congress amended the 1958 law and reduced the federal role in regulating dietary supplements.

The DSHEA defined a dietary supplement as a product (1) intended to supplement the diet and containing vitamins, minerals, herbs or other botanicals, amino acids, or combinations of these ingredients; (2) intended for ingestion in pill, capsule, tablet, or liquid form; (3) not represented as a conventional food or as the sole item of a meal or diet; and (4) labeled as a dietary supplement.

The DSHEA bans dietary supplements that contain ingredients that present a significant risk of illness or injury. It bars claims for dietary supplements when they purport to prevent, cure, or mitigate a specific disease (unless approved by the drug provisions of the Federal Food, Drug, and Cosmetic Act). Dietary supplements are required to have nutrition labeling and to be manufactured under conditions that ensure their safety. The DSHEA did not, however, require that the manufacturers of dietary supplements prove through testing that their products were safe or actually contributed to the health and well-being of their consumers. Rather, the FDA had the burden of proof that the products were unsafe before they could bar their sale.[40]

A Question of Safety—Claims and Counterclaims

Cell Tech marketing touted SBGA as "one of the planet's most perfect foods," with claims of increased energy and stamina, better moods, improved mental alertness, and better digestion. Claims of cured depression, allergies, and a plethora of other illnesses abounded. Reportedly, SBGA consumption produces a rush of energy.[41]

Andrew Weil, a nationally recognized expert on natural approaches to health, stated, "The fact that Super Blue Green Algae has a stimulant effect really bothers me. It seems quite possible that the product contains some sort of pharmacological agent, and it's worrisome that nobody knows what it is."[42]

There have also been many reported incidents of illness caused by SBGA, particularly diarrhea, headaches, numbness, and heart palpitations.[43] Under law, dietary supplements can be marketed without any testing for safety. The burden of proof that a product is not safe rests with the FDA. Although the FDA has received complaints about SBGA, until proof that SBGA when taken as directed presents a risk to users, the FDA is powerless to act.[44]

Cell Tech distributors were aware that these reactions could result from eating SBGA. Some noted in their pamphlets and newsletters that mild gastrointestinal illness is normal and a desirable side effect of SBGA's detoxifying, or cleansing, action.[45]

The National Council Against Health Fraud (NCAHF), however, noted that the concept of "detoxification" not only has no medical validity but can also be deadly. Lack of concern for side effects kept Herbalife salesman Bivian Lee from consulting a physician when he experienced a variety of adverse symptoms while learning to become a user of the products he intended to sell. He ignored the symptoms for more than two weeks before finally collapsing. The thirty-five-year-old retired professional football player died before he could see a doctor.[46]

The reported illnesses associated with eating SBGA have been attributed by some to the quality of the water in Upper Klamath Lake.[47] Additional concerns have centered on the water in the canals south of the lake. Cell Tech harvests the algae by trapping it in screens placed in canals that run from the lake through farmlands and residential and industrial areas. Speculation arose that the canal waters contained additional contaminants due to the runoff.[48]

Judith Mandelbaum-Schmid believed it was possible that the diarrhea, headaches, and other reported symptoms from algae eaters are caused by naturally occurring toxins in blue-green algae.[49] Evidence showed that exposure to sublethal levels of blue-green algae hepatotoxins are responsible for temporary stomach, intestinal, and liver problems in humans.[50]

Toxicity

The blue-green algae sought by processing companies and harvested from the lake belong to the species *Aphanizomenon flos-aquae* (AFA). Although this species is harmless, research has shown that many species of blue-green algae are toxic or poisonous. In the 1950s and 1960s the National Research Council in Ottawa, Canada, isolated the poisons produced by two of the most toxic blue-green algae, *Anabaena flos-aquae* and *Microcystis aeruginosa*.[51] The poison produced by the *A. flos-aquae,* a neurotoxin, was named anatoxin-a. The *M. aeruginosa* toxin, a hepatotoxin, was called microcystin.

These lethal toxins were defined by the symptoms they produced in animals. Neurotoxins interfere with the functioning of the nervous system and often cause death within minutes after the algae is eaten. Hepatotoxins damage the liver and can kill animals by causing blood to pool in the liver. Although the neurotoxins and hepatotoxins are the most dangerous, they are not the only poisons produced by blue-green algae. Cytotoxins are also produced; these poisons can harm cells but do not kill multicellular organisms.

Scientists worried that the toxic varieties of algae that grew alongside the *A. flos-aquae* in Upper Klamath Lake might be contaminating SBGA.[52] Although no human deaths had yet been traced to blue-green algae, concern existed about the modern fad of eating blue-green algae as a health food. Professor Wayne Carmichael pointed out that no guidelines required those marketing the algae to monitor their products for contamination by potentially poisonous strains. He noted that the safety of cyanobacteria is questionable because they are often gathered from the surface of an open body of water. Without using sophisticated biochemical tests, neither sellers nor buyers can distinguish toxic from nontoxic strains.[53]

During the 1996 harvesting season a crisis occurred when the toxic species of blue-green algae, *M. aeruginosa,* was found. "Upper Klamath Lake contained so much *Microcystis aeruginosa* . . . that the Oregon Health Department advised people to avoid any contact with the lake water and keep their pets and livestock away from it."[54]

Some people claimed that the *M. aeruginosa* is common only in Agency Lake, a smaller lake connected to the north end of Upper Klamath Lake, but the companies that harvested the algae directly from Upper Klamath Lake ceased operations until the *M. aeruginosa* had gone away. Cell Tech continued harvesting from the canals south of the lake, claiming that their processing and toxicity tests made it unnecessary for them to stop harvesting. Cell Tech's toxicity tests were performed by private laboratories and the results were not available to the public.[55]

State Regulation

Prior to 1997, the Oregon Department of Agriculture, responsible for ensuring the safety and wholesomeness of food products, had made no attempt to regulate the growing algae processing industry. In May 1997, because of concerns over the increase in *M. aeruginosa* during the 1996 harvesting season, department officials announced plans to begin regulating the blue-green algae industry starting with a standard for the purity of algae products. The department notified algae processing companies that it planned to require licensing and an inspection program for certain processing activities.[56]

In notifying processors, the Oregon Department of Agriculture conceded that the toxins were a worldwide concern.[57] Based on drinking water standards used in Canada, England, and Australia, the Oregon Department of Agriculture proposed to establish a maximum of one part per million of microcystin, the toxic substance produced by *M. aeruginosa*.[58] The department also stated its intent to require algae processing companies to make provisions for water monitoring, sampling methods, laboratory procedures, and a plan for recalling products already on the market that did not meet the standards. The department also notified the companies to be prepared to discuss the labeling of blue-green algae products as it related to consumption by children.[59] Officials expressed a special concern about the consumption of algae products by children since they are more susceptible to damage from toxins.[60]

Reported industry reaction to the Oregon Department of Agriculture's plans varied. International Aquaculture Technology, one of five companies that were cooperating in an aquaculture development council, supported the move. A separate association of three algae companies felt that the proposed plans were arbitrary. Another competitor thought the regulations were unnecessary. A consultant for Cell Tech stated that Cell Tech was willing to accept a reasonable amount of regulation, and that the company was trying to work with state officials to arrive at standards that would protect consumers and which would be achievable by the industry. It was also reported that industry officials were asking the state to ease the standard to as high as ten parts per million.[61]

In June 1997 officials of the Oregon Department of Agriculture and the Oregon Health Division met with about thirty representatives of the algae processing industry and representatives of the U.S. Food and Drug Administration to discuss the proposed standards. Media representatives were not allowed to observe the meeting. After the meeting Oregon Department of Agriculture officials commented, "We and the industry are working in a cooperative fashion to keep the industry in business and to protect the public. Once we've proposed a standard, there will be an open and public process. This is a complicated issue that is not easily reduced to sound bites."[62]

Media representatives criticized allowing industry comment before public hearings as creating the perception that the standards would be influenced more by the industry's ability to comply with the standards than what was safest for the public. They also criticized the Oregon agriculture and health officials as being too slow to recognize the public interest in developing health standards for algae products.[63]

The 1997 August Celebration

Thousands of Cell Tech distributors attended the 1997 "August Celebration" in Portland, Oregon. During the testimonials and ceremonies that took place at the celebration, this microbe was acclaimed as the answer to many of the world's health and nutritional problems.

However, Cell Tech was facing issues that could not be ignored—the foremost of which was the potential state regulation. The publicity resulting from the discussions surrounding the state regulation of the algae industry had focused public attention on the industry as a whole and fueled the ethical controversy surrounding its products. In addition, attention had been brought to bear on the children who were being fed algae as a dietary supplement. In light of these issues, Cell Tech faced many challenges in the coming years.

Case 10

The Interfraternity Council

Robert E. Stevens
David L. Loudon
Bruce E. Winston

Bill Conners, advisor to the Interfraternity Council, faced the challenge of developing a promotional plan to increase membership in the university's six social fraternities. Although the percentage of the male student body who were members of a campus fraternity was about 1.5 percent above the national average of 7 percent, other universities in the region had from 2 to 25 percent higher participation in fraternities (see Table C10.1). Bill felt that an effective promotional campaign could increase membership and help position fraternities as an important part of campus life.

Background

A fraternity is an association of men selected in their college days by a democratic process. A student expresses interest in a fraternity and, in turn, a fraternity expresses interest in a student in a membership recruitment process known as "rush." A mutual interest results in an invitation for membership, followed by a period in which the pro-

TABLE C10.1. Male Student Body Membership in Fraternities As a Percent of Total Male Student Body

Membership	Percent of total
Local	8.5
Regional	8.7-10.2
National	7.0

spective member "pledges" or undergoes a trial period to learn about the fraternity and its members as well as demonstrate at or above the required level for formal initiation into the fraternity.

Fraternities have existed in the United States since the early 1800s. Today, there are 61 national and international fraternities. Most fraternities place emphasis on four areas: (1) scholarship, (2) leadership, (3) philanthropy, and (4) social activities.

According to the National Interfraternity Conference, Inc. (NIC), the 1989 undergraduate membership in the sixty-one collegiate social fraternities in the United States was a record 400,000 students. This figure represents 300,000 undergraduate members and 100,000 new pledges or initiates. The percentage of membership is approximately 7 percent of the total male undergraduate population at U.S. universities and colleges.

Membership has been increasing in recent years, as has the number of chapters on campuses throughout the United States. In the 1989 *Fraternity Fact Book,* the National Interfraternity Conference provided the following reasons why record numbers of students are joining social fraternities:

- Develops interpersonal skills
- Offers mutual assistance and understanding
- Assists in orientation to college life
- Offers advice and counsel
- Encourages scholarship
- Increases social poise
- Provides leadership and business training
- Fosters high ideals

Supporting Information

Although there are nearly seventy national college social fraternities in existence, fifty-eight of them are grouped into an advisory body called the National Interfraternity Conference. This organization, which was formed in New York City on November 18, 1909, meets annually and concerns itself with many problems confronting the fraternities.

Fraternities have undergone many changes in organization. The National Interfraternity Conference indicates that there are nearly 2 million members of fraternities, with more than 7,000 active chapters. More than 2,800 of these chapters own their homes with a value of better than $150,000,000. Since World War II, nearly 100 colleges and universities have invited fraternities and sororities on their campuses; only one has eliminated them.[1]

Basic Expectations

In an effort to lessen the disparity between fraternity ideals and individual behavior and to personalize these ideals in the daily undergraduate experience, Nine Basic Expectations of fraternity membership have been established by the National Interfraternity Conference.[2] According to these expectations, a fraternity member will

- know and understand the ideals expressed in fraternity ritual and strive to incorporate them in daily life;
- strive for academic achievement and practice academic integrity;
- respect the dignity of all persons by not physically, mentally, psychologically, or sexually abusing or hazing any human being;
- protect the health and safety of all human beings;
- respect property of others by neither abusing nor tolerating abuse of property;
- meet financial obligations in a timely manner;
- neither use nor support the use of illegal drugs, and neither abuse nor support the abuse of alcohol;
- acknowledge that a clean and attractive environment is essential to both physical and mental health; therefore do all in his power to see that the chapter property is properly cleaned and maintained; and
- challenge all his fraternity members to abide by these fraternal expectations and will confront those who violate them.

A Few Statistics on Fraternity Men

- 71 percent of those listed in *Who's Who in America* belong to a fraternity.
- Of the nation's fifty largest corporations, fraternity men head forty-three.
- 85 percent of the Fortune 500 executives belong to a fraternity.

- Forty of forty-seven U.S. Supreme Court justices since 1910 were fraternity men.
- 76 percent of all congressmen and senators belong to a fraternity.
- U.S. president and vice president, except two in each office, born since the first social fraternity was founded in 1825, have been members of a fraternity.
- 63 percent of the U.S. president's cabinet members since 1900 have been fraternity members.
- An NIC report shows a majority of the 600 NIC fraternity chapters are above the All-Men's scholastic average.
- A U.S. government study shows that more than 70 percent of all those who join a fraternity/sorority graduate, while less than 50 percent of all nonfraternity/sorority persons graduate.
- Less than 2 percent of an average college student's expenses go toward fraternity dues.
- Over 85 percent of the student leaders on some 730 campuses are involved in the Greek community.
- Many celebrities were fraternity or sorority members, such as: Johnny Carson, Cindy Crawford, Michael Jordan, George Bush, George W. Bush, David Letterman, Bill Clinton, Anne Klein, Liz Claiborne, Jimmy Buffett, John Elway, Lou Gehrig, Martin Luther King Jr., Frank Gifford, Ted Koppel, Neil Armstrong, Amy Grant, Donna Mills, Elvis Presley, Jane Pauley, Faith Daniels, John Goodman, and Candice Bergen.[3]

The University's Six Fraternities

Bill was advisor to the six campus fraternities: (1) Delta Sigma Phi, (2) Delta Chi, (3) Kappa Alpha, (4) Kappa Sigma, (5) Pi Kappa Alpha, and (6) Sigma Nu. Fraternity membership represented about 7.5 percent of the male students enrolled at the university. Average costs for joining a fraternity at the university are shown in Table C10.2.

Research Data

As part of a marketing research class project, Bill worked with a student research team in conducting a survey of male students enrolled in courses at the university who were not members of a frater-

TABLE C10.2. Average Cost for Fraternity Membership

Fees for membership	Cost
One-time fees	
Pledging fee	$35
Initiation fee	135
Monthly fees	
Pledge dues	$30
Active dues	45

nity. The survey sought to gain insight into why these male students chose not to join. Bill furnished the group with a printout of all male students enrolled in the spring semester who were not members of a campus fraternity.

The research team working on this project drew a random sample of 150 students with local area telephone numbers. Of this sample, eighty students were surveyed using a questionnaire that sought (1) personal data on age, family income, high school activities, etc.; (2) awareness and knowledge of fraternities including the number on campus and cost of membership; (3) sources of influence on the decision not to join a fraternity; and (4) attitudes toward fraternities and fraternity activities.

The major findings of the study included the following:

1. Most respondents (70 percent) had little knowledge of the number of fraternities on campus or the cost of joining.
2. Juniors and seniors had more favorable attitudes toward fraternities than did freshmen and sophomores.
3. Most respondents (66 percent) had not read any material on fraternities before deciding not to join.
4. The most influential factor in the decision not to join was personal perception of fraternities (see Table C10.3).
5. Respondents saw fraternities as: (a) a good way to meet people, (b) helping people in the community, (c) being helpful when looking for a job, and (d) a brotherhood (see Table C10.4).

TABLE C10.3. Mean Scores on Level of Influence

Level of influence (descending order)	Mean value
1. Personal perceptions	2.6
2. Fraternity reputations	2.2
3. Finances	2.0
4. Peer influence	1.8
5. Family perceptions	1.8
6. Advertising/publicity	1.7
7. Religious beliefs	1.3

Scale: 1 = none; 2 = not too much; 3 = significant; 4 = most

TABLE C10.4. Mean Scores on Attitudinal Dimensions

Attitudinal dimensions	Mean value
1. You have to be rich to belong to a fraternity.	2.2
2. Fraternities are "rent-a-friends."	2.6
3. Fraternities are a good way to meet people.	4.3
4. Fraternities are a brotherhood.	3.6
5. Fraternities can help when looking for a job.	3.7
6. You do not need good grades to be in a fraternity.	2.6
7. You have to be a jock to be in a fraternity.	1.9
8. You have to do drugs to be in a fraternity.	1.6
9. You have to date sorority girls to be in a fraternity.	1.9
10. Only fraternity guys can date sorority girls.	1.9
11. Being in a fraternity is just for the time you're in college.	2.9
12. Fraternities help people in the community and on campus.	3.8
13. You have to drink to be in a fraternity.	2.2

Scale: 1 = strongly disagree; 2 = disagree; 3 = undecided; 4 = agree; 5 = strongly agree.

The student research team analyzed the responses in Table C10.4 by student classification. This analysis revealed a significant difference between the attitudes of juniors and seniors as compared to freshmen and sophomores. Juniors and seniors had more favorable attitudes toward fraternity membership than did freshmen and sophomores. The student research team concluded that continued exposure to fraternity members and their activities resulted in an increased positive attitude toward fraternity membership.

Promotional Plan/Budget

Bill was still undecided about (1) the target for marketing efforts, (2) what promotional strategy to undertake, (3) the content of promotional messages, and (4) how large a budget request to submit. The council did have about $5,000 accumulated over the past three years for development. He felt he could gain council approval to use this over the next three years. He also had access to the university-wide area telephone service (WATS) line so he could use telemarketing as a part of the promotional effort.

Case 11

Jill's House of Cakes

Phylis M. Mansfield
Jacquelyn Warwick

Jill sat looking around her kitchen imagining what it would look like twice as big, crowded with people, all making cakes. She had started out baking cakes for friends and family but somewhere along the line it had developed into a small but growing business. She wondered if growing was what she really wanted, and if her neighbors would let her expand her business in her home without complaint. Jill knew she needed to talk to someone with business experience, which was why she had called her friend Debbie, a business consultant, and invited her to lunch. They were to meet in thirty minutes to discuss Jill's future business plans. As she stood and picked up her car keys Jill sighed and mumbled to the empty kitchen, "What am I getting myself into?"

Home Business

Jill had always loved to bake, and her cakes were the talk of every family gathering. It became part of the family tradition to ask what her secret was to making cakes extra light and moist; but Jill, who thought it was flattering to have so many people ask her, would never tell how she accomplished the feat. Family members began to tell their friends who, in turn, started to ask Jill to make cakes for their special family occasions. Before she knew what had happened, she was making ten to fifteen cakes each month. Yet it was not until her best friend from college asked her to send a cake to Connecticut for a very special birthday that Jill found her niche in the market: mail-order cakes. After that, Jill began making three special-order cake packages per day for every major occasion and celebration (such as thank yous, congratulations, birthdays, anniversaries, Christmas, and Easter) for her friends and shipping them all over the continental United States.

A good share of Jill's business involved making and shipping birthday cakes, which brought in the most consistent cash flow, but not nearly what was needed to buy all the decorating supplies and ingredients for the different holiday seasons that were the biggest times of year for her business. Because of this, capital management was a constant concern since shortages of cash reserves were always a problem.

Even so, Jill's business appeared to be growing quickly in a world where people are all moving at a faster pace and want a gift that can be sent quickly and easily. Since many have moved toward the trend of impersonal, mail-order gift giving, Jill felt that what she provided was the unique opportunity to offer both: a gift sent by mail yet still a "personal" special occasion celebration package. Thus, the uniquely packaged gourmet cake becomes a wonderful alternative to the ever-familiar flowers or candy.

Price

Although Jill had been pricing her cakes at the $20 to $22 level, she was doubtful she could maintain that price with the new cost structure and higher level of competition. When assessing the price of the product, Jill determined she wanted her cakes to be priced below or consistent in price with other gifts that could be delivered to homes. She decided that the delivered cost of the cake should be at the mid- to upper-twenties range (including an 8.5 percent state sales tax and a standard shipping and handling charge for routine orders). To ensure price satisfaction and repeat purchases, Jill often put special party favors or other little treasures unique to the occasion in each box. These inexpensive items would also be included in the standard delivered cost of the cake.

Distribution

To keep customers satisfied, Jill promised that orders placed before noon would be shipped the same day. This usually worked, although sometimes when people called at 11:30 a.m. it presented a problem. Since 11:30 a.m. was so close to the deadline, if there was any problem in the kitchen the order would often not be sent the same day as promised. Her friends had always been very understanding about this, with the exception of one of her new neighbors, Elizabeth.

A bigger concern was with her delivery service provider. Although she called and stated she needed a refrigeration unit for her shipment, often the driver would come unprepared to pick up her delivery and would need to go back a second time before the cakes could be shipped. However, her husband told her she was worrying over nothing since they did not charge extra for the return trip and the delivery was still sent out on time; so, overall, Jill was happy with her current delivery system.

Competitors

Although her business was growing, Jill constantly worried over the competition in the marketplace. She knew by the number of catalogs she received every day in the mail that there were numerous decisions to consider before current or future customers made the purchase of a gift.

Jill knew that by using accessibility and free delivery as a weapon, local bakeries and gift shops in the area were all current competitors. Indirectly, all the catalogs and florist shops with their toll-free order numbers, as well as national toll-free florists, were potential competitors since they could add gourmet cakes to their product mix and quickly enter the market at any time. As of yet there were no local competitors in the surrounding communities. However, she knew other national companies, which sold cakes through their catalogs, direct-mail pieces, or through their stores, shipped into her area as well as throughout the United States. The constant national advertising campaigns from these large companies were of major concern to Jill since she did not have the same name recognition or money to compete on their level.

Current Operations

When Jill originally made her decision to expand her business, she asked her sister to help her during the day. Her sister readily agreed but spent a great deal of time chatting and catching up on family news and little time actually helping to produce cakes. Jill also asked her two older children to help her after school for a few hours each afternoon. Although not the best solution, it worked well for the first few weeks and then her children became involved in after-school activities and could no longer be counted on to be consistently available to help her in the kitchen. It was not until Jill had to make five cakes in one day and both children called to tell her they would not be home, that Jill decided she needed to seriously look for a stable workforce to help her make cakes.

As she explained her dilemma to her family they suggested she contact the Work Wagon, a nonprofit organization that found employment for adults who were homeless or in halfway houses by matching their abilities and skill levels to the employer's needs. Although it took a great deal of extra work on her part, Jill found the workers to be a relatively good, inexpensive labor force that was dedicated and willing to learn and work. She found that special care needed to be taken to ensure that workers were properly trained before operations would work smoothly and that often retraining was necessary. Jill also experienced the same concern with this group of workers that she had with her children; they often had health-related appointments or found other interests which kept them from consistently showing up when they were scheduled to work. In addition, many would often go back to their former living arrangements on the streets or would leave the city for other areas of the country.

Jill mulled over her current worker situation and product line schedule. With her one oven, she could bake two cakes at a time. She had performed a task and time assessment for the working day based on baking procedures, creating the boxes, and filling them with cakes and paper items. The task and time assessment found the estimated time for one complete package to be 2 hours and 55 minutes, with one hour at the end of each day devoted to specific decorating tasks and training.

Training was becoming a burden for Jill who was beginning to feel that all she did was train her workers, which was not why she had gotten into the cake business. She was not only doing the nightly ongoing training but she also had to train new employees. It took approximately three months of intense training before the new employees excelled at the tasks assigned to them. She was concerned about this since, in her mind, more time needed to be devoted to baking cakes and less time to training employees.

Promotional Activity

Although Jill had depended solely on word-of-mouth advertising to keep her business running, that was beginning to change. The Work Wagon featured her in the local newspaper as a smart, local businesswoman who hired many of their workers, teaching them a skill that would last them a lifetime. Through this simple publicity piece, Jill had seen her business almost double. She wondered what would happen if she began to advertise in that same local newspaper.

Thoughts of Expansion

While Jill was thinking over the leap to advertising in the local newspaper, her family was so enamored with her name in print and how much good her business was doing in the community that, over dinner one evening, they began to plant the seeds of expansion. Having taken a few accounting and marketing classes at the local community college a number of years before, Jill knew that to realistically think of selling cakes to people other than friends and family there were several things she would have to consider. She would have to review her cost and pricing situation, speak to the Work Wagon management or other sources about hiring more employees, and make numerous other decisions about the business. First, she would need to contact some contractors to discuss the costs of enlarging her kitchen. A preliminary but realistic estimate from her husband was $12,500 total. He had also learned that there were no zoning restrictions on expansion. Once she began to take expansion seriously, Jill realized she would need Debbie's help to establish a long-term strategic plan particularly focusing on marketing.

Jill's Research

Before Jill could develop any strategic plan to increase her cake business she decided to gain additional information by talking to people in her hometown about their likes and dislikes when ordering gifts over the phone or through the mail. To accomplish this task and to keep her costs down, Jill asked eight close friends to come and had each of them bring five other people. A total of forty people came, which Jill broke into four different "focus groups"; an adequate number, she thought, to give her the required information.

Results from Jill's focus groups suggested several potential marketing opportunities in three key areas: (1) local customers who are looking for unique gift ideas; (2) businesses who would purchase cakes for incentives or gifts; and (3) customers outside her local area.

Jill needed to decide on many issues as she attempted to put together a plan. One set of issues pertained to marketing. She needed to decide what customer target segments she should aim at and the extent to which these should be local, regional, and/or national. She was unsure how she should reach potential customers with her message, as well as what that message should be, and whether anything should vary based on the target group. Because of the good publicity she had already received in the media, she thought that this might be an important future component of any promotion plans she assembled. Moreover, she was not clear about how customers would contact her. Things were simple enough if she stayed local; but going national might complicate this process considerably.

Timing of her promotion and production plans also hinges on dates for important holidays during future years, although she did not know which ones were most relevant. In addition, Jill was not sure that she could continue her single price for cakes. Her decision on cake prices could vary from a one-price approach to having a price differential for special-order customization outside of holiday orders. She was aware that many businesses used price incentives such as coupons or frequent buyer plans, but she did not know whether this would be a viable approach for her business.

Jill estimated that during the first year of expanded operations she could sell an average of five cakes per day for the first three months, then increase by five orders per day quarterly, until she reached an average of twenty orders per day at the end of the first year. The second year, Jill hoped to double the first year's sales volume, and by the fifth year, she thought sales could reach fifty orders per day. Jill estimated that she would have to invest only $4,500 in advertising expenses to reach this sales level the first year, which she felt would drop to around the $1,000 range for succeeding years.

Jill estimated that she could produce cakes a total of 260 days each calendar year. She expected to pay wages of $5.25 per hour, for an eight-hour day to her workers, and a sales commission of 3 percent of sales. Administrative expenses were estimated at $1,500 per year. Her cost for shipping each cake is $3.00 unless a rush order is required, necessitating a 150 percent premium. Jill estimated the total production cost for 200 cakes as shown in Table C11.1 based on the supplies required. Table C11.2 shows the estimated production times for cakes.

Luncheon Meeting

Jill arrived at the restaurant before Debbie and, once again, wondered if she was doing the right thing by planning to expand her business. As she saw Debbie come through the front door with a big smile

TABLE C11.1. Total Production Costs for 200 Cakes

Business supplies	Per 200 cakes	Unit size	Unit cost
Baking supplies			
Pound cake mix	$42.72	50-lb. bag	$ 42.72
Glaze for lemon cake	35.57	50-lb. pail	35.57
Glaze for chocolate bunt	45.48	50-lb. pail	45.58
Chocolate chips	57.98	50-lb. box	57.98
Flavoring for lemon cake	15.00	12 oz.	15.00
Total baking supplies	$196.75		
Packing supplies			
Tissue paper	$26.00	400 sheet/box	26.00
Shredded paper filler	21.00	10 lb.	21.00
Streamers strings	3.51	3 oz.	3.51
Confetti	3.80	1-lb. box	3.80
Greeting card	200.00	100	100.00
Brochure	30.00	100	15.00
Hats	80.00	100	40.00
Horn	54.96	100	27.48
Balloon	12.50	144	9.00
Musical candle	400.00	36/box	72.00
Boxes	120.00	100	60.00
Silk screen	360.00	50	90.00
Total packing supplies	$1,311.77		

TABLE C11.2. Cake Production and Assembly Times

Activity	Time
Production times per cake	
Preparation time (start of each day)	15 minutes
Mixing time	5 minutes
Pouring batter in pans	5 minutes
Baking time	30 minutes
Cooling time	30 minutes
Glazing time	30 minutes
Drying time for glaze	60 minutes
Wrapping time	15 minutes
Clean-up time (end of each day)	30 minutes
Assembly time per ten cakes	
Folding boxes	10 minutes
Folding paper	10 minutes
Placing items in box	10 minutes
Shrink wrap	20 minutes

on her face, she knew her response would be positive. As Debbie sat down, Jill pulled out her notes and was anxious for them to be incorporated into the business plan she needed. Debbie now had the task of producing a thorough and workable marketing strategy recommendation for Jill that included pro forma income statements for years one, two, and five.

Case 12

Putting the Frosting on Cheerios

Cara Okleshen
Marilyn Okleshen

Introduction

After a series of new product failures along with negative publicity, the upper management at General Mills recognized the need for strategic change in order to improve profitability. In May 1995, as part of implementing that change, the board of directors of General Mills appointed Stephen Sanger as the CEO and chairman of the $5 billion company. Sanger's personal goals for the company included increasing earnings and creating growth through product innovation. General Mills planned to use Frosted Cheerios, the first in a series of proposed product introductions, as a template for future product growth.

In March 1995, Mark Addicks, appointed team leader, took on the task of launching Frosted Cheerios. Although Addicks was a novice in new product introductions, he was chosen to provide a fresh vision for the new promotion of a traditional brand. Addicks and his team immediately began their research by focusing heavily on ready-to-eat breakfast cereals but also looking at the introduction of other popular consumer products as well. Addicks stated, "We learned a lesson from venerable Coca-Cola in 1985 that reformulating a popular brand, a proven seller, was risky. Frosted Cheerios had to be differentiated from its rivals including other in-house brands and the cheaper store brand imitations such as Tasteeos."

Company Background

In 1995, the largest portion of General Mills' business was ready-to-eat breakfast cereal, and the company ranked second only to

Kellogg's as the largest dry cereal company in the United States and Canada. The company had experienced success since the 1920s when both Wheaties and its follow-up, Cheerios, hit the shelves. To further solidify its position, General Mills entered a joint venture with Nestlé (leading to the formation of Cereal Partners Worldwide), making its products available in over forty countries. Cereal Partners Worldwide's sales were approximately $2.5 billion in 1995, thus it proved to be a financially solid move for both companies.

Although General Mills was successful in the cereal market, in 1994-1995 the company confronted its share of problems, threats, and challenges. "The fiscal year 1995 was not business as usual," Sanger announced in the company's annual report to stockholders. Until 1993 General Mills' profits and earnings per share had increased annually, as shown in Table C12.1. A disappointing financial trend then developed as total profit declined in 1993 to $470 million from the previous high, $506 million, in 1992. Although earnings per share were $3.10 in 1993, earnings per share spiraled downward to $2.95 in 1994, concurrently with a decline in profit to $376 million. By the end of 1995, total profit increased to $476 million, but earnings per share continued to decrease, reaching $2.33. Upper management attributed the earnings decline to various causes. In 1994, traces of an unauthorized pesticide were discovered in some of its cereal products. For over a year, General Mills had been selling cereal contaminated with Dursban, a pesticide not approved for human con-

TABLE C12.1. General Mills Five-Year Summary of Profits and Earnings per Share (in millions, except per share data)

Category	1995	1994	1993	1992	1991
Sales	$5,027	$5,327	$5,138	$4,964	$4,657
Cost of goods sold (CGS)	2,123	2,012	2,003	1,967	1,819
Selling, general, and administrative expense (SGA)	2,008	2,351	2,191	2,126	2,075
Other expense	529	494	438	375	290
Net income	$476	$376	$470	$506	$473
Earnings per share	$2.33	$2.95	$3.10	$2.99	$2.87

sumption. A routine FDA inspection uncovered its use. Y. George Roggy, a General Mills contractor, had utilized the pesticide to cut costs. General Mills spent over $140 million on purchasing the contractor's grains, recalling contaminated products, and cleaning up the infected production plants. In addition, General Mills faced a contingent liability from a class action lawsuit on behalf of consumers, along with negative publicity from the disaster.

General Mills' management also reported that the declining trend in earnings was caused by a series of failed new product introductions traced back to 1991. Wheaties Honey Gold, Sun Crunchers, Sprinkle Spangles, Hidden Treasures, and Triples all captured less-than-expected market shares (cereals need at least 0.5 percent market share to be considered a success). The series of failed new product introductions were blamed on poor promotional efforts and a lack of emphasis on product innovation.

Consequently, General Mills' executives were concerned about the company's sagging profits and decided upon an aggressive plan to counteract a further decline in earnings. Management separated its restaurant division (including Red Lobster, Olive Garden, and China Coast) and Gorton Foods from its consumer foods division, placed more emphasis on expanding international activities, and realigned itself with grocery customers by stressing grocery category management and long-term consumer-targeted marketing. In its cereal division, promotional practices were changed by eliminating inefficient promotional spending, such as couponing and giving free samples to consumers, and replacing them with lower retail prices.

Competition

In 1995, four primary producers dominated the cereal industry: Kellogg's, General Mills, Kraft General Foods Post, and Quaker Oats, as shown in Table C12.2. Kellogg's and General Mills' brands dominated the list of the top ten ready-to-eat cereals (as indicated in Table C12.3). One aspect of intense competition within the ready-to-eat cereal industry is new brand introductions: only one out of five new cereal brands succeed. Over the past ten years eighty percent of the increase in cereal sales had been attributed to new brands. Of the top ten ready-to-eat cereals, General Mills' Honey Nut Cheerios, introduced in 1979, was the most recent entrant.

TABLE C12.2. Leaders in the Ready-to-Eat Cereal Industry in 1995

Company	Sales	Market share (%)
Kellogg's	$3 billion	36.2
General Mills	$2.1 billion	25.7
Kraft General Foods Post	$1.1 billion	13.6
Quaker Oats	$.65 billion	7.9

Kellogg's based its success in new product introductions on using a low-risk, long-term strategy of introducing line extensions rather than completely innovating new brands. For example, Nut 'N Honey Cornflakes was an expansion of the Corn Flake line, a line in production since 1898. Post could not introduce product line extensions because it had fewer total brands. General Mills had little success recently with its own new products, and accordingly reformulated its strategy with product line extensions.

Cheerios' Background

Original Cheerios, introduced over fifty years ago, was the second most popular cereal brand in the United States, with annual supermarket sales totaling $294 million in 1995. However, Cheerios' position declined from 1989 to 1994; its market share fell from 4.7 percent to 3.6 percent. In contrast, Kellogg's Frosted Flakes was the number one ranked ready-to-eat cereal, with annual sales of $334 million in 1995 and a 4.2 percent market share.

The Cheerios brand line consistently had been one of the five most popular cereals in the United States. Prior to the release of Frosted Cheerios, three variations of the original proved to be successful by achieving greater than 0.5 percent market share. In 1995, Honey Nut Cheerios was ranked fifth in popularity (with annual sales of $211 million); Apple Cinnamon Cheerios was thirty-third (with sales of $68.3 million); and Multi Grain Cheerios was thirty-fourth (with sales of $66.9 million). Frosted Cheerios, the most recent introduction, was a fourth generation spin-off.

Addicks stated, "The key to a strong spin-off was the Frosted Cheerios' ability to generate its own demand, while remaining similar enough to maintain a consistent perception with the original Cheerios product."

TABLE C12.3. Top Ten Selling Ready-to-Eat Cereal Brands in 1995

Rank	Brand	Company	Market share (%)
1	Frosted Flakes	Kellogg's	4.2
2	Cheerios	General Mills	3.6
3	Corn Flakes	Kellogg's	2.9
4	Raisin Bran	Kellogg's	2.8
5	Honey Nut Cheerios	General Mills	2.7
6	Rice Krispies	Kellogg's	2.7
7	Froot Loops	Kellogg's	2.5
8	Special K	Kellogg's	1.9
9	Corn Pops	Kellogg's	1.9
10	Lucky Charms	General Mills	1.9

Product Introduction

"Because we have twenty-two active projects at any time, the idea of putting frosting on Cheerios had been discussed within the company for more than twenty years," Addicks commented. Plain sweetened cereal represented the fastest-growing cereal segment, one in which General Mills had traditionally not competed. Recognizing an opportunity for growth, General Mills' executives wanted to penetrate this portion of the cereal market. In light of previous failures with new product introductions, management chose the Cheerios brand to jump-start sales. Of the twenty-two active projects, management decided to back the introduction of an extension of its most successful product, Cheerios.

More than $40 million was spent on introducing Frosted Cheerios. The start-up funds were allocated to advertising (40 percent), trade (in-store) promotion (28 percent), other promotions (28 percent), and product development (4 percent). Frosted Cheerios was positioned against plain sweetened cereals such as Kellogg's Frosted Flakes, Corn Pops, and Mini-Wheats. Addicks reflected, "More money was spent to launch Honey Nut Cheerios in 1979. Although the amount of money spent to introduce Frosted Cheerios ranked second in the company history, the launch was in first place in terms of volume and profit in the first-year category."

Plain sweetened cereal appeals to and is consumed by both children and adults. The product development team experimented with different degrees of sweetness for Frosted Cheerios, and chose one sweet enough to appeal to children yet still pleasant to adults. Cheerios' original version contained one gram of sugar and three grams of fiber, while Frosted Cheerios contained thirteen grams of sugar and one gram of fiber. Frosted Cheerios was designed to appeal 60 percent to children and 40 percent to adults. In April and May 1995, Addicks' team conducted research on the consumer acceptance of Frosted Cheerios. The results of in-home tests revealed that 88 percent of children would eat the product.

The Target Market

"Our idea for the start of the launch of Frosted Cheerios was to take a snack target, instead of the kids target. We wanted advertising, which was targeted toward adults and children, like Frito-Lay and Little Caesar's. Within a target market of households with children, the primary target was children, aged six to twelve years. Kids watch prime-time TV, along with the adults," said Addicks.

Addicks' team considered alternative markets and channels for Frosted Cheerios. Hispanics were targeted with commercials running on Spanish-speaking television channels. Radio commercials targeting African Americans were played on selected stations as well.

Communication

In line with its new approach to product introduction, Addicks' team reviewed seven versions of Frosted Cheerios' packaging in the process of choosing a design that differed from traditional General Mills' cereal boxes in a variety of ways. For example, General Mills had never before used the box's electric blue color, which conveyed newness and energy. The cereal on the front exploded from the spoon and implied excitement. The imagery broke away from the traditional static cereal box front. The box had a glossy finish, which distinguished it from other boxes on the shelf.

The communication goal was to break away from the cereal ad cliché that consisted of one or two people in a wood-paneled kitchen sitting around the table quietly eating breakfast. The ads resembled snack food advertising to evoke the feeling of opening the cereal box and starting a party. Frosted Cheerios' slogan, "Tastes So Good the Box Never Closes," complemented that idea of selling the product's "fun" taste. Addicks noted, "With regards to the advertising budget, we spent the most on mass advertising, and less on kids' direct advertising."

Network television served as the primary communication medium for Frosted Cheerios. Commercials aired in virtually every time slot including prime time. Commercial content was fast paced with high audio stimulation. The communication appeals were targeted to both children and adults. Advertisements ran on shows such as *Roseanne, Home Improvement,* and the *Late Show with David Letterman* to reach broad demographic populations. The team considered advertising via cable television an efficient means to reach a broader consumer base. The team selected a cable television children's channel, and purchased syndication rights to shows including *Bewitched, The Brady Bunch,* and *Rocky and Bullwinkle* to air commercials for Frosted Cheerios. Addicks said, "The advertising campaign was designed to surprise consumers with the idea that a consumer may never know who may be looking into a box of Frosted Cheerios."

The team considered various celebrities for its ads in an effort to create an enduring image of surprise and one that would stand out against other big brand names such as Tostitos, Nike, and Reebok. The team chose Chris Elliot (a comedian), Gilbert Gottfried (a fast-talking jokester), and Queen Latifah (a rap artist) as spokespeople. One ad featured Gilbert Gottfried shouting, "This cereal is louder than me!" The team used animated icons such as the caped canine Underdog, and the villainous Boris and Natasha from the *Rocky and Bullwinkle* series. One consideration that failed to make the cut was cross-dresser RuPaul, with an ad tag line of "Oh no. The box is empty. Talk about a drag."

Addicks' team considered unique promotion approaches to gain consumers' attention such as towing an iceberg into New York Harbor. (They used a similar idea when the company hired a disc jockey to broadcast from inside a 5,000-pound block of ice and pitch Frosted Cheerios for more than thirty-eight consecutive hours.) Advertisements for all "new" General Mills' cereals were placed on over fifty million milk cartons. Nutritional literature touting the health benefits of Cheerios for toddlers was distributed to physicians' offices. In conjunction with Frosted Cheerios' livelier packaging, consumers could order a pair of Joe Boxer shorts made out of material resembling the box front and including the advertising copy line.

Stocking Frosted Cheerios

The product came to market in half the time (six months) of past General Mills' product introductions. In September 1995, General Mills distributed Frosted Cheerios to grocery stores. Relying on the Cheerios brand name, Frosted Cheerios achieved national distribution with unprecedented speed because of the product's ability to gain sufficient shelf space. "Because the normal profit margins in grocery sales are one to two percent, we offered a special introductory deal to stores to feature Frosted Cheerios. When the special expired the grocery stores got to keep the extra profit," Addicks said.

John Hooley, president and CEO of Cub Foods, stated, "Although shelf space was at a premium, it wasn't a difficult decision to make room for this cereal." According to store managers, they had a hard time keeping the shelves sufficiently stocked with Frosted Cheerios. Some stores actually limited the number of boxes a customer could purchase. In the first week of availability the product gained a 0.44 percent market share, while in the first month it achieved 2.5 percent share. Frosted Cheerios ranked among the top five cereals in the United States with retail sales of $35.2 million, after being on store shelves for only eight weeks!

As with any brand extension, Addicks' team was concerned about cannibalization. Would the entire Cheerios line suffer? Their concern was quickly alleviated as the four established varieties of Cheerios sustained a combined market share of more than 8 percent during Frosted Cheerios' introduction. None of the previous Cheerios extensions were considered direct competitors of plain sweetened cereals. Addicks stated, "As a result, Frosted Cheerios stole very little from other Cheerios brands. With everything that we did, Cheerios' market share actually grew during the launch. In fact, Frosted Cheerios stole market share from Kellogg's."

Project Review Meeting

In January 1996, Stephen Sanger called for a meeting with Mark Addicks and his team to review Frosted Cheerios' progress in the market. Specifically, they were to evaluate the actions taken by the project team to date, analyze promotional strategies, and develop alternative courses of action for Frosted Cheerios in the future. The team and General Mills' upper management took many risks with the introduction of Frosted Cheerios, such as reformulating a brand extension, committing to a $40 million promotional budget for a product introduction, and attempting untried marketing communication strategies. Reflecting on Frosted Cheerios' penetration of the sweetened cereal market, Sanger and Addicks were left with lingering questions: Were the risks worth repeating again with other new products? Could the introduction of Frosted Cheerios serve as a template for other General Mills' products in order to drive the company toward increasing profits, growth, and success?

BIBLIOGRAPHY

Addicks, Mark. Telephone Interview. November 14, 1997.

Fiedler, Terry. "Soul of a New Cheerios." *Minneapolis Star Tribune,* January 28, 1996, p. D1+.

General Mills 1995 Annual Report.

General Mills 1996 Annual Report.

Gibson, Richard. "A Cereal Maker's Quest for the Next Grape-Nuts." *Wall Street Journal,* January 23, 1997, pp. B1-B2.

Goldman, Kevin. "General Mills to Launch Frosted Cheerios." *Wall Street Journal,* July 25, 1995, p. B9.

Goldman, Kevin. "General Mills to Push Frosted Cheerios." *Wall Street Journal,* October 2, 1995, p. B5.

Haran, Leah. "Promos Go Soggy As Co-Marketing, Intros Freshen Cereals." *Advertising Age,* September 27, 1995, p. 22.

Helliker, Kevin. "Old-Fashioned PR Gives General Mills Advertising Bargains." *Wall Street Journal,* March 20, 1997, p. A1.

Rickard, Leah. "General Mills Gathers Rewards of Change." *Advertising Age,* July 10, 1995, p. 4.

Case 13

Spencer's Supermarket

Robert E. Stevens
David L. Loudon
Richard W. Coleman
Bruce E. Winston

Ron Spencer, owner and operator of Spencer's Supermarket, was wondering if he had made the right choice when he began using plastic grocery bags to sack customers' groceries. Like many grocery stores of the same size, Spencer's used paper bags for years but made the switch to plastic because of the significantly lower price. This reduction in cost meant a better bottom line (see Table C13.1 for income/expense information).

Located in a midsized southern city, Spencer's Supermarket is typical of small, independent, family-operated supermarkets. Spencer's customers consist of two segments: (1) senior citizens from the local neighborhood areas, and (2) students from the nearby college. Ron Spencer believes that while the store's friendly, neighborly atmo-

TABLE C13.1. Income and Expense for Retail Grocery Operations in the $3 to $5 Million Sales Range

Category	Percent of operations
Net sales	100.0
COGS	77.2
Gross profit	22.8
Operating expenses	21.6
Operating profit	1.20

Source: Morris Associates, 1996

sphere attracts some of the customer base, others come because of the convenient shopping. The store is within walking distance of several neighborhoods.

Recently, some of his student customers asked for paper bags instead of the plastic because they believed the plastic bags were bad for the environment. At first, Spencer simply noted their requests without giving it a great deal of thought. However, when customer requests persisted, Spencer wondered if the students' attitude might be part of a trend. Over the next few weeks, Ron noticed the growing number of environmental claims for products as diverse as trash bags and deodorants. He became curious and decided to learn more about this environmental issue. As noted in Table C13.1, operating profits are relatively low in supermarkets and plastic bags were less expensive than paper.

Ron learned that some of his student customers participated in a consumer survey dealing with environmental concerns. This involvement led students to request the paper bags. The students gave Ron a copy of other research results as well as the students' own findings from the consumer survey (Box C13.1).

BOX C13.1. Summary of Consumer Survey

Study method: Telephone interviews completed with 100 local residents. A student team comprised of eight members collected the data as part of a class project in a marketing research class.

Findings:

1. Forty-nine percent of the respondents stated they considered themselves environmentally concerned consumers (ECC).
2. They were typically married, white, and under forty-four years old, and had under $30,000 annual income.
3. They reported that they were aware of environmental claims about products and looked for such information when buying.
4. These consumers also stated that they were willing to go out of their normal shopping routine and pay higher prices for "environmentally friendly" products.

Previous Research Findings

Academic research has examined environmental issues and the closely related issue of socially conscious consumers for almost twenty years. Much of the research on this topic has focused on identifying and more fully understanding the socially conscious consumer.

One of the first studies to consider the idea of the socially conscious consumer from a marketing perspective set out to determine which consumers comprised the market for products and services promoting social and/or environmental well-being. The hypothesis was that consumers exhibiting a high degree of social consciousness would differ significantly from consumers who did not. The study concluded that marketers could indeed segment the market based on consumer social consciousness. In addition, sociopsychological variables were better predictors of social consciousness than demographic variables.

Other research developed an "ecological concern index" that demonstrated the effect of various levels of ecological concern on consumers' cognitive maps for brands of laundry detergent. The study determined that ecologically concerned customers represented a viable market segment. The study determined that psychological rather than demographic attributes better defined this segment. The study showed that those who strongly believed that the actions of an individual consumer could make a difference also showed a greater concern for ecology.

A later study also showed that personality and attitude measures were better predictors of social consciousness than were demographic or socioeconomic attributes.

Socially and ecologically responsible consumers are distinguishable along both demographic and attitudinal variables with socially concerned consumers having a broader base of concerns than just the environment.

A New Dilemma

Ron decided to look further into the issue of which bag was better for the environment. Ron talked with Dr. Cynthia Green of the biology department at a nearby college. He explained to Dr. Green that he used to pay between four and five cents per paper bag ($40 to $50 per 1,000) but that he could purchase plastic bags between 1.8 and 2.0 cents a bag ($18 to $20 per1,000). This is a substantial cost reduction, although it might take more bags to carry a customer's purchase. Ron stated that the savings were significant to his store since the grocery industry operates on very low margins.

Ron told the professor of his surprise when the students complained about the negative environmental impact of plastic grocery bags. He went on to say that he was unsure exactly what the students meant by a negative environmental impact. Worse, he did not know if they were right or how to respond to such complaints. Dr. Green suggested that the students were probably referring to the fact that plastic bags are made from nonrenewable fossil fuels and degrade very slowly in landfills. In addition, the manufacturing production process for plastic bags adds to the pollution problem. She noted that plastic bags had become a "lightning rod" for people who wanted to be more environmentally conscious.

Just as Ron was about to conclude that the students were right in their concern over the negative environmental impact of plastic bags, Dr. Green described the environmental impact of using paper grocery bags. She explained that the brown Kraft paper bags used in most supermarkets are made of virgin paper, without contributions from recycled paper, and that the production of such paper pollutes the water, releases dioxins, contributes to acid rain, and consumes trees.

Dr. Green said that while a growing number of consumers have become convinced that plastic grocery bags are less environmentally friendly than paper bags, the opposite may be true. Dr. Green described the results of one research study on the entire range of environmental impacts of plastic and paper bags. This study found that from the time manufacturers extract the raw materials to the time bags are thrown away, a paper bag may actually damage the environment more than a plastic bag. Based on this type of life-cycle analysis, Dr. Green claimed that there was no overriding ecological reason to change from plastic to paper bags.

All of this information has put Ron in a quandary as to what strategy he should pursue.

Case 14

Lakewood Players

Jacquelyn Warwick

As the lights went down and the curtain was about to open, Bob Jones, chairman of the board of directors for the Lakewood Players, looked worriedly around the theater at the sparse audience. He had been concerned about ticket sales ever since the managing/artistic director, Scott White, had begun putting on what Jones considered "experimental" plays—plays with titles no one recognized, by unknown writers, and not considered well-written. This past season included plays such as *Inside Out,* and *Lloyd's Prayer,* as well as *The Crucifer of Blood* (see Figure C14.1). As the play was about to begin, Jones whispered to his wife, "We need to get more action in front of the curtain than behind the curtain."

History

The theater had not begun with experimental plays. In 1938, under the auspices of the Lakewood Arts Foundation, a small nonprofit group established themselves as the Lakewood Players and performed in the old Lakewood Theater while dreaming of the day they would have their own theater. This group of theater devotees produced several shows and was lauded as a "cultural asset" in the August 18, 1938, edition of the *Lakewood Log*. Performances were usually preceded by lavish dinner parties and followed by cast parties that were enjoyed fully by both the performers and their affluent hosts. The theater was part of the Lakewood social scene.

In 1960, heightened by the excitement of the coming Seattle World's Fair (1962) and all the activities that surrounded that event, the Villa Plaza Development Company donated land next to the Lakewood Mall for the construction of a theater. Money had already

FIGURE C14.1. Lakewood Players 1996-1997 Season

been raised and with the added help of two main company sponsors, Douglas Plywood Company and Weyerhaeuser, the Lakewood Community Theater was completed with no outstanding debt. Thus, the only expenses the organization paid regularly were the heat, lights, and water. Since the theater's completion, the Lakewood Players performed numerous well-known, well-written plays such as *Our Town, Oliver, Damn Yankees, The Nerd,* and *The Odd Couple.*

Jones knew there had been a great deal of enthusiasm before World War II and afterward one or two prominent people had helped the theater to establish an identity. Over the years more people had become involved, the number of plays per season had grown, the community had attended the plays, and the identity of the theater had become stronger.

Now Jones felt that community support seemed to be ebbing. Play attendance was down and the community did not seem to be realizing the value of the theater. The city of Lakewood, which should have held their 100th-year birthday party at the Lakewood Community Theater, instead held the celebration next door at the Lakewood Mall. To make matters worse, a volunteer representing the Lakewood Players got into a fight with others at the birthday celebration. In addition, new neighbors appeared. The city of Lakewood constructed a major bus transfer station between the mall and the theater, further alienating the two groups.

Organizational Structure

The Lakewood Players bylaws stated that the board of directors could not exceed fifteen members. Over the years, the board usually had no more than nine members. The current board consisted of a tightly knit group of only six which included four women who ranged in age from early thirties to mid-fifties and two men both over sixty. With the exception of one board member, they were all active in the workforce. The board had a problem getting new members who wanted to actively participate in decision making. Thus, they were considering initiating an "honorary board" for those who wanted minimal involvement, but would like to be associated with the Lakewood Players.

The only salaried employee was the managing/artistic director who reported directly to the board. The managing director had to be educated and have general knowledge of the theater. This position was considered full-time and involved many tasks (see Box C14.1) including researching and evaluating which plays would be offered for the coming season. If the managing director wanted other outside professional work while continuing to be employed by the Lakewood Players, the board needed to approve the request. White, the current managing director, was hired two years ago. The last managing director had stayed five years before moving back East to continue with his career in theater. White had started to recommend unknown, newer plays shortly after he arrived to entertain the people who already were

BOX C14.1. Managing/Artistic Director Duties

Duties to be met or overseen

Casting	Performance programming
Scheduling	Sound design/operation
Rehearsal	Stage management
Set design/construction/paint	Box office management
Lighting design/hang and focus/ repair/operation	Front-of-house management
Properties design/build/acquire	Concessions management
Costume design/build/acquire	

Duties unrelated to the plays

House cleaning	Grounds/property/signage
Physical plant	Contracting talent (supplemental)
Errands	Community events
General theater tech/rigging	
Capital improvements	

Duties requiring ample attention

PR/marketing	Hiring teachers
Art/design	Registration
Copy	Phone reception
Production	Class project production
Distribution	Education management
Advertising	Curriculum planning
Press releases	Reviews

coming to the theater and to draw in the twenty- to forty-year-olds who were not attending.

The managing director oversaw three distinct groups of individuals. First, the play directors who worked as subcontractors and were paid a nominal amount for their work. Usually, there was a different play director for each show. Second, two very separate groups of volunteers: those who volunteer to act in the plays and go through auditions, and those who did everything from costume design to taking tickets and painting the building.

The majority of volunteers were high school or college students ranging in age from fifteen to twenty-five. Many were involved in drama classes at school, and the theater gave them a viable outlet to become involved in the arts. At the start of the season, there is a rich source of volunteers but the managing director needs to set aside quality time to get volunteers doing meaningful tasks. When this does not happen, the volunteers become frustrated, and this frustration is turned toward the managing director. The managing director then gets irritated which simply adds to the frustration level of the volunteers. At this point many may leave with a bad taste in their mouth over their theater experience.

Performances at Lakewood Playhouse

The managing/artistic director made all decisions concerning which plays would be offered each season. White contacted local directors, actors, and writers, as well as board members, to be on a reading committee. These volunteers read and suggested plays the theater could perform. Board members chose not to attend. White rejected the feedback to perform well-written plays with dynamic roles. Members of the committee felt White was choosing plays that were not well written. The play selections were passed to the board for approval but the board was not actually part of the decision loop. There was simply an expectation of implied approval once the board received the list for the coming season.

For many years the age range of the audiences who attended the Lakewood Community Theater was approximately fifty to sixty years old. Although Jones did not attend all the plays, he believed that in the past two years, the audiences were closer to being in their forties. Jones had also observed that the audiences attending the plays seemed to be the same regardless of which play was running. Given the theater's 150-seat capacity, the board considered plays that had an average of eighty to ninety attendees per night as good plays. However, a "red flag of distress" went up when the average attendance was only thirty to fifty people per night.

The Lakewood Community Players' season ran from October 1 through the June 30 with six plays, each typically running four to five weeks. There were two-week breaks between plays so the next play in the sequence could be advertised before it actually started. The plays were performed each Thursday, Friday, and Saturday night with special Sunday matinees.

Candy bars, cookies, coffee, and soda were served before each play and during the intermission. Opening night included a special "board of director's buffet" in which a light meal was served and the audience could stay to meet the actors.

When White first began his job and attendance was low he went to the board and asked, "If this play isn't successful, why not just close the doors?" The defensive response of the board came quickly, "Shut the doors? Never! The play will go on until the end!" White did not point out that on Broadway, if a play does not do well, the doors are closed. While White was at this meeting he also suggested cutting down the number of weeks a play ran. White assumed that if a play ran for three weeks instead of five, the same people would attend but in a shorter time frame. The board rejected this idea also.

Financial Information

Ticket prices varied. Opening night performances, which included the board of director's buffet, were ten dollars per person. An average performance was nine dollars for adults, eight dollars for military personnel, and seven dollars for senior citizens and students. Four options were available for purchasing season tickets.

Organizations also had two options for hosting a performance. A specific performance could be hosted for $400, which would allow the entire organization to attend but would also allow open admission for others. An organization could also host an "exclusive" performance at a cost of $500. Currently, only one group consistently purchased one performance of each play in this manner. The organization allowed open admission during these performances.

Organizations could also sponsor a play in one of two ways: support a play for a single night's run for $1,000, or sponsor a single play's entire run for $2,000. Usually, six to eight organizations regularly sponsored an entire run of a play. As the managing director, it was White's job to contact local organizations to attain these sponsorships. The board members did realize, however, that it was equally their responsibility to establish strong contacts in the community to help White solicit funds.

Several area arts organizations were available for assistance, including the Washington State Arts Commission, Pierce County Arts Commission, and the Tacoma Arts Commission. The Tacoma Arts

Commission, as well as other organizations, requires a theater to have a minimal budget of $50,000 as well as a budget audit before an application for a grant is considered. Jones considered the audit a stumbling block since the Lakewood Players had the required budget but could not seem to get the required budget audit. Jones stated, "You need to make sure where the money is going but the audit has to be in an acceptable form. We have two CPAs on our board but they won't do it; they can't since there is the issue of conflict of interest. We need to go to an outside source and get this done, but in the meantime we aren't applying for grants."

Competition

The theater had three main competitors that the board thought were all similarly priced. The Tacoma Little Theatre and the Tacoma Musical Group were both approximately ten miles away. The Performance Circle, which performed in Gig Harbor, was approximately thirty miles away. The Lakewood Players did not consider ACT, a theater in Seattle, to be a competitor because it presented professional touring plays and the Lakewood Players were all volunteer actors.

Promotional Activities

The theater did its main advertising by distributing pamphlets during several different times of the year. A summer educational mailing, another in the fall promoting season ticket purchases, and finally a reminder pamphlet was sent out before each of the six plays. These pamphlets were distributed using a database consisting of 3,000 to 5,000 households of past season ticket holders, donors, and volunteers.

A description of the current play was listed in the feature "Art Tix" which ran every Friday in the local paper, *The News Tribune*. An advertisement was also placed in the *Lakewood Journal/University Place Journal,* another smaller local weekly paper. The board was considering placing an ad even when no plays were running just to keep the theater in front of the public eye, but nothing had been decided concerning that proposal.

Jones also liked the idea of posters being placed all around the community. He felt that this was very educational and would keep the public informed of what was playing. Jones and White had several discussions on this form of advertising. White could not see the benefit of using the posters and often claimed that it did not seem to matter whether they used them or not; it did not seem to change the attendance for a play.

There seemed to be no interest in developing informational material that board members, or other volunteers, could pass out to friends, family members, or the community at large, explaining the presence of the theater. Also, although board members were involved in organizations such as the Lakewood Chamber of Commerce, they had not built strong theater-related ties with this group.

1996-1997 Performance Assessment

Lakewood Players' handbills proclaimed, "Don't miss this year's Season of Dreams!" but given audience turnout, it appeared that some did. Six plays were offered, all of which were considered "experimental" (plays with unknown titles and/or authors). The season began with a well-attended play, *The Crucifer of Blood,* a thrilling but not well-known Sherlock Holmes mystery adventure. This was followed by *Charlie and the Chocolate Factory,* an adaptation of *Willy Wonka and the Chocolate Factory.* This play was also well attended; however, a majority of those who attended were the family and friends of the children who were performing. This production was followed by *Dark Side,* a space adventure that was touted to contain "edge-of-your-seat tension." Although many thought this play was well done, it did not do well at the box office. *Inside Out,* a "chic comedy that fits all sizes," was performed and was considered very successful. However, for *Graceland,* attendance was low. (Jones' conclusion: "Elvis may be a big hit in the South, but he does not draw people in our area.") *Lloyd's Prayer* was said to be "a side-splitting, hair-raising, falling-down funny" comedy and was the final event of the season. Again, it was not well received by the audience and numbers were low. Overall, this season, as well as the last, was not what the board had expected.

Board Meeting

Many weighty issues were discussed at the last board meeting. The biggest concern was low play attendance. Someone suggested that the Lakewood Players had lost their identity. The board members indicated that they all thought it stemmed from the plays that had been run the past two seasons. The overwhelming answer: change back to well-known plays such as the 1994-1995 season and the problem would be resolved. Although all agreed, Jones seemed willing to "leave the door open a bit" by suggesting that there could still be room for a new but well-written play if it was not a "cutting-edge" play.

A board member suggested that the Lakewood Community Theater be used all the time. Others quickly agreed that it needed to be used year-round for activities when there were no performances. As this topic came to an end, a very serious discussion took place concerning the Players' community outreach program that many on the board termed as "not great" and "in need of help." The conversation revolved around the need to cultivate new people and enhance community relations. Some members thought the Players needed to educate the public, especially young people, to get them enthused about the theater.

Finally, the discussion turned to the decision of whether they should replace White and hire another artistic director. After assessing many different issues, no decisions were made by the board, and the meeting was adjourned. They agreed to meet the following month to decide on a course of action. Jones now had to develop his own plan to recommend at the next meeting.

Case 15

BCH TeleCommunications

Marlene M. Reed
Rochelle R. Brunson

As the Prague police car pulled away from the curb in front of 156 Sokolovska, thirty-two-year-old Jeff Welker bit his lip to hold back the tears. It was bad enough that his partner had left the country and taken all of the $150,000 in cash they had in the BCH TeleCommunications checking account; but to compound matters, this was one of his oldest and dearest friends. In addition to the money, his partner had also taken some important legal documents that were necessary for running the company. It was July 1996 and the business was just beginning to take off.

Jeff's partner had simply left a letter on his desk telling him that he was leaving because the partnership had caused him great frustration, and he was going to Poland and taking the money with him. As he left his spartan office on the second floor of an older building in the northeast section of Prague, Jeff reflected on the course of his life.

Preparation for Prague

For as long as he could remember, Jeff had wanted to go into hospitality management. When he completed high school in Glendale, California, he entered Glendale Community College and ultimately completed an associate's degree in business management with a concentration in food management.

After researching a number of schools that offered bachelor's degrees in hospitality management, Jeff decided to enter the program at the University of Nevada at Las Vegas (UNLV). During his time at the university, he established many close relationships—including friendships with managers and directors of hotels in Las Vegas.

With the conclusion of his work at UNLV, Jeff interviewed with a number of companies and ultimately accepted a job as assistant convention director at a Sheraton Hotel located in the Los Angeles area. Within the next three years, Jeff was promoted several times.

Early Entrepreneurial Speculations

Jeff's family had some wealthy friends in California who had offered financial support to any venture Jeff might be involved in. He filed this away in the back of his mind just in case something interesting did come along. After a couple of years, Jeff was transferred to the Sheraton Hotel in San Diego. He soon became friends with an older man who was a real estate developer in Los Angeles and Hawaii.

Jeff began contemplating putting together a project for a hotel in Hawaii. For the next two years, he worked concertedly on this plan. He even selected a parcel of land in Hawaii, talked to the owner about his interest in putting a hotel there, and developed an aerially shot video of the land to show to potential investors. In addition, he had a graphic artist overlay a sketch of the proposed hotel onto a photograph of the land. Jeff was now twenty-six years old, had enough pledges to build a hotel in Hawaii, and envisioned that his lifelong dream was about to become a reality.

However, this dream was not to be. He had made friends with a young lawyer from New York named Charles. Charles was tired of working grueling hours in a large law firm and planned to quit his job and start a business of his own. Jeff was understandably startled when Charles asked him one day, "Have you ever thought of building the hotel somewhere else for about one hundred times less money?" He continued, "Do you know anything about the Yugoslavian Riviera?" Jeff admitted that he knew almost nothing about Yugoslavia, and he certainly did not know it had a riviera. However, by a strange twist of fate, the travel section of the local newspaper had a twelve-page article on the Yugoslavian Riviera the following weekend. Jeff read each word carefully and began doing some research on this part of the world. He went back to his investors and told them about this new opportunity, and they became as excited as he was. Charles and Jeff began applying for visas; unfortunately, it was late 1990 and early 1991 and war broke out in the country before they could get there. This forced them to scrap the whole idea and begin all over.

Four months later, Charles suggested that they continue to concentrate on Eastern Europe where doors of opportunity were beginning to open for entrepreneurs. He proposed that they consider starting a bar and grill in Prague, Czechoslovakia, which was the gateway between Eastern and Western Europe. Jeff knew a bit more about Czechoslovakia although he had never been there. Other circumstances in his life at the time caused him to rethink the future. He had left Sheraton and gone with Marriott Hotels, and Marriott was in the process of restructuring. Jeff became uncomfortable with the changes he saw taking place and decided Charles's idea was not so bad after all. He quit his job and began serious research on the new project. It was now April 1992.

Research for the Venture in Prague

Although a formal business plan was never developed, Jeff and Charles did spend some time researching the proposed project in Czechoslovakia. Charles had decided that in addition to the bar and grill that Jeff would run, he would like to start an import-export business in Prague because he had always been enamored by this type of operation and had a hunch that such a business might work in this country newly opened to Western goods.

They needed to know the type of goods not presently available in that country. First, they did some research at the library of the University of California at San Diego and visited the Czech Consulate in Los Angeles. Then they flew to Washington, DC, and talked to representatives at the Czech Embassy, the United States Department of Commerce, EXIM (Export-Import) Bank, the IMF (International Monetary Fund), and anywhere else they could get information on the country and the economic climate there. At the Czech Consulate and Embassy they were told there was a great need for used blue jeans and used computers in the country at that time. Charles's law firm had a one-person office in Prague, and that lawyer also assisted them in understanding the country.

Jeff and Charles began exploring names for their embryonic company and decided to use an acronym for the company title. After brainstorming for days, they finally arrived at BCH—an abbreviation for "beach"—a place where Jeff had spent some of the best years of his life. In November of 1992, Jeff and Charles arrived in Prague to launch their business operations. Jeff secretly wondered just where BCH Enterprises would take these two entrepreneurial friends.

Economic Developments in Czechoslovakia

In November 1989, Czechoslovakia experienced what would later be referred to as the Velvet Revolution. In response to the pleas of students and nurses, the socialist government finally stepped down and handed the country over to the people. Great social, political, and economic changes subsequently occurred in the newly freed nation. The disintegration of the former Council for Mutual Economic Assistance (Comecon) was one of the most significant factors for change. The National Assembly elected Václav Havel president of Czechoslovakia on December 29, 1989. Havel came from a family that had a long history of business and cultural activity. In spite of major difficulties under the former socialist government, Havel became one of the most celebrated of all Czech contemporary playwrights.

The primary constraint to any reform efforts on the part of Václav Havel and his new government was the fact that all industrial and agricultural production was owned by the state or state-dependent collective farms. In February 1990, the new minister of finance, Václav Klaus, proposed a coupon privatization project. By paying only a small administration fee, all Czechoslovakian citizens were given the opportunity to obtain a coupon book, which could be used to purchase shares in certain privatized concerns. The first coupon books were sold on May 18, 1992, with the result that 70 percent of the population became shareholders. Following this was a project titled Small Privatization which singled out smaller service and trade premises from state property and sold them at auction.

Another constraint to reform was the less-than-rapid integration of Czechoslovakia into the community of Western European states. Exporters in the Western European countries were delighted with the new opportunity to sell their goods in Czech markets, but they were reticent to buy Czech goods. The former socialist economy was strongly oriented toward Comecon (a planned economy) and the former Soviet Union. This had a negative effect on domestic production and caused the country to be noncompetitive in world markets. The central planning commission stressed heavy industry and neglected the service sector entirely. Because of this, the Czech economy suffered a decrease in exports when Comecon was dissolved, and there was a loss of Eastern markets for their goods.[1]

In January 1993, Czechoslovakia split and became the Czech Republic and Slovakia. With the collapse of markets in Eastern Europe the country began to develop a greater orientation toward the markets of Western Europe, and more foreign firms began to enter the domestic Czech market[2] (see Figure C15.1).

According to one source, by the end of 1994, 65 percent of the gross domestic product in the Czech Republic was from contributions of private sector business activities (both domestic and foreign). However, even though a whole range of laws and decrees had been promulgated which purported to encourage the formation of small business, a proper legal system to defend private property and enterprise and enforce contracts had not been implemented.[3]

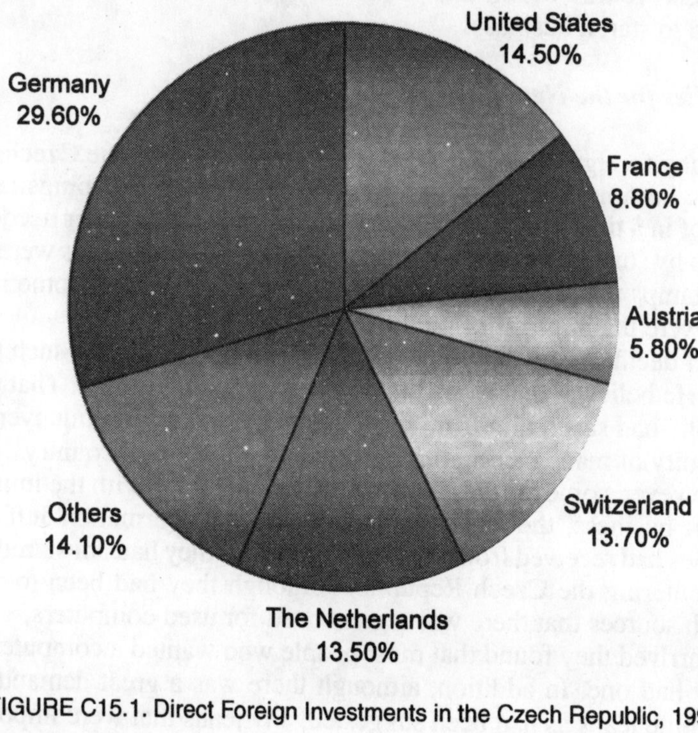

FIGURE C15.1. Direct Foreign Investments in the Czech Republic, 1995

For one thing, the government bureaucracy had become a major barrier to the creation of new enterprises. The former state-owned banks were very slowly being privatized and new banks from other countries were beginning to enter the country. The experience of one company in Russia was very similar to experiences of entrepreneurs in the Czech Republic. This new small business received the required twenty-seven documents—many requiring notarizations—after a loan approval and before the money could be disbursed.[4]

Two separate Czech economies appeared to be developing by the middle 1990s. One was the economy in which new Czech entrepreneurs were attempting to start up new ventures and having great difficulty getting loans (except at 30 percent interest) and breaking through the "old-boy" network, which was a residual of the socialist state. The other sector, which represented companies from Western countries that had access to banks outside the Czech Republic and well-skilled lawyers to assist with the bureaucracy, was experiencing great success.[5] It was within this economic climate that Jeff and Charles hoped to start a business.

Hurdles for the New Business

Many foreign companies that made investments in the Czech Republic became frustrated with the difficulty of getting things taken care of in a timely manner. Every contract or piece of paper needed a stamp by someone to make it official. Sometimes the stamps were paper stamps that could be purchased at a post office, and sometimes they were the imprints of a rubber stamp.

Jeff decided very early that he would not be daunted by such hurdles. He believed that he had to do everything on his own. That philosophy had saved him from many hours of anxiety fretting over the difficulty of maneuvering through business in his new country.

However, some hurdles became insurmountable. With the import-export business, the hurdle was the incorrect information Jeff and Charles had received from sources with whom they had consulted before entering the Czech Republic. Although they had been told by Czech sources that there was a great need for used computers, when they arrived they found that most people who wanted a computer already had one. In addition, although there was a great demand for used blue jeans as had been suggested, any jeans that were imported were either stolen at the border or, if they made it past the border, were burdened with a heavy duty by the Czech government. BCH could not make a profit with prohibitive duties on their products.

Jeff and Charles faced more obstacles with the renovation of a building for their bar and grill. They signed a contract for a stated amount with one construction company only to have them come back later and suggest, "We forgot to put doors and windows in our contract; and also there is water damage in the walls, and we have to fix that." They let this company go and signed a contract with another construction company who later said to them, "Oh, we must add an additional $80,000 to the contract for electrical wiring, elevators, and stairs."

Jeff and Charles began to understand that the signing of contracts meant nothing, and the project would go well beyond their budget. They knew they could not continue to ask their investors to pour money into a black hole, so they gave up. Jeff and Charles lost more than $40,000 on this project. Their deal with investors was that the investors would put $250,000 into the project, but they wanted Jeff and Charles to invest (and be willing to lose) the first $50,000. Jeff wondered if part of their problem might have been that neither of them spoke the Czech language and depended upon translators for all transactions.

An Introduction to Callback Services

Jeff began doing some hospitality management consulting in Eastern Europe since tourism had become a big business after the demise of communism. One of the biggest expenses of the business was the telephone bill. The Czech Republic had a metered charge for local as well as long-distance calls, and the long-distance calling fee at the time was $3.50 a minute. Jeff first used AT&T, then Sprint, then another carrier, but the costs were still quite high.

On a trip back to the United States, Jeff read in a magazine about a company providing callback service for international calling. He called a representative of the company and asked him to explain callback services. The representative explained the process to him in the following way: "You call from Prague to our computer in New York to a specially assigned telephone number, and you hang up before our computer answers. After this, the computer calls you back and offers you a dial tone, and then you dial as if you were in the United States." The representative's explanation was, "International rates in the United States are so much cheaper than the rest of the world that they give you discounted rates."

Of course, when Jeff tried the process, it did not work exactly as the representative had said. In Czechoslovakia in 1992, only one out of ten phone calls worked. In addition, 99 percent of telephones in Czechoslovakia had rotary dials. To use the service, they needed a Touch-Tone phone. They brought one from the United States and then had to get an adaptor to make it work.

One day the CEO of the company that offered callback services called them and asked if they would like the license for the company for Eastern Europe. Jeff immediately responded that they would not be interested because the service did not work. Then the CEO responded, "Would you be interested if we got the service working?" Jeff said they might be interested, and so the CEO got an engineer on the phone to listen to their complaints.

Jeff was uncomfortable with the prospect of selling. However, Jeff also realized that although he was doing hospitality consulting, his partner was not doing any consulting work and this new venture might bring some money into the company. Also, since they would primarily be speaking with representatives of Western companies, language would not be a hindrance. The growing number of Western companies doing business in the Czech Republic provided an excellent customer base for this service.

As much as Jeff hated the idea of calling people and convincing them that they needed to buy their service, he and Charles reluctantly accepted the licensing and marketing agreement for Eastern Europe. This would be the first company to offer such services in Eastern Europe.

Charles began immediately working on the project in May 1993; within four months, he had signed up sixty people. When Charles went back to the United States for two weeks, he asked Jeff if he would follow up with some companies that he had sent information to and see if they were interested in the callback services.

First, Jeff called people who had recently signed up and asked about the service. The service from Czech Telecom (the former Czech monopoly) was so bad at the time that it took ten tries to get one call through. The people Jeff called who were using the service said they got their calls through seven out of ten times. As one might imagine, they were very pleased with the service. In addition, all of the companies that Charles had sent information to wanted to sign up for the service. All of this happened within thirty minutes, and Jeff was astounded.

After completing the calls, Jeff picked up the English-language newspaper, *The Prague Post.* He saw some ads placed by large multinational companies that were doing business in the Czech Republic. On a whim, Jeff picked some of the companies at random and called them to explain their callback services; the common reply was, "How fast can you send information and have a meeting with us?" Jeff hurriedly sent the information to the companies, met with them soon afterward, and very quickly signed them up for the service.

He was doing so well with the large companies that when Charles returned he said he would continue to work with the multinationals and Charles could stay with the smaller companies. Charles concurred with this suggestion. At this juncture of the operations, they decided that it would be appropriate to name the portion of the business dealing with callback services BCH TeleCommunications (see Box C15.1).

Competition for BCH

The biggest competitor for BCH TeleCommunications was the state-owned Czech Telecom. In the former centrally planned economy of Czechoslovakia, the government had a monopoly in all industries. There was no private enterprise. In the 1980s, the U.S. telephone monopoly, AT&T, agreed to break up into a number of smaller regional local calling companies which allowed competition for the long-distance calling market. The transition in Czechoslovakia was hampered because the legal and economic infrastructure necessary to move to a free market system was slow and cumbersome. Czech Telecom refused to believe that it would be possible for another company to compete with them.

Soon after BCH TeleCommunications began offering callback services, the Czech government and Czech Telecom came to Jeff and Charles and threatened to kick them out of the country. They presented the young men with official documents with the required

BOX C15.1.
BCH TeleCommunications DirectDial Services

BCH DirectDial Services provide international telephone services that can save you up to 42% on your international calls.

There are many added values when using *BCH DirectDial Services:*

- Best rates
- No monthly fees
- Direct dialing to all countries worldwide
- 24-hour unbeatable customer service
- Many different kinds of connections to fit the needs of customers
- Detailed call record every month for free
- Easy billing in CZK, USD, or by major credit card

Joining ***BCH DirectDial Services*** is easy. We will need only this information:

- Where the client wishes billing information to be sent
- The currency the client wishes to pay with
- The local numbers to be connected

This routing creates two billings for each call:

- The first is charged by the local telecom
- The second is charged by ***BCH*** at tremendous discounts

BCH DirectDial Services is one of many top-quality services offered by BCH TeleCommunications. Please call us for more information about ***DirectDial*** and the many other attractive products and services available form Central Europe's leader in discount international telecommunications.

number of stamps on them and said, "You must leave the country in sixty days." Jeff and Charles consulted with their Czech lawyer who said, "They may make your life more difficult, but you have done nothing wrong." These two relatively naive young Americans soon discovered that competition may come in a thousand different disguises, and some may actually threaten your well-being or your life. Jeff mulled over the truth that every entrepreneur must know his or her competition well and understand how to survive in the midst of competition.

Often, when Jeff would give information about the company to potential customers, they would ask, "This is great. Does it break any laws?" Jeff would assure them that it did not; however, when these same customers called Czech Telecom, the company would claim callback services were illegal.

Jeff became aware later that other countries—including the United States—did not always view this new process as enthusiastically as he did. Often, the established operator community in a country publicly and legally took a dim view, claiming in various ways that the services actually constituted wire fraud. The operator community was especially troubled by revenues they were unable to collect on the use of their assets, and they also suggested that it circumnavigated their international conventions for settlement.

Argentina and several African countries had attempted to block the switching techniques that enable callback hardware to capture identification codes and reroute calls.[6]

Jeff was also aware that there was growing interest—even in the Czech Republic—in substitute products and services such as e-mail and fax messages. These were both low-cost alternatives to long-distance calling and competitors for callback services. In fact, the telephone companies themselves seemed to have a bright future. Unlike BCH, they were not tied to the one product for long-distance communications. In 1995, the world spent 60 billion minutes communicating by phone, fax, and e-mail, four times the amount spent in the previous decade.[7]

An issue raised with this type of operation was international comity. International comity is based on the principle of respect. "Comity is implicated where domestic and foreign laws conflict. When a conflict occurs, a country must decide whether to respect the foreign law or to enforce its own domestic law. In making such a decision, the domestic body balances domestic public interests against international considerations. The domestic body is under no obligation to abide by the foreign law; the decision of whether to respect foreign law is entirely discretionary."[8] Jeff reasoned that these potential problems might put a constraint on callback services.

The Company Grows and Takes on More Staff

BCH soon began to represent other telecommunications companies such as Sprint, DirectNet, AxCom, and Dial International (DIT), which did not have representatives in Eastern Europe. They also expanded the operations of BCH TeleCommunications into Poland, Slovakia, and Hungary in July 1993. Jeff, meanwhile, expanded his hospitality management consulting into Slovakia and Hungary. The company was doing so well that the Office of the Ministry of Finance identified BCH as one of the top new companies in the country and sought Jeff's advice on ways to help Czech entrepreneurs succeed (see Box C15.2).

Jeff speculated that their company did well not only because of the cheaper telephone services that they offered but also because of the good technical support they provided their customers. The company hired an engineer just to work on technical problems and help with plans for future expansion of the business. Jeff found it interesting that over 50 percent of their new business came from referrals by satisfied customers.

The company also had an excellent staff of people working with them. One was a young lady named Ivana Svobodova. She had come to work for them in 1994 as a receptionist and within months had worked her way up to sales associate and finally became a director of the company. When Ivana had a free minute, she read everything in the office about the operations of the company. When people called the company, Ivana could answer their questions and actually began to sell the company's services over the phone without a meeting. She soon became the person on the staff that Jeff most depended upon to give a realistic assessment of his ideas for the operations in the Czech Republic. She was a native of the country and knew better than he what would work and what would not work there. An added benefit was that Ivana was a native and could assist with Jeff's learning of the Czech language, and she was also a trustworthy translator.

Crisis for Jeff Welker

By January of 1995, Jeff noted that their callback service operations had grown by 150 percent since they had become involved with it two years ago. He had heard that callback services in general were growing at a rate of 15 percent a month. BCH operations were grow-

BOX C15.2. Financial History of BCH

1992

Revenues from restaurant	0*
Revenues from consulting	0
Total revenues	0
Expenses of restaurant	$15,000
Profit (loss)	($15,000)

- *Restaurant*—No money was generated from the restaurant because contract disputes prevented the building from being completed. The owners spent much of this year finding a place to build (location, architect, contractor, etc.).
- *General*—In addition, they used most of their time getting themselves established in the business community (networking and getting involved in the expatriate community).

1993

Revenues from consulting	$10,000
Revenues from telecom	50,000
Total revenues	60,000
Expenses of restaurant	35,000
Expenses of telecom	12,000
Expenses of consulting	1,000
Profit (loss)	$12,000

- *Consulting*—Company established a hospitality and communications consulting arm of the firm. The primary targets were the hospitality industry and the service industry (real estate, law firms, and grocery stores).
- *Telecom*—At the beginning of this year, the company broke into the telecom market offering discount callback services. BCH was the first to offer such services in the region, and

(continued)

*Numbers are rounded off to the nearest thousand.

(continued)

gained about 100 customers in the first year. They worked out of Jeff's apartment and began a full advertising/marketing campaign.

1994

Revenues from consulting	$25,000
Revenues from telecom	105,000
Total revenues	130,000
Expenses of consulting	3,000
Expenses of telecom	154,000
Profit (loss)	($27,000)

- *Consulting*—This part of the business grew well and kept Jeff busy all of the time. The company expanded its activities into Slovakia and Hungary (for specific clients). Much of this revenue (which was almost pure profit) was supporting and paying many of the company's past bills and financing the marketing efforts of the telecom division.
- *Telecom*—This project continued to grow very rapidly. At the end of the year, the partners decided to work on their own. Instead of making a commission for another firm, BCH would actually buy and sell their own international time from large telecom carriers. In addition, they took on a third partner for additional expansion. He was an expatriate who had lived in Prague for two years. They added four full-time sales staffpeople and moved into a large office complex. They added one postgraduate (from graduate school on a one-year internship) to assist with the think-tank process of expanding. They were actively marketing their services in Hungary.

1995

Revenue from consulting	$31,000
Revenue from telecom	175,000
Total revenues	206,000

(continued)

(continued)

Expenses of consulting	3,000
Expenses of telecom	217,000
Profit (loss)	($14,000)

- *Consulting*—This division continued to generate revenue that was used to support the expansion efforts of the telecom division. The partners had decided that it was not necessary to continue to grow this division but to maintain it and use it as a networking effort to further support the telecom division.
- *Telecom*—The company moved to a less expensive private office. BCH added two more postgraduate interns. They expanded their services portfolio to include an international calling card. This proved to be successful for the next two to three years. The sales team grew by two, and then they added two full-time customer service staffpeople. At the end of the year, their third partner was asked to leave the firm, and this added a large financial burden to the bottom line because of his severance costs. The company expanded into Poland and established a full office. One of the partners was stationed in Poland 85 percent of the time. BCH began working with a total of three telecom service providers. These were firms through whom they bought and sold telecom time. This allowed BCH to add more services to its portfolio.

1996

Revenues from consulting	$17,000
Revenues from telecom	180,000
Revenues from glass/crystal	3,000
Total revenues	200,000
Expenses of consulting	1,000
Expenses of telecom	39,000
Expenses of glass/crystal	70,000
Profit (loss)	$90,000

(continued)

(continued)

- This was a year of great change.
- *Consulting*—This division basically was winding down its activities, and the company began to concentrate all of its efforts on the telecom division. This had been very enjoyable for Jeff and a good moneymaker, but he no longer had enough time for all of its activities.
- *Telecom*—There was much unrest in this division as it continued to grow. All three interns left the firm because they were disgruntled with the overall direction and management of BCH. One of the primary partners—Charles—decided to depart BCH on a permanent basis; and as he did, he removed all of the financial assets of the firm and left the country. This brought on an enormous financial burden to the company operations. At the end of the year, there were only two employees on the payroll. Three additional employees stayed on for four months without pay.
- *Glass/Crystal*—BCH decided to start up a new project of exporting glass and crystal to the United States and Canada.

ing in Poland and Hungary, and Charles wanted to take over the business operations in Poland. However, Charles became increasingly unhappy and frustrated in the business and in his relationship with Jeff, so he left a letter for Jeff telling him he was leaving the business and taking $150,000 in cash with him. It was now July 1996, and Jeff felt that the rug had been pulled from under him. He normally had a very positive outlook on life, but this setback seriously discouraged him.

With no money in the bank and all of his legal documents gone, Jeff considered filing for bankruptcy. Under the former socialist state, "bankruptcy" was a word that no one mentioned. Central planning had always provided an easy way out for money-losing enterprises. Under the new government, bankruptcy was beginning to play a role; however, the process was not working well. Usually, for struggling companies, a hint of the possibility of insolvency meant scrambling to hide assets before creditors noticed. The 1991 Bankruptcy and Settlement Act was based on rules dating back to the Austro-Hungarian Empire. The Act had already been amended ten times, and parliament, bankers, and unions were wrangling over proposed amendments again.[9] The average bankruptcy period in the Czech Republic, from start to finish, was six years.[10]

Jeff also had to take a hard look at the future of callback services. Although these services had been extremely profitable until now, he wondered about the growth of alternative means of communication. Total revenues for callback services in 1994 were $200 million and in 1995 were $350 million; they were projected to grow to $500 million in 1996, $1 billion in 1997, and to $2 billion by 1998.[11] A recent article had also suggested a possible saturation of this market. The author reported that in1990 there were only six callback operations in North America, and at the present time there were over 200—all offering consumers in dozens of foreign countries cheaper (and even illegal) international phone and fax calls.[12]

In addition, the U.S. Federal Communications Commission (FCC) had taken notice of the disparity in international dialing rates and was considering new pricing rules that would force foreign carriers to lower their rates or face possible punitive measures. The FCC saw competition by the callback services as an additional means of encouraging other nations to comply.[13]

Jeff wondered to himself how he could survive and make the business prosper with no money to pay his staff or creditors. He also wondered if this would be a good time to move into a related business that would have greater prospects for profitability in the future. Although Czech Telecom was still a monopoly, now 27 percent owned by Swiss and Dutch investors, by the year 2000 the monopoly was to be broken up and competition from other companies would be welcomed.

Notes

Chapter 1

1. American Marketing Association, Board of Directors (1985).
2. Gale, Bradley T. and Buzzell, Robert D. (1989). "Market Perceived Quality: Key Strategic Concept." *Planning Review,* March-April: p. 11.
3. Gale, Bradley T. (1990). "The Role of Marketing in Total Quality Management," Quest for Excellence Conference, Washington, DC.
4. Boyd, Harper W. Jr., Walker, Orville C. Jr., and Larreche, Jean Claude (1995). *Marketing Management.* Chicago: Irwin, pp. 453-454.
5. "GM Brings Its Dealers Up To Speed" (1998). *Business Week,* February 23, pp. 82-84.
6. Wrenn, Bruce (1997). "The Market Orientation Construct: Measurement and Scaling Issues." *Journal of Marketing Theory and Practice,* 5(3): 31-54.
7. Best, Roger (2000). *Market-Based Management.* Upper Saddle River, NJ: Prentice-Hall, p. 7.
8. Ibid., p. 18.
9. Wiley, Jack W. (1991). "Customer Satisfaction and Employee Opinions: A Supportive Work Environment and Its Financial Costs." *Human Resource Planning,* 14: 117-123.
10. Kotler, Philip (2003). *Marketing Management,* Eleventh Edition. Upper Saddle River, NJ: Prentice-Hall, pp. 26-27.
11. Harrell, Gilbert and Frazier, Gary (1999). *Marketing*. Upper Saddle River, NJ: Prentice-Hall, p. 4.

Chapter 2

1. Lehmann, Donald R. and Winer, Russell S. (1997). *Analysis for Marketing Planning*. Chicago: Irwin, pp. 118-119.
2. Sullivan, Allanna (1995). "Mobil Bets Drivers Pick Cappuccino Over Low Prices." *The Wall Street Journal,* January 30, p. B1.
3. Available online at <http://www.claritas.com/i3_communications_energy/SUB/i3_case_cox_2.html>.
4. "Claritas: A Beacon of Data to the Marketing World," available online at <http://www.claritas.com/6_news _events/SUB/news_articles_links.html>.
5. Available online at <http://www.sric-bi.com/VALS/about.shtml>.

Chapter 3

1. Flax, Steven (1989). "How to Snoop on Your Competitors." *Fortune,* May 14, p. 29.

2. Montgomery, David B. and Weinberg, Charles B. (1979). "Toward Strategic Intelligence Systems." *Journal of Marketing,* 43(fall): 44-45.

3. Ibid., p. 47.

4. Kopp, Norel M. (1989). "Corporate Sleuthing." *World,* (spring), pp. 2-3.

5. Kopp, Norel M. (1989). "Firms Step Up Their Watch on Rivals." *Marketing News,* 23(January 2), p. 17.

6. Word Communications Web site: <http://1198.110.248.165/namexico/0908 seville.htm>.

7. Porter, Michael E. (1985). *Competitive Advantage.* New York: The Free Press.

8. Porter, Michael E. (1979). "How Competitive Forces Shape Strategy." *Harvard Business Review,* March-April: pp. 137-145.

9. Cringely, Robert X. (2001). "Big Game." *Worth,* July/August, p. 45.

10. Aaker, David A. (2001). *Strategic Market Management,* Sixth Edition. New York: John Wiley and Sons, Inc., p. 70.

11. Kotler, Philip (2003). *Marketing Management,* Eleventh Edition. Upper Saddle River, NJ: Prentice-Hall, pp. 254-272.

12. Adapted from Lynn, Robert A. (1987). "Anticipating Competitive Reaction: Marketing Strategy in the 1980s." *Journal of Consumer Marketing,* 4(1): 8-9.

13. Ibid., pp. 9-11.

14. Kahaner, Larry (1996). *Competitive Intelligence.* New York: Simon and Schuster, Inc., p. 23.

15. Ibid., pp. 31-35.

16. Ibid., pp. 201-208.

17. Kopp, "Corporate Sleuthing," pp. 2-3.

18. Kopp, "Firms Step Up Their Watch on Rivals," p. 17.

19. Adapted from Kahaner, *Competitive Intelligence,* pp. 53-122.

20. Hershey, Robert (1980). "Commercial Intelligence on a Shoestring." *Harvard Business Review,* September-October: 23-30.

21. Adapted from Oxenfeldt, Alfred R. and Moore, William L. (1978). "Customer or Competitor: Which Guideline for Marketing?" *Management Review,* August: 43-48.

Chapter 5

1. Drucker, Peter F. (1974). *Management: Tasks, Responsibilities, Practices.* New York: Harper and Row Publishers, p. 75.

2. Ibid., p. 101.

3. Abell, Derek F. (1978). "Strategic Windows." *Journal of Marketing,* July: 21-26.

Chapter 6

1. Much of this section is based upon Best, Roger J. (1997). *Market-Based Management.* Upper Saddle River, NJ: Prentice-Hall, pp. 123-127.

2. Kotler, Philip (2003). *Marketing Management,* Eleventh Edition. Upper Saddle River, NJ: Prentice-Hall, p. 280.

3. "Databased Marketing" (1994). *Business Week,* September 5, pp. 56-62.
4. Cravens, David W. (1997). *Strategic Marketing.* Chicago: R.D. Irwin, pp. 192-197.

Chapter 7

1. Best, Roger J. (1997). *Market-Based Management.* Upper Saddle River, NJ: Prentice-Hall, pp. 368-369.
2. Pride, William M. and Ferrell, O.C. (1997). *Marketing.* Boston: Houghton Mifflin Co., p. 550.
3. Bonoma, Thomas V. (1985). *The Marketing Edge: Making Strategies Work.* New York: The Free Press.
4. Kotler, Philip (2003). *Marketing Management,* Eleventh Edition. Upper Saddle River, NJ: Prentice-Hall, p. 22.
5. Steingraber, Fred (1990). "Total Quality Management: A New Look at a Basic Issue." *Vital Speeches of the Day,* May, pp. 415-416.
6. Aaker, David A. (2001). *Strategic Market Management,* Sixth Edition. New York: John Wiley, pp. 288-302.
7. Nutt, Paul C. (1986). "Tactics of Implementation." *Academy of Management Journal,* 29(2): 230-261.
8. Dickson, Peter (1997). *Marketing Management,* Second Edition. Fort Worth: Dryden Press, p. 671.
9. Hobbs, John M. and Heany, Donald F. (1977). "Coupling Strategy to Operating Plans." *Harvard Business Review,* May/June: 119-124.
10. Deshpande, Rohit and Webster, Frederick E. (1989). "Organization Culture and Marketing: Defining the Research Agenda." *Journal of Marketing,* 53(January): 3-15.
11. O'Reilly, Charles (1989). "Corporation, Culture, and Commitment: Motivation and Social Control in Organizations." *California Management Review,* summer: 9-25.
12. Adapted from Collins, James C. and Porras, Jerry L. (1994). *Built to Last.* New York: Harper Business, p. 136.
13. Dickson, *Marketing Management,* pp. 646-659.
14. Chandler, Alfred (1962). *Strategy and Structure.* Cambridge, MA: MIT Press, p. 113.
15. Certo, Samuel and Peter, J. Paul (1990). *Strategic Management.* New York: McGraw-Hill, p. 124.
16. Kotler, *Marketing Management,* pp. 496-497.
17. Ibid., pp. 498-499.

Chapter 8

1. Stewart, Thomas (1997). "A Satisfied Customer Isn't Enough." *Fortune,* July 21: 112-113.
2. Kotler, Philip (2003). *Marketing Management,* Eleventh Edition. Upper Saddle River, NJ: Prentice-Hall, pp. 684-685.
3. Ibid., pp. 695, 697.

4. Kotler, Philip (1984). *Marketing Management: Analysis, Planning, and Control,* Fifth Edition. Englewood Cliffs, NJ: Prentice-Hall, pp. 765-766.

5. Ibid., p. 766.

6. Kotler, *Marketing Management,* Eleventh Edition, p. 697.

7. Ibid., pp. 698-699.

Case 9

1. Ross, G. "Algae Turns into Money." *Jefferson Monthly,* February 27, pp. 8-11, 35.

2. "Super Blue Green Algae," available online at <http://www.ggold.com/ggold/sbga/sbga.htm>, April 1, 1997.

3. "Fast Facts on Super Blue Green Algae," available online at <http://chatlink.com/~algae/facts.html>, April 1, 1997.

4. "The Ray Cassano Tape," Cell Tech distributor's promotional audiotape. Kimberly Bright Cassano Enterprises, 1993.

5. Poe, R. (1995). "Rich Niches," *Success,* 42(3): 20-23.

6. Ibid., p. 20.

7. Ibid., pp. 20-23.

8. Ibid., p. 20.

9. PR Newswire 1 (1997). *Self,* February 24.

10. Poe, "Rich Niches," pp. 20-23.

11. "The Color of Money" (1996). *Oregon Business,* 9(9).

12. Ibid.

13. Poe, "Rich Niches," pp. 20-21.

14. Ibid., p. 20

15. Ibid., p. 21.

16. Kollman, Daryl (1996). *Letter from Daryl.* Cell Tech, Klamath Falls, Oregon, December, p. 1.

17. Ross, "Algae Turns into Money," pp. 8-11, 35.

18. "Algae, from Lake to Capsule, Proves Source of Controversy" (1986). *Oregonian,* March 18, p. 14.

19. PR Newswire, *Self.*

20. Ibid.

21. "Cell Tech: A Window of Opportunity for the Whole World" (1996). Cell Tech, Klamath Falls, Oregon.

22. Ibid.

23. Ross, "Algae Turns into Money," pp. 8-11, 35.

24. "Cell Tech: A Window of Opportunity for the Whole World."

25. Ibid.

26. Ibid.

27. "Prices." Cell Tech distributor Web page, available online at <www.illuminates.com/clients/algae/price.html>.

28. "Cell Tech: A Window of Opportunity for the Whole World."

29. "Commission Considers Dietary Supplement Health Claims" (1996). *Chemical Marketing Reporter,* February 26, p. 26.

30. "Flash Reports: Herbal Supplements" (1997). *Supermarket Business,* June, p. 85.

31. Ibid.

32. "The Cell Tech Business Opportunity." Cell Tech distributor Web page, available online at <http://webcom.com/~cfravel/ctbizinf.html>, April 15, 1997.

33. "Distributor Kits." Cell Tech distributor Web page, available online at <http://www.illuminatus.com/clients/algae/dist.html>, April 15, 1997.

34. "What's Wrong With Multi-Level Marketing?" Available online at <http://www.best.com/~vandruff/mlm1.html>, April 15, 1997.

35. "Multi-Level Marketing." United States Postal Inspection Service Web page, available online at <http://www.usps.gov/websites/depart/inspect/pyramid.htm>, April 15, 1997.

36. Carmichael, W. W. (1994). "The Toxins of Cyanobacteria." *Scientific American,* January, pp. 78-86.

37. Ibid., p. 80.

38. Ross, "Algae Turns into Money," pp. 8-11, 35.

39. Ibid., p. 8.

40. "Dietary Supplement Health and Education Act of 1994." (1995). U.S. Food and Drug Administration Center for Food Safety and Applied Nutrition, December 1, 1995.

41. Mandelbaum-Schmid, Judith (1997). "Blue-Green Algae." *Self,* March, pp. 145-148, 169.

42. Ibid., p. 146.

43. PR Newswire, *Self.*

44. Ibid.

45. Ibid.

46. Information for Prudent Consumers from the National Council Against Health Fraud, Inc., "Blue-Green Algae," available online at <http://www.bios.niu.edu/plant/sims/NCAHF1.html>, April 3, 1997.

47. Ibid.

48. Ibid.

49. Ibid.

50. Carmichael, "The Toxins of Cyanobacteria," p. 84.

51. Ibid.

52. Mandelbaum-Schmid, "Blue-Green Algae," pp. 145-148, 169.

53. Carmichael, "The Toxins of Cyanobacteria," p. 86.

54. Ibid.

55. Mandelbaum-Schmid, "Blue-Green Algae," p. 168.

56. "Algae Rules Put in Place" (1997). *Herald and News,* May 23, pp. 1-2.

57. Ibid., p. 1.

58. Ibid.

59. "ODA Announces Plans to Regulate the Algae Industry" (1997). *Basin Business,* Klamath County Chamber of Commerce, June, pp. 1, 2, 15.

60. "Standards Proposed for Algae Purity" (1997). *Herald and News,* June 17, pp. 1-2.

61. Ibid., p. 1.

62. Ibid., p. 1.

63. "State Should Involve Public Sooner on Algae Standards" (1997). *Herald and News,* June 20, p. 4.

Case 10

1. Available online at <http://athens.cac.psu.edu/fraternities/psdelt/nic.html>.

2. Available online at <http://worldmall.com/erf/lxa/lxa8.txt>.

3. Available online at <http://www.unm.edu/~greeks/stats.html>.

Case 15

1. Jac, Radomin (1999). "An Overview of the Czech Republic," *Czech Republic Business Guide,* pp. 2-6.

2. Pokorny, Jiri (1994). *The Czech Lands 1918-1997.* Prague, Czech Republic: Prah Press, pp. 41-46.

3. Levitsky, Jacob (1996). *Small Business in Transition Economies.* London: Intermediate Technology Publications, Ltd., pp. xiii-xxv.

4. Wallace, Elizabeth (1996). "Financial Institutional Development—The Case of the Russian Small Business Fund." *Small Business in Transition Economies,* pp. 76-84.

5. Weston Stacey, personal communication, April 10, 2000.

6. Liebmann, Lenny (1997). "The Siren Song of Callback Services." *International Business,* March, pp. 37-38.

7. Morton, Peter (1996). "Dialling for Dollars: Callback Companies Give Consumers Great Long Distance Rates, but They Pluck Revenues from Foreign Phone Systems." *Financial Post,* October 19, p. 16.

8. Silber, Seth C. (1996). "The FCC's Call-Back Order: Proper Respect for International Comity." *The George Washington Journal of International Law and Economics,* pp. 97-125.

9. "Tunnel Vision" (2000). *Business Central Europe,* April, p. 39.

10. Zivnustkova, Alena (2000). "Losing the Bankruptcy Battle." *Prague Business Journal,* April 24, p. 1, col. 2-4.

11. McClelland, Stephen (1995). "Learning to Love Callback." *Telecommunications,* July, pp. 40-41.

12. Scheele, Michael J. (1995). "You Can't Beat the Price." *Telephony,* April 24, pp. 65-70.

13. Shiver, Jube Jr. (1996). "FCC, Phone Firms Take Notice As Callback Industry Expands." *The Los Angeles Times,* December 13, p. D-1.

Index

Page numbers followed by the letter "f" indicate figures; those followed by the letter "t" indicate tables.